TITANIC

The Exhibition

WITH TEXT BY

JOHN P. EATON AND CHARLES A. HAAS

DISCARD

WONDERS

THE MEMPHIS INTERNATIONAL CULTURAL SERIES
A DIVISION OF THE CITY OF MEMPHIS, TENNESSEE

IN ASSOCIATION WITH

RMS TITANIC, INC.

TITANIC

The Exhibition

PUBLISHED BY
LITHOGRAPH PUBLISHING COMPANY,
A DIVISION OF LITHOGRAPH PRINTING COMPANY

WONDERS
The Memphis International Cultural Series

© 1997 WONDERS
THE MEMPHIS INTERNATIONAL CULTURAL SERIES,
A DIVISION OF THE CITY OF MEMPHIS, TENNESSEE
ALL RIGHTS RESERVED.

PRINTED IN THE UNITED STATES OF AMERICA

LIBRARY OF CONGRESS CATALOG CARD NUMBER: 97-60525

ISBN 1-882516-06-0 (HARDCOVER)
ISBN 1-882516-07-9 (PAPERBACK)

PROJECT MANAGER: RUSS GORDON

CATALOGUE PRODUCTION: CURATORIAL ASSISTANCE, LOS ANGELES
DIRECTOR: GRAHAM HOWE
EDITOR: GARRETT WHITE
GRAPHIC DESIGN: KAREN BOWERS
EDITORIAL STAFF: KAREN HANSGEN, DIANNE WOO
DIGITAL IMAGING/GRAPHIC DESIGN: PHILIP GOLDWHITE
PHOTOGRAPHER: PHILIPP SCHOLZ RITTERMANN

PRODUCTION COORDINATOR: CONNIE REEVES
COLOR SEPARATIONS AND PRINTING:
LITHOGRAPH PRINTING COMPANY

FRONT ILLUSTRATION:
BOY HAWKING NEWS OF THE SINKING OUTSIDE OCEANIC HOUSE, THE LONDON HEADQUARTERS OF THE WHITE STAR LINE.

FRONTISPIECE:
E. D. WALKER, *TITANIC LEAVING SOUTHAMPTON*, OIL ON CANVAS, 1996. COURTESY OF THE ARTIST.

RIGHT:
TITANIC IN NO. 3 SLIPWAY AS SEEN FROM ALBERT QUAY ACROSS THE RIVER LAGAN.

CONTENTS PAGE ILLUSTRATION:
TITANIC IN THE DOCK AT SOUTHAMPTON, GOOD FRIDAY, APRIL 5, 1912.

CONTENTS

THE EXHIBITION

WONDERS: The Memphis International Cultural Series, a division of the city of Memphis, is renowned for bringing the world's great art, history, and culture to American audiences through the development of large-scale exhibitions. The organization's six previous exhibitions have featured some of the most important historical figures of all time. Napoléon, Catherine the Great, Ramesses II, the Ottoman sultans, the Etruscans, and the emperors of ancient China have each been the focus of WONDERS exhibitions, which together have attracted more than two million visitors to the city of Memphis.

The tragic story of *Titanic* is of a more recent past. It is more than just the account of perhaps the most memorable maritime catastrophe of the twentieth century. *Titanic* is a lasting symbol of the great age of immigration that brought the hopes and dreams of so many to our shores. The Edwardian age was a time of rising expectations and technological achievement, and *Titanic* remains a powerful symbol of that era. It was the largest, grandest object conceived by humankind, and its terrible loss appeared, at the time, to signal the end of a promising age of optimism.

Since the 1985 discovery of *Titanic*'s resting place two and a half miles beneath the surface of the North Atlantic, many of the world's foremost scientists, archaeologists, and maritime scholars have expressed concern over the acceleration in the deterioration of the wreck site. Experts feel that if the present rate of decline continues, *Titanic* will be an unrecognizable hulk in as little as twenty years. Fortunately, the site's court-appointed salvor-in-possession, RMS Titanic, Inc., has diligently sought to preserve and protect the site from unscrupulous treasure hunters who certainly would have descended upon this most historic of shipwrecks. No one, however, can protect it from the ravages of time and the sea.

RMS Titanic, Inc., has employed the most advanced undersea archaeological methods to research and document the site. The four artifact recovery expeditions (1987, 1993, 1994, and 1996) have all been conducted in association with one of the premier oceanographic institutions, the *Institut Français de Recherche et Étude de la Mer* (IFREMER), headquartered in Paris, France. IFREMER provided its research vessel, *Nadir*, and its companion submersible, *Nautile*, one of the few vessels in the world capable of operating at depths exceeding 12,000 feet. Object restoration has been performed by Électricité de France (EDF) in Paris, and LP3 Conservation in Semur-en-Auxois, Burgundy, using techniques specially developed for the restoration of *Titanic* artifacts.

WONDERS has sought to promote awareness of and education in the world's diverse cultures by displaying actual objects reflecting individuals and events that have had a significant impact on human history. As one sage put it, it is our mission "to guard their memory and tell their tale." WONDERS is honored to have been selected by RMS Titanic, Inc., to develop an exhibition that will ensure that *Titanic*, its survivors, and those who were lost are never forgotten. It is our desire to present the *Titanic* story in a historically accurate and reverent manner, and to promote further study and research into this influential event.

E. D. Walker, Titanic Starting on Sea Trials, *oil on canvas, 1994. Courtesy of the artist.*

Letter from
SURVIVORS

The legendary saga of RMS *Titanic* is a story known the world over. But for the four of us, who personally lived through that tragedy, it is more than a story—it is a moment in time when our lives were forever changed. In that moment, we became inextricably linked to one another and to *Titanic*.

On this, the eighty-fifth anniversary of that fateful night, the public will have the opportunity to share in this monumental tragedy through the sensitive and respectful display of objects recovered and conserved from the great ship. As survivors of this disaster, we are pleased to see the memories of the ship and of the loved ones we lost so long ago preserved in such an accurate and dignified manner.

Millvina Dean

Michel Navratil

Edith Haisman*

Eleanor Shuman

*Edith Haisman passed away on January 20, 1997, at the age of 100.

James A. Flood, RMS Titanic Queenstown Bound,
acrylic on canvas, 1994.

MAYOR OF MEMPHIS

F ew subjects have fascinated the public as *Titanic* has. The tragic story of the grand ocean liner "that would not sink" has an appeal that has reached across the eighty-five years since her sinking and touched people of all ages, races, and cultures.

With the premiere of *TITANIC*, the sixth exhibition organized by WONDERS: The Memphis International Cultural Series, the public will once again be captivated by the story of this magnificent ship. More than 300 artifacts recovered from the North Atlantic wreck site and more than seventy-five objects from several of the largest private *Titanic* memorabilia collections in the world tell the tale of the ship,

her passengers, and her crew in a way it has never been told before.

Perhaps the most significant objective this exhibition can accomplish is to preserve the memory of the victims of this historic disaster. Their stories of courage and grace in the face of death are the most valuable lessons of the tragedy. Through them, we learn more about ourselves and about the limits—and triumphs—of human endeavor.

Thanks to the efforts of RMS Titanic, Inc., the salvor-in-possession, we also have visual reminders of this great tragedy. I would like to express my thanks to the company for its loan of objects recovered from the ocean floor. Thanks also to Denis Cochrane, John Eaton, and

W. K. and Rita Haines, who have contributed items from their personal collections of *Titanic* memorabilia.

Without the generous support of businesses, organizations, and individuals from the community, a project such as the WONDERS series cannot succeed. I would like to thank the Memphis City Council, the Memphis and Shelby County Port Commission, International Paper, the Kroger Company, Coca-Cola, Federal Express Corporation, Delta Air Lines, ICI Acrylics, and Universal Outdoor for their ample support. Very special thanks also go to the 2,000 volunteers whose time and effort are vital to the operation of each WONDERS exhibition.

I would especially like to express my gratitude to Jon Thompson, Director of Cultural Affairs for the city of Memphis, who has put countless hours of effort into making this world premiere exhibition possible. He and the dedicated staff at WONDERS have committed themselves to making this exhibition a success for our city.

W. W. Herenton

Dr. W. W. Herenton
Mayor, City of Memphis

Simon Fisher, Dusk, Cherbourg Harbor, April 10, 1912, *oil on canvas, 1994. Courtesy of the artist.*

In late 1994, WONDERS began the odyssey that has culminated in this marvelous exhibition and in the impressive catalog you see before you. At that time, Dr. Stephen Deucher of the National Maritime Museum in Greenwich, England, introduced Glen Campbell, Director of Operations and Administration at WONDERS, to the principals of RMS Titanic, Inc., the salvor-in-possession of the *Titanic* wreck site. During two years of negotiations, an association was formed that has resulted in the first comprehensive *Titanic* exhibition in history.

Our departure from the typical WONDERS format, which usually focuses on fine art from around the world, has produced a historical exhibition that explores one of the most compelling events in history. A true icon of the twentieth century, *Titanic* and the tragic events of her short life have grown to mythical proportions in the decades since her sinking.

WONDERS is a nonprofit, nonpartisan division of the city of Memphis. As such, we have endeavored to produce as principled an exhibition as possible on this sometimes controversial subject. We decided early in the process that the exhibition should relate the dramatic story of *Titanic* in a reverent and respectful manner from its birth in Belfast, to its death near Halifax, Nova Scotia, and the subsequent recovery and conservation of objects from the ship and the belongings of crew and passengers. We especially wanted to preserve the memory of those who became unwitting players in the most famous maritime drama in history. To accomplish this, we assembled a team of experts from around the world. Historians, architects, designers, model and mount makers, photographers, writers, editors, and publishers worked tirelessly to produce the results you see today.

We will be forever grateful to Bill Gasparrini, chairman of the board, and George Tulloch, president, of RMS Titanic, Inc., for their desire to share with the world the treasures gathered through ten years of diligent effort.

A very special thanks to Denis Cochrane, who granted us access to his extensive collection of *Titanic* material, without which we could not have told the complete story.

No other city in the United States can match the WONDERS record of having provided its citizens with a succession of quality major exhibitions. Through the vision of Mayor W. W. Herenton and the Memphis City Council and critical funding from the Memphis–Shelby County Port Commission, WONDERS has been able to deliver once again. Unfaltering leadership and the generous participation of our patrons, sponsors, and contributors are the keys to the success of a cultural series that has become the envy of cities across the country.

To the dynamic staff at WONDERS and the legion of volunteers whose reward comes from knowing they have given their all in achieving another world-class performance, I express my praise, respect, and humble thanks. To have had the privilege to work behind the scenes during this latest and most crucial period in the life of this great ship, *Titanic*, has been the experience of a lifetime. I am very proud to have had a small part in properly presenting *TITANIC: The Exhibition*.

Jon K. Thompson

Jon K. Thompson
Director of Cultural Affairs
City of Memphis

Letter from
RMS Titanic, Inc.

Eighty-five years after *Titanic* arrived in Southampton for her maiden voyage, we at RMS Titanic, Inc. are proud that our work with WONDERS is at last ready to share with the world through *TITANIC: The Exhibition*, the largest show of *Titanic* artifacts ever displayed.

The night of April 14, 1912, is one of the saddest in history. Scholars have often turned to Shakespeare and the literature of ancient Greece in an attempt to express the magnitude of *Titanic*'s tragic sinking. RMS Titanic, Inc. was founded to preserve the memory of *Titanic* and the events of that night for present and future generations. Artifacts from the ship, gathered and conserved through great effort, will remain a vital witness to the reality of the ship and to the circumstances of her sinking.

The present exhibition draws from one of the world's most astonishing collections, containing more than 5,000 *Titanic* objects that have been carefully chosen on the basis of diversity, message, and voice. From the ship's

The French three-man submersible Nautile *aboard the research ship* Nadir.

mighty whistles to the coffee mugs of the crew, the selection reflects the people of the more than forty nations represented on board, helping us to appreciate our common heritage and understand something of the enormity of *Titanic*'s loss.

We welcome this opportunity to express our deepest gratitude to the many people around the world who have labored tirelessly to realize this goal. The process of discovery, recovery, conservation, and exhibition of artifacts from *Titanic* has involved so many good men, women, and children that to single out a few would be a disservice to the unrecognized efforts of so many others.

The tragic sinking of *Titanic* should have been prevented. Her greatest lesson to all of us is safety first; few gambles merit the risk of human life. We hope that this magnificent exhibition of artifacts will provide an opportunity to consider *Titanic*'s many legacies, and we wish to extend our thanks to all who visit for helping to preserve *Titanic*'s memory.

RMS Titanic, Inc.
New York, New York

INTRODUCTION

The ocean liners of the early twentieth century were among man's noblest creations. Steel. Glass. Wood. Iron. Textiles. Ceramics. Precious metals. Ship designers applied every human craft with skill and ingenuity to bring form and vitality to vessels that were international spectacles of engineering and aesthetic achievement.

Once launched, each liner assumed a life of its own, an indefinable personality that differed from all others and followed it through a life span of twenty-five years or more.

Ships lost in their early years of operation are fairly common. After the initial headlines, most are quickly forgotten. Rare, indeed, is the ship, particularly a liner, lost during its maiden voyage.

There is, however, one magnificent liner whose brief, unfulfilled life and tragic end place it forever among history's best-remembered ships. Its design, construction, and fitting-out marked a milestone in the art of shipbuilding. The opulence of its interiors and the beauty and comfort of its furnishings made it the most outstanding liner of its era. The ship's name . . . *Titanic*.

Titanic was, as many thought, a symbol of the culmination of human technical achievement through the previous century. But on the night of April 14, 1912, the fifth night of her maiden voyage from Southampton to New York, the ship struck an iceberg in a calm sea and sank in two hours and forty minutes, with the unbelievable loss of 1,523 of its 2,228 passengers and crew.

Today, only a handful of survivors remain. There are no longer any living crew, no first-class passengers. The ship, discovered in 1985 after lying in darkness for seventy-three years two-and-a-half miles beneath the surface of the Atlantic, has since been seen by only a few dozen people. Yet even after the most catastrophic end the sea can inflict, the care taken on the smallest details of the liner's construction is still visible in the scattered evidence on the ocean floor. Many of these artifacts, including objects once dear to the ships's passengers, have been recovered and restored as a memorial to *Titanic* and to those who died.

One day, the corrosion engulfing *Titanic* will cause the great hull to collapse, and the artifacts retrieved from the site—gathered with archaeologically correct methods, handled with care, and skillfully preserved—will provide the only tangible evidence of history's most famous shipwreck, on display for future generations and not just for the privileged few who have dived to the wreck.

Titanic was designed for comfort rather than speed, and intended for many years of useful service. Even while the ship was being built, her owners knew there were faster and larger liners on the way. Within two years of her loss, her great length and bulk would be exceeded by two other liners, Cunard's *Aquitania* and the Hamburg-American Line's *Imperator*. But at the time of her launch on May 31, 1911, *Titanic* was the largest manmade moving object ever constructed.

Simon Fisher, The Last Sunset, *oil on canvas, 1997.*
Courtesy of the artist.

chapter one

ORIGINS

Detail from the cover of a White Star Line passenger list.

Titanic was the crowning achievement of the White Star Line of Liverpool, one of the world's premier shipping companies, and Harland and Wolff of Belfast, one of the world's greatest shipbuilders. Both had long and distinguished histories, and both brought decades of commercial experience and engineering expertise to their joint plan to build the largest, most luxurious ocean liners ever conceived.

Early in 1868, thirty-one-year-old sailing ship owner Thomas Henry Ismay of Liverpool purchased the assets of a bankrupt Australian shipping company, the White Star Line. Several months later, he decided to turn his acquisition into a steamship line. Legend

Downshire House, the London home of William James Pirrie, where, over dinner in 1907, Pirrie and White Star Chairman Joseph Bruce Ismay devised a plan to build three immense transatlantic liners.

holds that the decision was reached over a game of billiards at the home of Liverpool financier Gustav Christian Schwabe, uncle of Gustav Wolff, who was a junior partner of Harland and Wolff. Schwabe promised to back Ismay financially in the new venture, under one con-

dition: The ships would be ordered from Harland and Wolff.

Ismay accepted the offer, and negotiations and fund-raising for the new company began. White Star was registered under its corporate name, Oceanic Steam Navigation Company, Ltd., on September 6, 1869. Initial capital was £400,000 ($2,000,000) in shares of £1,000 ($5,000).

The first steam vessels built for the company—*Oceanic, Atlantic,* and *Baltic*—entered service in 1871 within a few months of one another. Their compound engines consumed less coal than comparable liners owned by other companies, and their passenger accommodations offered vast improvements over those of earlier liners. Cabins, equipped with electric call bells, were nearly double the size of the industry standard, and for the first time, the dining saloon was large enough to fit all passengers in a single sitting.

The White Star Line

Registered as a British company on September 6, 1869, the Oceanic Steam Navigation Company, Ltd.—better known as the White Star Line—earned a reputation over the next sixty-five years as one of the most progressive shipping firms, calling at the ports of six continents.

Thomas Henry Ismay founded the White Star Line in 1868.

The company's vessels, almost all built at Harland and Wolff shipyards in Belfast, Northern Ireland, and bearing names ending in -*ic*, were instantly recognizable by their livery (black-topped buff funnels, black hulls, red "boot topping") and their house flag, a red swallow-tailed pennant emblazoned with a brilliant five-pointed white star.

White Star Line vessels achieved many firsts. They were the first to place "saloon" (first class) passengers amidships; the first to provide gas lighting; the first to offer a Turkish bath and extra-tariff à la carte restaurants; the first to exceed 20,000 tons, later 40,000 tons; the first to have permanent indoor swimming pools; and the first to provide staterooms with private promenades. Neither did the company confine itself to passenger trade; its numerous cargo vessels were successfully employed worldwide.

Most of White Star's fleet was remarkably successful; several held the Blue Riband for fastest Atlantic crossings, while

William Imrie became Thomas Ismay's business partner in 1870, and thereafter the White Star Line was managed by the firm of Ismay, Imrie and Company.

Joseph Bruce Ismay became chairman of the White Star Line upon the death of his father, Thomas, in 1899.

(Left) Simon Fisher, The Last
Meeting, *oil on canvas, 1994.*
Titanic *and* Olympic *at Belfast,
March 1912. Courtesy
of the artist.*
*(Below) Built by Harland and
Wolff and launched in 1899, the
White Star Line's* Oceanic II *was
the largest liner of its day.*
*(Bottom) These brass buttons,
recovered from* Titanic, *were
used to fasten the uniforms of
White Star employees.*

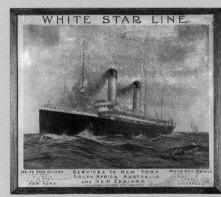

others—including *Titanic*'s sister ship *Olympic*—are considered high points in ocean liner evolution. As with all major shipping companies, however, White Star was not immune to calamity. Although *Titanic* is undoubtedly the most famous, other White Star vessels also suffered mishaps, from being struck by lightning to suffering attack by German divebombers to capsizing due to ice in the rigging.

Ironically, the end of the company was much less dramatic. In 1934, both White Star and its greatest rival, the Cunard Line, asked the British government for financial assistance in building new vessels. The government agreed, but only if the two rivals merged. The first new passenger ship to result from this merger would herself become immortal—RMS *Queen Mary*, now a tourist attraction in Long Beach, California.

The final White Star passenger ship, the motor vessel *Britannic*, ended her days in a Scottish scrapyard in December 1960. But a remnant of the company's extensive fleet survives today. Nearly nine decades after her launch in 1911, the tender *Nomadic*, which ferried passengers out to *Titanic*'s side in Cherbourg Harbor, still operates in Paris under her original name as a floating restaurant moored on the River Seine, across from the Eiffel Tower.

To most, *White Star* and *Titanic* are synonyms for disaster, but to shipping enthusiasts worldwide, *White Star* is synonymous with beauty, innovation, and quality.

*William James Pirrie, later
Lord Pirrie, joined Harland
and Wolff as an apprentice
draftsman in 1862. He
became a partner in the firm
and managed it successfully
into the next century after
Edward Harland's death in
1895. (Above) Lord Pirrie—
wearing the uniform of an
Irish Privy Councillor—and
Lady Pirrie in front of their
Belfast home.*

*(Center of page) This shallow dish, displaying the
White Star logo, may have
been used in* Titanic's *third-
class table settings.*

A fourth sister, *Republic*, joined the fleet in 1872, followed that same year by two slightly larger vessels, *Adriatic* and *Celtic*. Although it concentrated on the lucrative Atlantic trade, White Star also provided passenger and freight service between England and South America, Australia, and New Zealand, as well as trans-Pacific service between San Francisco and ports in the Far East.

The company continued to expand its North Atlantic passenger fleet, adding *Britannic* (1874), *Germanic* (1875), *Teutonic* (1888), *Majestic* (1890), and *Cymric* (1898). In 1899, a second *Oceanic* was launched. Dubbed the "Ship of the Century," she was the culmination of the art of nineteenth-century shipbuilding. *Oceanic II* was also the last White Star vessel whose construction was supervised by Ismay. He died on November 23, 1899, a few months after the ship's triumphant maiden voyage.

Upon Ismay's death, his thirty-seven-year-old son, Joseph Bruce, became chairman

This water carafe, brought up from the wreck site, might have been seen on any of the tables in Titanic's *dining areas. The White Star logo is etched into the crystal.*

of the White Star Line. The younger Ismay had entered the company's service in 1880 and became a partner on January 1, 1891. Painfully shy, he had an intense dislike of personal publicity and assiduously avoided it. He developed a brusque and sarcastic manner, and those who knew him only casually were taken aback by his overpowering personality.

In an unpublished biography of J. Bruce Ismay, Wilton J. Oldham writes that Ismay's personal style frightened subordinates "out of their wits, making contact between him and [them] an ordeal for all concerned. This did not, however, apply to those who knew him well, who realized that this was a front, which concealed the sensitive, kindly man behind the public image." An article in the *Times* of London described Ismay as having "deep feeling and sympathy for the 'underdog'" and as being "always anxious to help anyone in trouble."

Among Thomas Ismay's most influential

Harland and Wolff

Founded in January 1862, Harland and Wolff has had a distinguished record of shipbuilding that spans more than 130 years. The birthplace of *Titanic*, the company's yards at Queen's Island in Belfast, Northern Ireland, have produced a veritable parade of vessels, from tiny tenders to monstrous tankers.

After serving as general manager of the Robert Hickson shipyard in Belfast for four years, Edward J. Harland bought the company in 1858 at the age of 28, with assistance from G. C. Schwabe of Liverpool.

Yard number 1—the company's first vessel—was *Venetian*, a 29-foot, single-screw iron barque of 1,508 gross tons built for Britain's Bibby Line. Yard number 73, *Oceanic* of 1870, marked the beginning of an exclusive long-term relationship between Harland and the White Star Line. The yards would build more than seventy-five White Star vessels and agreed never to construct vessels for companies in direct competition with White Star.

At its height, more than 15,000 were employed at the yards; today the number is about 3,000. Although the company still receives the most inquiries about yard number 401, *Titanic*, it has produced more than 1,800 vessels, including cargo vessels, tankers, naval warships, special-purpose vessels, and of course passenger ships, including *Canberra* of Falklands War fame. The company continues to diversify, providing design services and technical assistance in a variety of maritime- and land-based projects around the world.

A photograph from the June 1912 issue of Engineer *shows a Harland and Wolff shop (above) as it appeared during the building of* Titanic. *Hundreds of blueprints required to build the ship were drawn at Harland and Wolff's Queen's Island drafting office (below).*

Gustav Wilhelm Wolff, nephew of G. C. Schwabe, became a partner in Harland's new company on April 11, 1861. The company name was officially changed to Harland and Wolff on January 1, 1862.

legacies was his plan for four large liners to replace the company's aging tonnage. In the design of these vessels, cargo and passenger capacities were to be increased, and speed was to be sacrificed in exchange for superior accommodations. The first of these liners was *Celtic* (1901), then the world's largest liner at 21,000 tons and 681 feet in length. *Cedric* (1903), *Baltic* (1904), and *Adriatic* (1907) followed.

American financier J. P. Morgan had created International Mercantile Marine (IMM) with an original capital investment of $120,000,000. This huge conglomerate already owned a number of transatlantic lines and had secret agreements with Dutch and German shipping interests. Morgan wanted to add the White Star Line to IMM, and on February 4, 1902, a provisional agreement was reached with a purchase price in excess of $50,000,000. Two years later, when IMM chairman Clement Griscom fell ill,

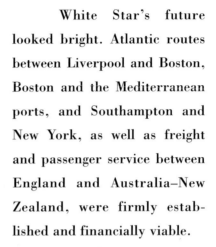

In a bid to control all of the North Atlantic steamship lines, American financier J. P. Morgan formed International Mercantile Marine (IMM), a vast shipping trust that soon included the White Star Line's parent company, Oceanic Steam Navigation. Morgan made Oceanic's chairman, J. Bruce Ismay, the new president of IMM.

Morgan asked J. Bruce Ismay to take over. Ismay was given the title of IMM president and managing director while remaining chairman of White Star.

White Star's future looked bright. Atlantic routes between Liverpool and Boston, Boston and the Mediterranean ports, and Southampton and New York, as well as freight and passenger service between England and Australia–New Zealand, were firmly established and financially viable.

Soon, however, vigorous competition from White Star's main rival, British-owned Cunard, materialized on the Atlantic route to New York. In 1905, construction began on Cunard's *Lusitania* and *Mauretania*, modern liners that would outpace anything in the White Star fleet. The two ships had almost simultaneous maiden voyages—*Lusitania* in September 1907, *Mauretania* in November 1907—and raised the record crossing speed by two knots. At more than 31,500 tons and 762 feet in length, they

Simon Fisher, The Lusitania at Liverpool, oil on canvas, 1992. Courtesy of the artist.

Built by the Cunard Line, White Star's greatest rival, with financial assistance from the British government, Lusitania and her sister ship Mauretania were the largest and fastest liners in the world at their launch in 1906. White Star's Olympic-class liners would surpass them in size and comfort if not in speed.

were the world's largest vessels by a substantial margin.

Their premier service threatened, White Star's directors turned to Harland and Wolff. Upon its founding in 1859, Harland and Wolff had employed forty-four men and covered a site of 3-3/4 acres. By 1907, the firm employed thousands and occupied dozens of acres. Of the sixty-five steam vessels owned or chartered by White Star, fifty-six had been built at the Harland and Wolff yard.

Control of the company's present and future was in the hands of one man, William James Pirrie, created a baron in 1906 and Viscount Lord Pirrie in 1921. Born May 31, 1847, in Quebec, Canada, Pirrie joined Harland and Wolff at age fifteen as an apprentice. His character and resourcefulness led to a partnership in 1874, appointed by the company's founder, Edward Harland. Pirrie's bold ambition and energy stimulated the firm's progress, and the company grew to occupy a significant place in the shipbuilding industry.

When Sir Edward Harland died on December 24, 1895, Pirrie had already moved up the ladder to the position of managing director. He became controlling chairman upon Gustav Wolff's retirement in 1906. As chairman, Pirrie solicited all new business, discussed

preliminary plans with clients, and managed the company's finances. His cousin and brother-in-law, Alexander Carlisle, was chief designer as well as a partner and ran the yard's day-to-day operations.

In the summer of 1907, the Pirries entertained Ismay and his wife, Florence, at their London home, Downshire House, Belgrave Square. After dinner, reportedly over port and cigars, the two men discussed the competition presented by Cunard. Pirrie suggested it was time for White Star to build its own "thousand foot" liners. A fortnightly round-trip service could be pro-

The size of the new Olympic-class liners necessitated construction of a new deepwater White Star Line dock at Southampton. Meanwhile, in New York, J. P. Morgan convinced the city to extend the line's New York pier (above) at its own expense.

Titanic's Belfast dock (right) as it appears today.

vided by two liners. Why not offer the weekly service that three liners could provide?

The men immediately began sketching designs for the three great liners. In keeping with White Star tradition, the emphasis would be on comfort and style. Although the vessels would exceed speeds of 20 knots, unprecedented safety and luxury would be stressed over record-breaking transatlantic crossings.

On September 11, 1907, White Star publicly announced its agreement with Harland and Wolff to build two large liners that would compete with Cunard's *Lusitania* and

Mauretania. White Star's sixty-sixth and sixty-seventh steamships would approach 900 feet in length. This required Harland and Wolff to enlarge its building slips, and two massive new gantries were erected in a space formerly occupied by three slips. A 200-ton floating crane, the world's largest, was also acquired. Because the new slipways could accommodate no more than two hulls, only the first two of the three planned *"Olympic* class" vessels were announced to the public.

Early in 1908, White Star issued £1,500,000 ($7,500,000) in new shares to help pay for the liners. Pirrie himself designed the hulls, while Carlisle designed the interior. Ismay and Pirrie studied various combinations of funnels, masts, and superstructure to determine the final appearance of the liners. On July 31, 1908, a contract letter was signed authorizing construction.

Building the great ships of the early twentieth century demanded imagination and outstanding leadership. At age thirty-nine, Thomas Andrews, a Harland and Wolff managing director and coordinator of *Titanic's* construction, had both qualities. Andrews was born in 1873 to an affluent Irish family. His mother, Eliza, was the sister of William Pirrie, who would go on to become Harland and

Wolff's principal owner. Andrews's love of ships and engineering led to a premium apprenticeship with the company in May 1889.

The requirements of his apprenticeship were rigorous. From May 1889 to May 1894, he was employed for months at a time in each of the yard's principal departments. This culminated in an eighteen-month assignment to the drawing department. Andrews's progress was swift. After completing his apprenticeship, he worked as an assistant in the repair department and quickly became head of the department. In 1900, he was promoted to construction manager, and four years later he was named assistant chief designer. The enterprising young man became head of the design department in 1905, working directly under Pirrie. He was given the title of managing director in 1907.

Andrews displayed immense kindness and patience toward his employees. His skill and knowledge rivaled that of anyone in the profession. When he brought his talent to bear on the creation of *Titanic*, he grew familiar with her every plate, every bulkhead, every corridor. Andrews came to know the great ship as no one else knew her.

chapter two

DESIGN & CONSTRUCTION

The keel for *Olympic*, first of the White Star Line's great ships, was laid in slip 2 on December 16, 1908, at the shipyard of Harland and Wolff. Her yard number was 400. Three and a half months later, on March 31, 1909, the keel was laid in slip 3 for yard number 401, *Titanic*.

Section by section, the two enormous hulls began to take form in the slipways. Ribs and cross girders reached skyward. Steel plating, poured and rolled in Scotland, was transported across the Irish Sea to Belfast. A cavernous space was made in each hull to hold two mammoth engines and twenty-nine boilers, fabricated in the Harland and Wolff shops.

Workers Leaving Harland and Wolff's Queen's Island shipyard along Queen's Road, with Titanic *in the background, May 1911. Among them were many of the most skilled ship builders in Europe.*

The hulls of Titanic *(left) and* Olympic *under construction, viewed from the high-level staging.*

Demarcations of the interior decks could be seen fore and aft. Two orders were placed, one in September 1910 and one in March 1911, for special tableware and glassware from United Kingdom suppliers. Because the china and crystal might be used aboard other White Star liners, no ship's names were engraved, only the company logo.

Olympic was launched on October 20, 1910. She was opened for public viewing prior to sea trials, which concluded on May 30, 1911. The following day she departed Belfast for Liverpool, site of White Star's main office. After another brief public viewing, *Olympic* sailed to her home port, Southampton, where she was again opened to the public. Thousands visited her before she left Southampton on June 14 for her successful maiden voyage.

The day *Olympic* departed for Liverpool, *Titanic* was triumphantly launched at Queen's Island. Friday, May 31, 1911, was clear and bright, and the yard quickly filled with employees' friends and families, who had come to watch the launch. During its construction, the hull had rested on wood pilings. On launch day, these pilings were cut and knocked away by shipyard workers until the ship's immense weight rested on only two enormous hydraulic triggers.

Although no formal ceremony was held in accordance with White Star policy, a group

Port bow view of Titanic (right) in no.3 slip prior to launch. Olympic (left) prior to launch with Titanic, fully shell plated at last. (Below) A 1911 souvenir edition of The Shipbuilder devoted solely to Olympic and Titanic.

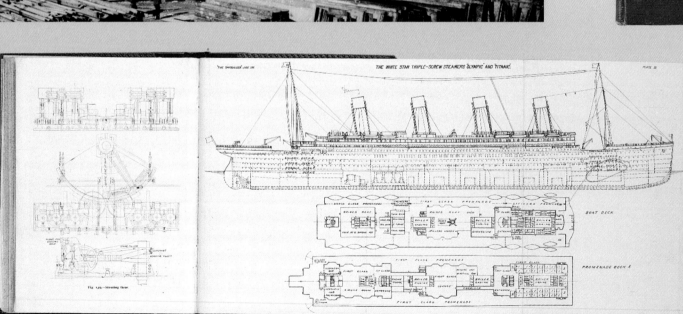

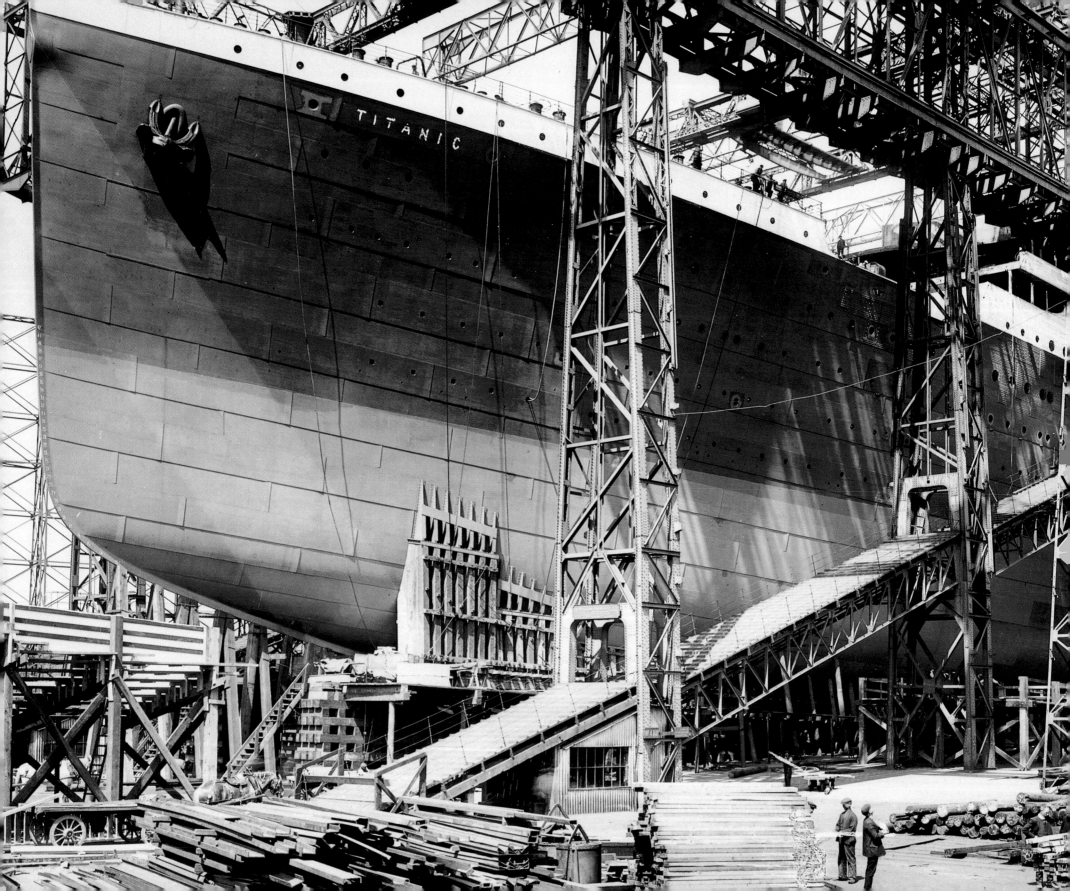

Launching a Ship

Many who have seen the 1958 film *A Night to Remember* may recall the dramatic scene in which a woman proclaims, "I name this ship *Titanic*. May God bless her and all who sail in her." She then cuts a ribbon, a bottle of champagne is smashed on the bow, and the newly christened liner begins its breathtaking journey down inclined ramps into the sea.

In reality, however, it didn't happen quite that way. For *Titanic*, there was no christening ceremony, no champagne. The White Star Line did not believe in formal launching ceremonies. As one shipyard worker put it, "They just builds 'em and pushes 'em in." The vessel being launched in the film's opening moments is actually the *Queen Mary*. Contemporary newspaper accounts indicate that *Titanic*'s launch was filmed and shown in British cinemas shortly afterward. The footage apparently has not survived. Either it was destroyed in the war, or, more likely, it was a casualty of the fragile nitrate film then in use.

Although ship christenings today are star-studded media events, the majestic sight of a ship hurtling down a ramp stern-first is a thing of the past. Such a procedure poses great danger to shipyard workers, spectators, and the ship herself. Instead, a floating-out ceremony has become the norm. Modern ships are built in special dry docks. Once the ship is constructed, valves are opened, permitting water to flood the dock's interior gradually. Eventually, the water lifts the ship gently off its keel blocks, and she is towed to a dock where fitting out is completed and the liner is prepared for departure.

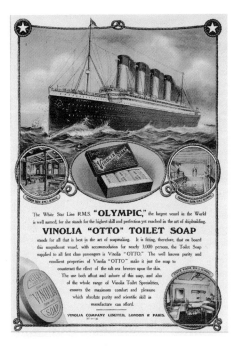

(Below) A 1912 ad for Vinolia "Otto" soap—first-class luxury at sea with the best of soaps.

Titanic's two main reciprocating engines (above) nearing completion in Harland and Wolff's engine works erecting shop. Titanic in gantry (opposite, top) viewed from across the River Lagan prior to launch; port stern view (opposite, far left) on slip prior to launch; port stern entering water (opposite center); port bow three-quarter profile of Titanic afloat immediately after launch.

of dignitaries gathered on a specially erected stand at the hull's bow. Among them was Harland and Wolff Chairman William James Pirrie.

Tens of thousands of excited, chattering Belfast citizens crowded the shoreline along the River Lagan. Specially chartered ferries and harborcraft plied the river for a closer look. A hushed silence fell as the raising of a red flag at the stern and the firing of a single red rocket

indicated that the moment had arrived.

Foremen and supervisors made their final reports. There was a gesture from Pirrie, and another red rocket was fired. At 12:13 P.M. the triggers were released. *Titanic*'s hull began to move down the slipway, her course smoothed by 22 tons of tallow and soap. In just over two minutes, the ship entered the River Lagan. *Titanic*'s life afloat had begun.

The liner was then towed to her berth

A twenty-horse team (above) pulls a fifteen-and-a-half ton anchor, one of three carried by Titanic; another anchor (left) ready for delivery at the factory. Workers install the sixteen-foot diameter center propeller (below left); one of Titanic's four twenty-two-foot diameter funnels emerging from the factory (left).

Titanic's 29 boilers seen here in the Harland and Wolff shop (left), were 15' 9" in diameter and weighed nearly 100 tons.

Workers forging the ship's massive anchor lines (below).

for outfitting. Electricians, shipfitters, plumbers, fabricators, and their assistants set to work installing conduits, bulkheads, piping, and flooring. From boiler rooms to passenger cabins, *Titanic*'s interior gradually took shape.

By August 20, 1911, the foremast was in position. Outfitting was delayed, however, when sister ship *Olympic* returned to the builder on October 6, 1911, following a collision with the British navy cruiser HMS *Hawke* near Southampton on September 20. Workers were diverted to White Star's already proven income producer, *Olympic*, causing the delay of *Titanic*'s original sailing date of March 20, 1912. Her maiden voyage would now commence on April 10, 1912.

Work on *Titanic* progressed rapidly despite the delay. On November 30, 1911, the keel was laid in slip 2 for yard number 433. Originally named *Gigantic*, this third "*Olympic* class" vessel was launched on February 26, 1914, as *Britannic*.

About two months prior to departure, *Titanic* was placed in dry dock for hull maintenance and painting, then removed two weeks later for lifeboat installation. Sixteen boats and four collapsibles provided seating for

North Atlantic Rivalry

Though remembered primarily for their first-class finery, the early twentieth century's most famous ocean liners—and countless smaller vessels—were built because of immigrants. Crossings by the rich and famous were well publicized, but the big news focused on the hefty profits shipping companies made from selling tickets to millions of steerage passengers.

Traffic across the North Atlantic hit its zenith during a time of great advances in the shipbuilder's art, when *Titanic* and her two sister ships were conceived and built. From 1900 through 1915, more than 10,250,000 immigrants entered the United States through the port of New York alone. To keep up with the growing demand, shipping companies in Great Britain, France, and Germany built increasingly larger and faster vessels to bring these "huddled masses" to the New World, augmented by smaller ships flying the flags of Holland, Sweden, and Italy, among others.

Britain's Cunard Line ordered two vessels of its own, each about 50 percent larger and significantly faster than anything else afloat at that time. Named *Lusitania* and *Mauretania*, the 32,000-ton pair entered service in 1907. In response, the White Star Line came out with *Olympic*, *Titanic*, and later *Britannic*. Each was 50 percent larger than *Lusitania* and *Mauretania*. But while Cunard's pair were built with fine hull lines permitting speeds of 26 knots, White Star's trio featured broader beams and speeds of 21 to 22 knots. In 1914 Cunard completed its own trio with *Aquitania*, which slightly eclipsed *Olympic* in size and speed.

France's Compagnie Générale Transatlantique furthered the competition with its lovely *France*. Though smaller than the Cunard and White Star ships, she was France's largest vessel and nearly as fast as the Cunarders. Germany's Hamburg-America Line commissioned *Imperator*, *Vaterland*, and *Bismarck*, each weighing more than 50,000 tons and each, in turn, the world's largest vessel.

The First World War brought the competition to a halt, and plans for even larger and faster ships were shelved or abandoned. *Lusitania* and *Britannic* were destroyed in the war, and the German trio were later awarded to Britain and the United States as war reparations. Shipbuilding would hit another high point during the late 1920s to the mid-1930s, when new giants such as *Queen Mary*, *Normandie*, *Bremen*, *Europa*, and *Conte di Savoia* took their places as passenger liners on the North Atlantic run.

(Left) Simon Fisher, Aquitania Departing Pier 54 New York, *oil on canvas, 1995. Courtesy of the artist.*

Titanic's *watertight doors (below) between the engine and boiler rooms were closed from the bridge moments after the ship struck the iceberg. Float valves were also designed to close them automatically.*

1,178, which exceeded British Board of Trade requirements—still determined at the time by ship tonnage rather than passenger capacity—by 17 percent.

On February 24, 1912, during an eastbound Atlantic crossing, *Olympic* lost a blade from her port propeller. After deboarding passengers at Southampton, she arrived in Belfast for repairs on March 1 and remained for six days. It marked the only time the three sisters—*Olympic*, *Titanic*, and *Gigantic-Britannic*—were together at the yard.

After *Olympic* was repaired, the finishing touches were made to *Titanic*'s exterior. *Olympic*'s first-class passengers often complained of being splashed with ocean spray at the bow as they walked along the promenade deck. White Star chairman J. Bruce Ismay personally gave the order to construct a glass enclosure over *Titanic*'s forward promenade deck. The enclosure became the most prominent feature distinguishing *Titanic* from *Olympic* in photographs. With this and other improvements, including carpeting and hardwood furnishings and expanded first-class passenger space, *Titanic* outweighed *Olympic* by more than 1,000 tons.

Now, as then, it is difficult to comprehend *Titanic*'s proportions:

Tonnage: 46,329 gross, 21,831 net
Displacement: 66,000
Overall length: 882 ft. 9 in.
Beam: 92 ft. 6 in.
Molded depth: 59 ft. 6 in.
Height (waterline to boat deck): 60 ft. 6 in.
Distance from keel to top of funnel: 175 ft.
Horsepower (reciprocating engines): 30,000 indicated
Horsepower (turbine engine): 16,000 shaft
Cruising speed: 21 knots
Top speed (estimated): 23 to 24 knots

The hundreds of shell plates used in *Titanic*'s construction averaged 6 feet in width and weighed between 2.5 and 3 tons each; the largest measured 36 feet in length and weighed 4.5 tons each. More than three million rivets secured the plating, and their total weight exceeded 1,200 tons. The ship was powered by two enormous reciprocating engines whose exhausts operated a large turbine. Steam for the engines was provided by five single-ended and twenty-four double-ended boilers to produce a working pressure of 215 pounds per square inch. The boilers' steel shell plating was 1-11/16 inches thick.

Three propellers, two wing and one center, drove and maneuvered the ship. Cast in

Three-quarter profile of Titanic (top left) at outfitting jetty with funnels up but unpainted; port view (center left) as water is about to be drained from the graving dock; port stern view of Titanic (below left) in the graving dock, where propellers were fitted and final paint was applied.

manganese bronze, the three-bladed wing propellers measured 23 feet, 6 inches in diameter, and the four-bladed center propeller, driven by the turbine, was 16 feet, 6 inches in diameter. Condensers, air and oil pumps, large sirocco fans, water pipes, and storage tanks were vital components of the complex life-support system of *Titanic*.

Many of the ship's significant features were fabricated right in Harland and Wolff's own Queen's Island yard. A significant number of components, however, came from elsewhere in the United Kingdom and from other countries and had to be assembled at the yard. The logistical challenges were staggering, and employees worked day and night to complete *Titanic*'s fitting out. Due to the coal strike of 1912, only 1,880 tons of coal were received for her 6,600-ton-capacity bunkers. More coal was hastily transferred or purchased from the holds of other ships. During the last two weeks of March, the ship's engineering and deck officers arrived, accompanied by sailing department heads and senior crew members.

The largest moving object ever built at that time, *Titanic* became a media sensation, thrilling readers of newspapers, magazines, and technical journals around the world. Each day of her three-year construction and outfitting

Port profile of Titanic (above) during outfitting at Thompson's deepwater dock, promenade deck still open. Lifeboats (left) under construction at Harland and Wolff.

The painting at left, E. D. Walker's Titanic Leaving Belfast for Sea Trials, April 2, 1912 *(oil on canvas, 1983), depicts the scene photographed above, taken as the ship was pulled by tugs through Victoria Channel to Belfast Lough. Courtesy of the artist.*

brought new word of innovative design and groundbreaking installation. News releases and pamphlets published by Harland and Wolff and brochures, postcards, and posters prepared by White Star trumpeted new standards of luxury, safety, comfort, and convenience. Though not actually stated by her builder or owner, *Titanic*'s invulnerability was nevertheless strongly implied.

Titanic was finally ready for sea trials and formal receipt by White Star. The liner departed Queen's Island at 6 A.M. on Tuesday, April 2, and proceeded down Victoria Channel and out into Belfast Lough, assisted by the Alexandra Towing Company's tugs *Huskisson*,

Starboard profile of completed ship (above) in Belfast Lough with tugs.

(Left) Stern view of Titanic *in Belfast lough with tugs.*

(Right) E. D. Walker's Sea Trials Completed, April 2, 1912, oil on canvas, 1983. Courtesy of the artist.

Herbert J. Pitman

Third Officer Herbert J. Pitman, a seventeen-year veteran at sea, came to Titanic from White Star's Oceanic, which was still docked due to the recent coal strike. Pitman, pictured at left in his White Star Line uniform in a photograph published in the Daily Mirror shortly after the disaster, reported to Liverpool per White Star orders, and traveled to meet Titanic at Belfast along with officers Boxhall, Lowe, and Moody. Pitman went from his quarters to the bridge after the collision, later assisting with lifeboats and eventually departing on First Officer Murdoch's orders in charge of lifeboat number 5.

After the sinking, Pitman continued to serve the White Star Line, eventually sailing as a purser when eye problems prevented him from serving on the bridge. Part of the Denis Cochrane Ocean Liner Memorabilia collection, the two signal flags below belonged to Pitman during his career at sea. Pitman was a member of the freemasons. The leather freemason pouch (above) still contains his mason apron.

Among the heaviest objects yet recovered from the debris field, this unrestored bollard (left and below left)—sometimes refered to as a bitt—was used to secure lines aboard the ship when docking. It measures 6.7' x 2.5' x 3.4' and weighs nearly two tons. The bollard (below) as it was brought aboard the French research vessel Nadir.

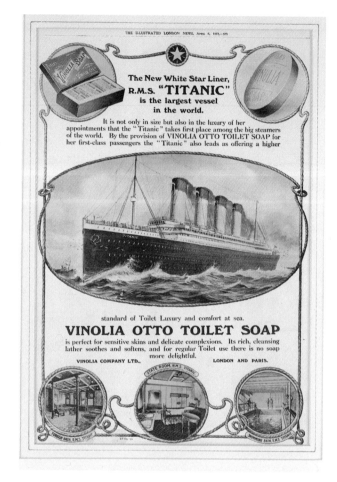

Herculaneum, Hornby, and Herald. Once the tugs cast off, the ship embarked on a series of starts and stops and turned in circles of various sizes at various speeds. After the results of the trials were compared and discussed, the liner sailed 40 miles on the Irish Sea. At sunset she returned to the lough and anchored off Belfast Harbor.

Titanic received certification from the British Board of Trade. Additional galley equipment and first-class lounge furniture was brought aboard, and the ship was turned over to her proud owner.

Shortly after 8 P.M., Titanic began her 570-mile journey across the Irish Sea and through St. George's Channel, made her way around England's southernmost tip into the English Channel, and arrived in Southampton at the White Star Line's new deepwater dock on April 4. The great ship moored at berth 44, facing outward, poised for her maiden voyage.

Titanic *leaving for trials in the Irish Sea, April 2, 1912 (above left). An advertisement for Vinolia "Otto" toilet soap (above), furnished to first-class passengers aboard* Titanic. *A lone man—Captain Smith?—walking down the 187-yard-long lower promenade deck (right).*

chapter three

DEPARTURE

The second-class passenger list for Titanic. *Of the 271 second-class passengers on board, only 119 survived.*

When Harland and Wolff's work crews were diverted from the completion of *Titanic* to the repair of *Olympic*, the impact of the move was soon felt. One week before her scheduled April 10 departure, *Titanic* was not ready to receive passengers. Many first- and second-class staterooms had exposed pipes and conduits, carpeting had not yet been laid, walls stood unpainted, and kitchen equipment was still being installed. In addition to the bustle of workers in nearly every part of the ship was the scramble to load supplies, including staggering amounts of food, tableware and glassware, linen, and vases for fresh flowers.

Throughout the week, cargo arriving dockside was quickly transferred to the liner's deep holds. Nothing unusual was on the ship's cargo manifest, only the high-grade commercial foodstuffs and consumer goods routinely transported by North Atlantic express liners. Among these goods were ostrich feathers, lace, shelled walnuts, books, ribbons, gloves, cheese, cognac, vermouth, anchovies, and seventy-six cases of dragon's blood, a plant product used in varnishes and photoengraving.

In this atmosphere of organized chaos, it was deemed unwise to bring visitors aboard. Contrary to White Star policy, which normally allowed tours of new ships prior to maiden voyages, proceeds from which were donated to charity, visitors were not allowed aboard *Titanic* at Southampton. It was hoped this would be rectified upon the ship's return. As a salute to the citizens of Southampton, however, *Titanic* was "dressed." On Good Friday, April 5, 1912, signal flags were flown on a line extending from stem to stern. It was the only time the colorful display was rigged aboard the ship.

Recruitment of the crew began the fol-

Simon Fisher, Arrival at Southampton, oil on canvas, 1995. Courtesy of the artist.

Advertisement for return voyages of Olympic *and* Titanic *from New York.*

Among the few photographs of Titanic's *brief voyage are several taken by Father Francis M. Browne, a 32-year-old teacher and candidate for the priesthood who debarked at Queenstown. At left, passengers board the boat train to Southampton at London's Waterloo Station.*

(Right) Titanic *at Southampton, Good Friday, April 5, 1912.*

lowing day. Job hopefuls jammed the company hiring hall and the town's local union halls. The national coal strike that had disrupted British shipping since February had at last been settled, but although coal was now available, most ships had not yet been replenished, and there was general unemployment, even for regular crews. To them, *Titanic* represented desirable employment. The White Star Line's fleet and officers were popular among Southampton's sailors, and *Titanic's* captain, Edward J. Smith, was particularly well liked. Company officials had no difficulty signing on a full complement the first day. There were even a number of standbys.

White Star demanded the best shipboard workers on the North Atlantic, and the 328 stewards and stewardesses who boarded *Titanic* were no exception. Most hailed from the Southampton area, others from London, Liverpool, and towns and cities throughout the country. Many were married and looked forward to the stability that came with White Star employment.

Of *Titanic's* 280 stokers, coal trimmers, and engine greasers, many were barely literate; others signed the ship's articles with an X. Later, some of the most dramatic and articulate written and oral accounts of the disaster would be composed by these workers.

The senior members of the sailing department were outstanding men in their own right. Chief Surgeon Dr. William Francis Norman O'Loughlin was as respected for his professional skill as he was for his affability and his charm as a raconteur. Joseph Bell, one of Britain's best marine engineers, had served aboard White Star ships since 1885. Chief Steward Andrew Latimer was a man of graciousness and talent.

Titanic's command consisted of her master, Edward John Smith, popularly known as E.J., and seven officers: Chief Officer William M. Murdoch, First Officer Charles H. Lightoller, Second Officer David Blair, Third Officer Herbert J. Pitman, Fourth Officer Joseph Groves Boxhall, Fifth Officer Harold G. Lowe, and Sixth Officer James Paul Moody.

(Far left) A group photo of Titanic officers and staff, probably taken at Queenstown. Four are identified on the photograph: Captain Smith, seated at left; Dr. William F. N. O'Laughlin, Chief Surgeon, also seated; First Officer Murdoch, standing at left; and Chief Purser Hugh W. McElroy, second from left.

(Left) Captain Edward John "E.J." Smith, "a natural born leader and fine seaman."

(Bottom left) First Officer William M. Murdoch, who was in command on the bridge when Titanic struck the iceberg.

Titanic's departure from Southampton, April 10, 1912.

The required boat drill aboard Titanic *before departure involved a simple crew muster and the lowering of two lifeboats to the water.*

Five had previously served on *Oceanic*. They ranged in age from twenty-six to thirty-nine and drew monthly salaries of $37 to $100. Except for Lowe, who came over from *Belgic* on the Australian run, all were experienced in North Atlantic weather and navigation.

Without a doubt, *Titanic* was regarded as a superior assignment. Promotion was based on regular evaluations by the captain and White Star's marine superintendent, Charles A. Bartlett. An officer worked his way through the system until he was given his own command or reached what the company considered his maximum level of competency.

"When anyone asks me how I can best describe my experiences in nearly forty years at sea," Captain Smith told an interviewer in New York on May 16, 1907, "I merely say 'uneventful.' You see, I am not very good material for a story." Despite his modesty, Smith's career was exemplary. He was born in Hanley, Staffordshire, England, on January 27, 1850, and educated at local schools. At nineteen he signed on as an apprentice with a firm of sailing ships and joined the White Star Line in 1886 as *Celtic*'s fourth officer. As he moved up through the ranks, he served faithfully in White Star's Australian and Atlantic trades and commanded *Majestic* as a troop ship during the Boer War.

Beginning with *Baltic* in 1904, he commanded each new company liner on her maiden voyage.

Contrary to popular belief, *Titanic* was not intended to be Captain Smith's last command. He had been scheduled to stay with the liner until the maiden voyage of *Britannic*, planned at that point for 1915.

Captain Smith, his wife, Eleanor, and his daughter, Helen, resided at "Woodhead," Winn Road, Southampton. Smith's annual salary was $6,250, supplemented by a $1,000 bonus if no ship under his command was involved in an accident during the year. As described by British historian Geoffrey Marcus in his book *The Maiden Voyage*, the captain was a "big, broadshouldered, grey-bearded man, generally regarded as the *beau ideal* of a Western Ocean mail boat commander. His personality radiated authority, tact, good humor, and confidence. He had a pleasant, quiet voice, and a ready smile. A natural leader

and fine seaman, Captain Smith was popular with officers and men alike."

Henry Tingle Wilde, *Olympic*'s chief officer, did not sail when the ship departed Southampton for New York at noon on April 2. He boarded *Titanic* on the morning of April 4. Although not officially assigned to her staff, he worked with the crew night and day to prepare the liner for sailing. Captain Smith spoke with Marine Superintendent Bartlett and arranged to have Wilde assigned as chief for *Titanic*'s first voyage. Wilde had been Smith's chief aboard *Olympic*, and his knowledge of *Titanic* and her staff would serve him well in the future, when he might likely assume command of the liner.

Wilde's assignment resulted in some shuffling of the crew. One day before departure, Chief Officer William M. Murdoch found himself demoted to first officer, First Officer

A set of three copper-alloy whistles was attached by an armature to each of Titanic's four funnels. The photo above depicts the configuration of the whistles. Three chambers (left) were recovered from the debris field. The small whistle (far left) created the highest pitch of Titanic's three-note voice. In the center, the large whistle, measuring 16 inches in diameter, produced the lowest pitch. The medium-pitch whistle is shown at left. The large and small chambers came from the first, or forward, funnel; the medium chamber was originally attached to the second funnel.

Six tugs helped Titanic *maneuver from berth 44 at Southampton (above left). As the propellers began to revolve (above right), the ship moved downstream.*

Charles H. Lightoller became second officer, and Second Officer David Blair was returned to *Oceanic.* The roster of junior officers—Pitman, Boxhall, Lowe, and Moody—remained unchanged.

April 10, 1912, sailing day, began with a 5:18 sunrise. Although the weather had been cold the previous night, the air temperature soon climbed through the 40s. By noon it was a still cool but pleasant 50°. Brisk north-northwest winds drove clumps of clouds through the clear blue sky.

The crew came aboard early in the morning and signed the roster, or sign-on list. The 8-to-4 watch in the engine room went to

their stations, as did kitchen, dining room, and bedroom stewards. Captain Smith boarded at approximately 7:30 A.M. and proceeded directly to his cabin, which lay forward on the deck's starboard side, immediately aft of the bridge. There he received the sailing report and prepared to meet throughout the morning with White Star and Board of Trade officials.

The boat train carrying second- and third-class passengers departed London's Waterloo Station at 7:30 A.M. and arrived dockside shortly after 9:30 A.M. Passengers began boarding almost immediately, first in a trickle, then in a torrent. Stewards worked quickly to keep up with the flow. Many passengers had never been on a ship. Mothers balancing infants on their hips tried to keep their other children together. Single men, particularly those in third class, came back on deck after seeing their bunks, adding two-way traffic to the activity. The shrill cries of children, the sharp slam of cabin doors, the clatter of footsteps on uncarpeted corridors, and the murmur of hundreds of voices filled the ship's interior.

Many of the third-class passengers were seeking a better life in the New World. Mothers and children were traveling to join husbands and fathers in America; immigrants were en route to farms in the United States and Canada; two Welsh boxers were headed for a series of prize-fights; men with large families planned to open businesses in America; and a group of Chinese seamen were on their way to join a ship in New York. In second class were small-business owners, teachers, and *Titanic*'s orchestra. The

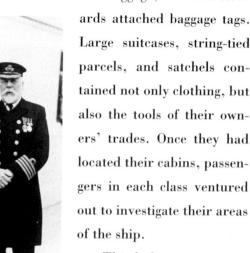

Captain Smith (right) with purser Herbert W. McElroy, taken outside the officers' quarters. Later, as Titanic *was sinking, McElroy told his staff to refuse demanding passengers their valuables and urge them into their life vests instead.*

bandsmen, traveling as passengers, were under contract to a Liverpool employment agency.

As they boarded the ship, many passengers carried their own luggage, to which stewards attached baggage tags. Large suitcases, string-tied parcels, and satchels contained not only clothing, but also the tools of their owners' trades. Once they had located their cabins, passengers in each class ventured out to investigate their areas of the ship.

Third-class quarters and public rooms were plain but adequate. Slatted benches and wood chairs provided simple, unadorned comfort. Linoleum tiles covered the floors. A small, open-air promenade area, aft, was furnished with benches from which passengers could enjoy the view. The long tables in the white-enameled dining saloon seated more than 470 passengers. The accommodations were far from luxurious, but the camaraderie of travel-

When a passenger aboard Titanic *checked his or her valuables at the purser's office, a tag such as this one, recovered from* Titanic, *served as a claim check.*

This restored leather travel bag, also recovered from the site, might have been carried by a passenger in any class.

Passenger Profile

A veritable floating city, *Titanic* carried passengers and crew from a wide cross section of the world's population. Although the majority of the ship's passengers were American or British, many Swedes were traveling in third class. Canada was also well represented, as was Ireland.

Another significant group in third class were Syrians. Other countries represented included Argentina, Austria-Hungary, Belgium, Bulgaria, China, Croatia, Denmark, Finland, France, Germany, Greece, Italy, Japan, Norway, Peru, Portugal, Russia, South Africa, Switzerland, and Turkey. Despite the babble of many tongues, *Titanic* had but one interpreter on staff, Mr. L. Muller.

ABOARD TITANIC

- First class passengers: 337
- Second class: 271
- Third class: 712
- Oldest passenger: 74-year-old Johan Svensson of Sweden.
- Youngest passenger: 2-month-old Elizabeth Gladys (Millvina) Dean, the youngest living survivor today.

LARGE FAMILIES ABOARD TITANIC

- Asplunds (3 adults, 5 children)
- Fortunes (6 adults)
- Goodwins (2 adults, 6 children, all lost)
- Kinks (4 adults, 1 child)
- Lefebres (1 adult, 4 children, all lost)
- Panulas (2 adults, 5 children, all lost)
- Rice family (1 adult, 5 children, all lost)
- Sages (2 adults, 9 children, all lost)
- Paulssons (1 adult, 4 children, all lost)
- Skoogs (2 adults, 4 children, all lost)

THE CREW

- Men: 885
- Women: 23

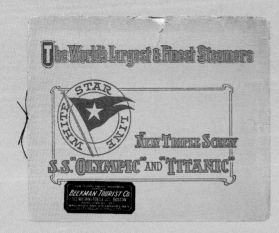

This advertising brochure (left), printed by White Star circa 1911, contains sketches of Olympic and Titanic interiors, along with an illustration comparing the two ships to the architectural wonders of the world.

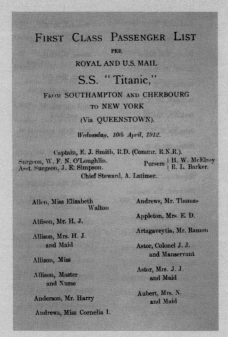

First-class passenger list. Of the 337 first-class passengers, 199 were saved.

Mr. and Mrs. George D. Widener of Philadelphia. Captain Smith enjoyed dinner at a party given by the Wideners in the à la carte restaurant on the evening of April 14.

(Left) A nickel and copper-alloy cooking pot from one of Titanic's kitchens.

(Right) A glass candy dish used in first class. (Far right) A ceramic mug emblazoned with the White Star Line logo.

sions were two starboard aft freezers on the orlop deck, one for westbound meat, the other for eastbound meat. A separate room was reserved for thawing.

Titanic's crew also fared well in the midst of such plenty. Diets for shipboard workers were established by the British Board of Trade, which specified everything from minimun weekly quantities of meat and vegetables to a ration of tea.

Because Titanic's hull broke in two between the third and fourth funnels in an area near the galleys, many utensils and tableware items were found in the debris field. Those recovered to date represent a small sample of the varied equipment that helped to make every meal aboard the great White Star liners a special one.

This porcelain cup-and-saucer set (right) was one of many that graced the ship's first-class dining saloon. (Far right) A faience pot with floral decoration and the White Star logo.

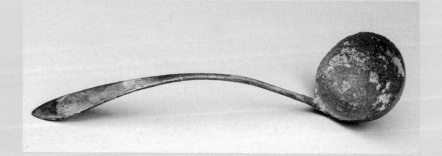

The plain design of this silver-plated ladle hints at its function as a kitchen or third-class utility serving piece.

(Left) A nickel and copper-alloy cooking pot from one of Titanic's kitchens.

(Right) A glass candy dish used in first class. (Far right) A ceramic mug emblazoned with the White Star Line logo.

This porcelain cup-and-saucer set (right) was one of many that graced the ship's first-class dining saloon. (Far right) A faience pot with floral decoration and the White Star logo.

sions were two starboard aft freezers on the orlop deck, one for westbound meat, the other for eastbound meat. A separate room was reserved for thawing.

Titanic's crew also fared well in the midst of such plenty. Diets for shipboard workers were established by the British Board of Trade, which specified everything from minimun weekly quantities of meat and vegetables to a ration of tea.

Because Titanic's hull broke in two between the third and fourth funnels in an area near the galleys, many utensils and tableware items were found in the debris field. Those recovered to date represent a small sample of the varied equipment that helped to make every meal aboard the great White Star liners a special one.

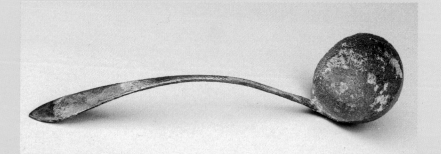

The plain design of this silver-plated ladle hints at its function as a kitchen or third-class utility serving piece.

ing with family and with people from the same country more than compensated for the lack of opulence. For some, these modest surroundings were an improvement on those from which they came.

The cabins, library, dining saloon, and open deck space in second class provided amenities unheard of in first-class accommodations of twenty years earlier. While more passengers were assigned to a given space than in first class, second-class cabins and rooms were tastefully appointed.

Shortly before 11:30 A.M., the first-class boat train arrived dockside after its 140-minute trip from Waterloo Station. Many second- and third-class passengers crowded the open decks and rails to watch the first-class travelers board. After climbing the gently sloping gangway, first-class passengers walked through twin metal doors that opened to the sumptuous entrance hall on the forward B deck. The hall's oak paneling was illuminated by natural light that flooded through an elegant iron-and-glass

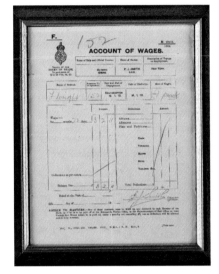

White Star provided stable employment, and hired only the best staff. This account of wages was for Titanic *crewman Fred Wright, for service on* Olympic *under Captain Smith. Wright did not survive.*

dome. The sunlit air was warm, and the hall was filled with the aroma of newly polished wood and metal. Travelers were greeted upon entry, many by name. The three elevators in first class were in constant use as stewards escorted passengers to their cabins.

From deep in the ship, a gentle vibration began reverberating softly but continuously through every cabin and corridor. The awesome power of *Titanic*'s mighty engines was about to be unleashed.

By noon, it was nearly time to sail. Captain Smith and harbor pilot George Bowyer stood on the bridge. Bowyer had been a pilot at Southampton Harbor for thirty years and would accompany the ship through the port. The ship's officers were at their stations fore and aft. Orders received from the navigating bridge via the docking bridge telegraph were relayed by Third Officer Pitman to First Officer Murdoch, who oversaw the boatswain and his crew as they manned the mooring lines and tugboat hawsers.

(Illustration preceding pages) Simon Fisher, Titanic Arriving Cherbourg, Wednesday, April 10, 1912, *oil on canvas, 1996. Courtesy of the artist.*

This claim check, along with a clarinet, a diary, and items indicating a trip from New York to Australia, was recovered from the luggage of Howard Irwin, who does not appear on Titanic *passenger lists. A friend, Henry Sutehall, was lost on* Titanic. *Irwin's fate remains a mystery.*

The tender Nomadic (right), which carried first- and second-class passengers to Titanic *at Cherbourg, survives as a Paris restaurant moored on the River Seine.*

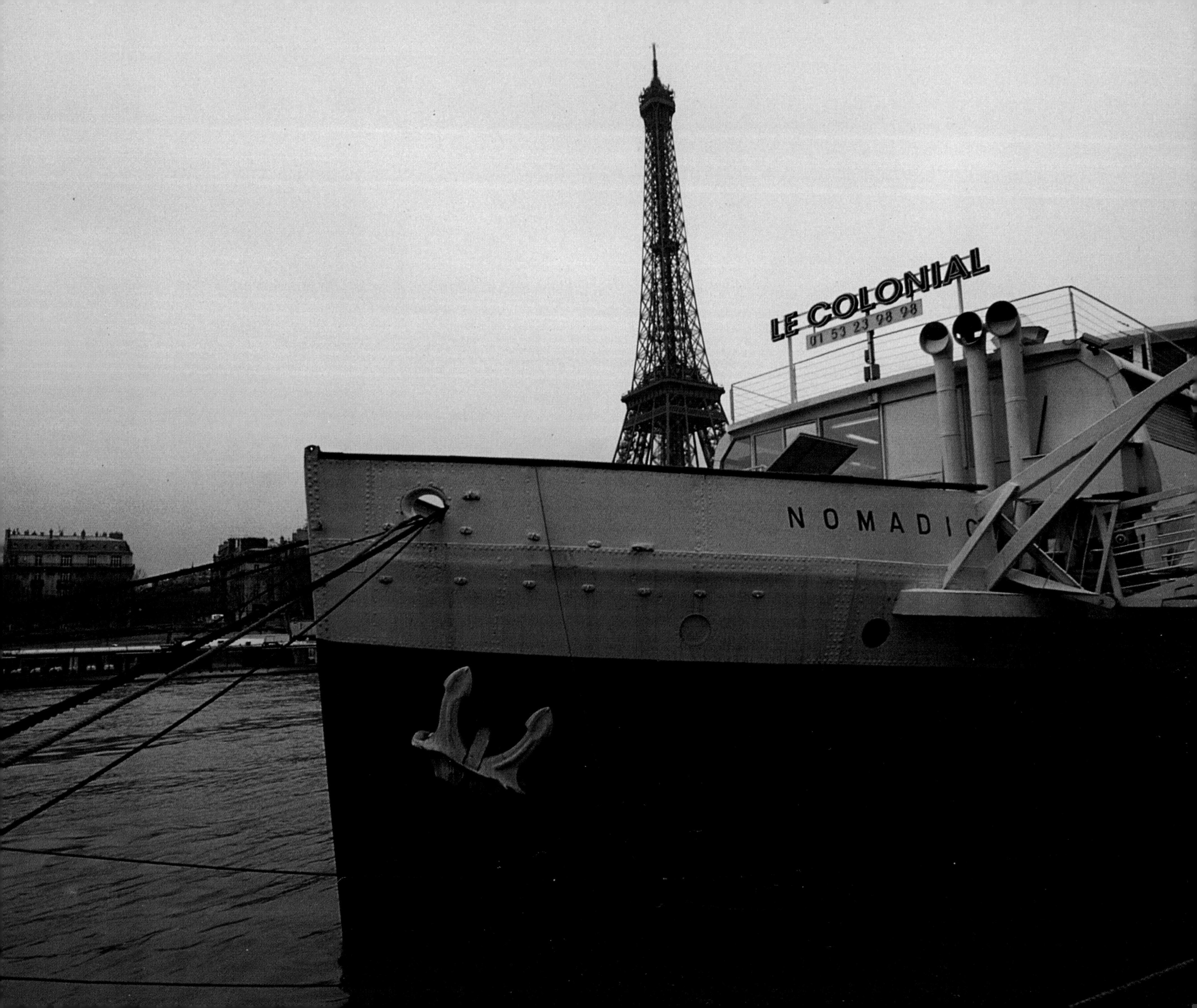
LE COLONIAL
01 53 23 98 98
NOMADIC

Three blasts of the liner's mighty whistles on each of her four funnels sounded across the harbor and the city of Southampton. Sixth Officer Moody was prepared to haul in the narrow aft gangway when six figures came running down the dock: two stokers, Shaw and Holden; Brewer, a trimmer; and three brothers, Bertram, Tom, and Alfred Slade. After signing on early that morning, the men had gone to a nearby pub to enjoy a pre-sail drink or two. As they rushed toward the dock entrance, their path was blocked by a long freight train.

Moody hesitated. Should he lower the gangplank? He did not, and the six men looked on as *Titanic*'s great hull moved away from the dock's edge. On board, the six had already been replaced from among a muster of standbys. The remainder of standbys were discharged and left the ship a short while later.

Loosed from her fore and aft moorings and held fast by six tugs, the immense liner was pulled away from the dock and into a turning circle at the end of the pier. After maneuvering her through a 90° turn to port, the tugs cast off. A bell in the engine room indicated "ahead slow," and *Titanic* set off down the River Test.

Downriver, a near disaster lurked. Moored at berth 38, out of service due to the recently ended coal strike, were the liners *Oceanic* and *New York*. The massive water displacement brought by *Titanic*'s passing caused the mooring ropes on *New York* to slacken, then tighten and snap, and the smaller liner's stern began to arc toward *Titanic*. A collision was averted only by the quick thinking of pilot Bowyer, who had been with Captain Smith aboard *Olympic* during her September 1911 collision with HMS *Hawke* at Southampton, also caused by *Olympic*'s passing. Bowyer signaled "stop engines" and then "full a' stern." As an added precaution, Captain Smith ordered the starboard anchor partially lowered. The master of the tug *Vulcan*, which moments before had helped to move *Titanic* from her berth, hurriedly threw a line aboard

White Star tender Traffic *(far left), which carried third-class passengers to* Titanic *at Cherbourg; (near left) Michael V. Ralph,* Cherbourg Departure, *acrylic on canvas, 1992. Courtesy of the artist.*

Emigrants waiting to embark at Queenstown (right). All third-class passengers were required to be examined by a doctor prior to boarding.

New York. The line broke. A second line held, and *Vulcan* pulled *New York* clear of *Titanic,* which was already backing up. At one point the two liners were separated by only a few feet.

After more than an hour's delay, *Titanic* recommenced her journey. The American flag, symbolizing the liner's final destination, billowed from the foremast as *Titanic* moved into open water. Pilot Bowyer was dropped off at the Nab Light Vessel. Ship's bugler P. W. Fletcher went from deck to deck, summoning passengers to lunch. The vessel steamed across the English Channel toward her first stop: Cherbourg, 67 miles southeast.

A lifeboat slung out from Titanic's *deck at Queenstown (left). In the last known photograph taken of him, Captain Smith looks down from above.*

(Right) Titanic *off Cowes after leaving Queenstown, one of the last known photographs of her.*

Larry S. Anderson

chapter four

LIFE ON BOARD

At a speed of 15 knots, it would take more than four hours for *Titanic* to cross the English Channel. In the first- and second-class galley and in the two pantries adjacent to the first- and second-class dining saloons on D deck, Chef Proctor and his staff of sixty-eight cooks, bakers, and butchers and eleven pantrymen were in the midst of serving the midday meal. They had been preparing the luncheon since early morning.

Stockpots, saucepans, and a variety of frying and sauté pans simmered and boiled atop large coal-fed ovens and stoves. Passengers dined on scrumptious steak-and-kidney pie, fillet of plaice, and roast Surrey capon. Platters of lobster, shrimp, roast beef, and Cumberland ham were attractively arranged for the buffet. A consommé jardinière was ladled out of huge silvered tureens on service tables throughout the dining saloons.

Below, on F deck, a typical lunch was

A bronze cherub (above, detail) was found in the debris field near the stern section of the wreck, indicating that it may have come from the aft grand staircase.

served to third-class passengers from a separate galley and in two dining rooms. The menu was not fancy but satisfying: rice soup, corned beef and cabbage, boiled potatoes, and for dessert, peaches and rice.

The ship continued toward Cherbourg, where 274 passengers waited to embark. Many had departed at 9:40 A.M. from Gare St. Lazare in Paris for the six-hour ride to the coast on the Train Transatlantique. Upon arrival, however, they were informed that embarkation on the two White Star tenders to *Titanic* would be delayed by at least one hour.

By 5:30 P.M., passengers had assembled, somewhat grumpily, at Cherbourg's Gare Maritime. One-hundred-and-seventy-two first- and second-class travelers boarded the tender *Nomadic*, while 102 third-class passengers—predominantly Russians, Serbs, and others from the Near East—filled barely one-quarter of the available space on the tender *Traffic*. Shortly after 6 P.M., *Titanic* appeared around the point of the roadstead. At 6:30 P.M. the anchor was dropped as the ship's starboard side faced the shore.

Nomadic discharged her 142 first-class

Larry S. Anderson, Grand Staircase, watercolor on paper, 1996. Courtesy of the artist.

(Illustration preceeding spread) The most lavish feature of first-class accommodation was the forward grand staircase. Crowned by a wrought iron and glass dome, the staircase featured polished oak panelling and elaborate gilt balustrades. The centerpiece of the staircase was a clock on the uppermost landing flanked by classical figures representing Honor and Glory crowning Time.

Placed throughout Titanic's open deck spaces were a number of wooden benches with ornate, delicately handcrafted copper-alloy supports. The wooden sections of the benches found in the debris field have long since been degraded by bacteria or devoured by shipworm mollusks, but the copper-alloy supports have endured (right).

(Far right and following page) Hank Blaustein, Boat Deck of the Titanic, April 11, 1912, Queenstown, watercolor on paper, 1993. Courtesy of the artist.

First-Class Staterooms

Titanic's *lavish first-class state-rooms B64 (right), B57 (below center), and B60 (below, far right).*

(Below) Initials on the exterior of this box indicate that its owner may have been first-class passenger Richard L. Beckwith.

(Above) First-class suite bedroom B59.

(Right) This gilded grille covered a heating duct in first class.

A black bow tie (top) was indispensable for a gentleman's dinner dress aboard Titanic.

(Above) A fashionable 18-karat gold pocket watch.

One of the most stunning pieces of jewelry recovered from the ocean floor is this sapphire-and-diamond ring (left). Also shown is an 18-karat gold ring featuring one large and 76 small diamonds. An inscription indicates that it was presented to its unknown owner on June 9, 1910.

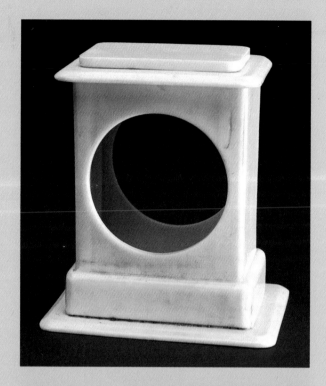

(Center left) A pair of gold, onyx, and diamond cuff links.

An imitation ivory mirror holder and hair brush set (bottom right) bears the inscription, "Royale Ivoire France." The set, along with a clock case (top right), are made of an early plastic called Bakelite.

A fountain pen (left) with a 14-karat gold nib bears an American patent date of February 27, 1906.

The design of this silver-plated lamp (above), a prominent feature of many first-class cabins, dates back to a time when many state-rooms were lit by candles. The gimbal mounting ensured that the candle remained level no matter how rough the seas.

(Right) Cuff links and a box in which to store them were a standard feature of any gentleman's wardrobe.

passengers through the double-door entrance into the reception room forward on D deck. Thirty second-class passengers boarded through an entrance aft on E deck. After *Traffic* arrived, third-class travelers entered through a large door forward on E deck. Many second- and third-class passengers had to walk more than two-thirds of the ship's length to reach their cabins. First-class passengers were more fortunate; most of their state-rooms were located adjacent to the D-deck entrance.

Fifteen first-class and nine second-class passengers deboarded the ship at Cherbourg. Their names were not on any published White Star Line passenger list, though they did appear on the company's ticketing list.

Around 8 P.M., the tenders departed for their onshore stations. Ten minutes later the anchor was drawn up. Using her wing propellers to make a tight reverse turn, *Titanic* headed seaward under darkening skies toward her next destination, Queenstown, on Ireland's southeastern coast.

Night descended on the brilliantly lit

ship as passengers strolled the decks prior to the evening meal. Some paused to sit on the wooden benches along each promenade and gaze out at the passing sea. First-class strollers on A deck aft walked by the Verandah Café and Palm Court. Its cheery lights and ivy-laden trellises beckoned them to enjoy a pre-dinner drink. With the disappearance of the warm land air, the spring night turned cool.

At 7:30, P. W. Fletcher's bugle announced the dinner hour. As first-class passengers descended the grand staircase to the D-deck reception room, the ship's orchestra regaled them with popular musical compositions of the day and standard salon music. A festive air ensued as ladies and gentlemen, elegantly clad in formal attire, gathered around the wicker settees and barrel chairs upholstered in stunning peacock blue. The meal was no doubt enlivened by the consumption of a portion of the 1,500 bottles of wine, 850 bottles of spirits, and 20,000 bottles of beer, ale, and stout packed in storage rooms far below.

Due to fatigue from a long journey to

First-Class Promenades

It is difficult to determine who owned this bracelet (below), which originally held 26 gems; two are missing. At least two ladies called Amy were aboard Titanic. There was also a woman named Amelia and another named Amanda.

(Below right) A silver hairpin with a chinese ideogram.

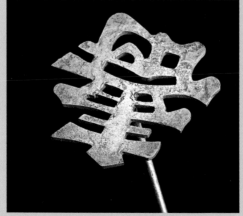

The entrance (above) to the private first-class promenade of the starboard suite B51, 53, and 55, the most palatial accommodation on Titanic. (Right) Private promenade for suites B52, 54, and 56, occupied by Bruce Ismay.

S.S. "TITANIC"
PROMENADE DECK

Second-Class Staterooms

(Right) An illustration of a typical second-class stateroom.

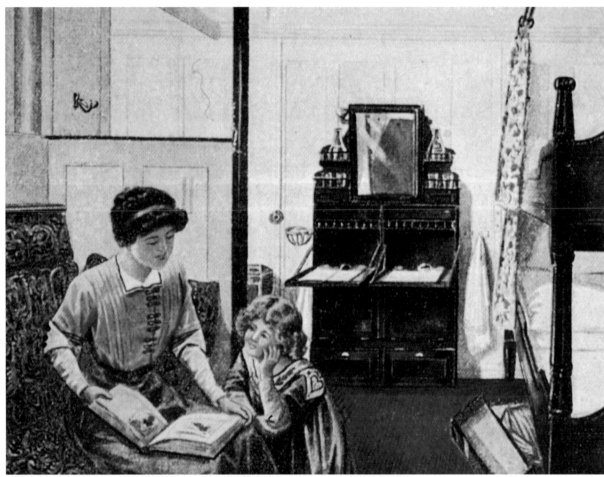

This basin (above) was once attached to a wooden cabinet found in Titanic's second-class cabins. Each morning, a steward poured fresh water into a tank in the cabinet's upper compartment. Passengers filled the basin, washed, then tipped the basin into the cabinet, emptying the used water into the tank below for collection by the steward.

Few staterooms had flushing lavatories, even in first class, so chamber pots (left) like these (9.25" x 7.67" x 4.52") were used in passenger cabins.

Ceiling light sockets were surrounded by sculpted ceramic fixtures (above). Among other places on the ship, the pattern on these fixtures was found in the second-class lounge.

(Below) A necklace made of gold nuggets.

the docking station and to the hurried activity involved in boarding a great liner, the first night out was usually a short one for passengers. *Titanic*'s first night out was no different. Save for some inveterate card players huddled in the smoking rooms and a few younger passengers renewing old friendships and perhaps trying to form new ones, the onboard activity quickly quieted down following the evening meal. By 11 P.M., the corridors and public rooms were still, save for creaks in the felt caulking and the ever-present murmur of the mighty engines.

Dawn the next day was clear and bright. Early risers took a dip in the plunge bath on the starboard side of F deck, adjacent to the first funnel's uptake. They then exercised in the gymnasium or played squash in the court on G deck under the helpful tutelage of staff squash professional Fred Wright. Breakfast, served between 8 and 10 A.M., was well attended. The sea was smooth and the liner was not

This porcelain sprinkler is among the most poignant objects from the wreck site. It was either a treasured souvenir or a gift en route to the New World.

rolling. During the course of the morning, *Titanic* made a number of turns to adjust her several compasses, leaving behind a serpentine wake in St. George's Channel.

Near morning's end, *Titanic* slowed to pick up the harbor pilot at the light vessel, then approached the entrance to Queenstown Harbor. About two miles from the town quay, *Titanic* dropped anchor off Roche's Point. Soon the smoke from *America* and *Ireland* could be seen trailing in the distance as the two tenders moved toward the stationary liner.

A party of six—Lily Odell, her daughter and son, two brothers named May, and a young teacher, Francis Browne, who was studying for the Jesuit priesthood—prepared to disembark. A seventh man, Mr. Nichols, also readied himself to depart.

The tenders, ferrying 120 passengers and mail destined for America, were soon alongside *Titanic*. Seven second-class and 113

Third-Class Cabins

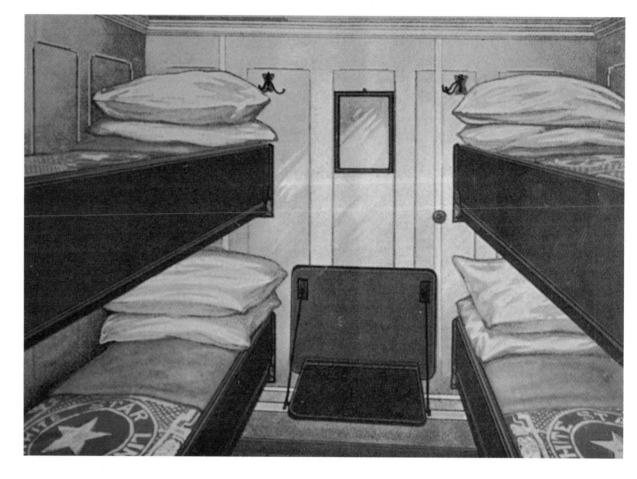

Third-class cabins like the one illustrated at right were small but agreeable. Titanic's third-class accommodations were the most comfortable of any liner of its day.

This leather suitcase (right) might have been carried by a passenger in any class. Organic materials begin to shrink once exposed to air and must be kept wet prior to restoration and conservation. Titanic's passengers included craftsmen of all trades. Their tools (far right) were as varied as their occupations. This and other tools were found in the luggage of a passenger who was probably a leather worker.

This thick-walled drinking glass was used by crew members in working and living quarters.

third-class passengers boarded. Among the latter there was an air of sadness: Many of these travelers were leaving behind not only their beloved countries, but also their mothers, fathers, families, and lifetime friends.

Joining one of the returning tenders and socializing with those on board was *Titanic* crew member John Coffey, a twenty-four-year-old stoker who happened to reside in Queenstown. His absence was not noted for many hours.

As *Titanic* weighed anchor and began her departing turn, passengers bid farewell to their homeland and loved ones. The sound of Irish pipes emanated from *Titanic*'s aft deck; third-class passenger Eugene Daly was playing the dirge "Erin's Lament." Shortly after 1:30 P.M., *Titanic*'s voice was heard as the "three hails of farewell" resonated from the brass throats of her twelve whistles.

The pilot was again dropped off at the light vessel, and *Titanic* made a wide, sweeping

From a long, thin silver chain hangs a pendant on which are embedded 68 clear gems, with an additional six gems on the connecting loop.

starboard arc and headed back down St. George's Channel. Afternoon faded to twilight as the green hills of Ireland began to vanish from sight astern. A French fishing trawler, a link to the Old World, passed close to the enormous liner and dipped her colors in salute. *Titanic* responded with a whistle blast, ordered by the watch officer.

The Old World slipped away as the ship turned her bow westward, the gentle Atlantic swells surrounding the liner as she moved toward her fate.

Even before disaster struck, *Titanic*'s unprecedented scale, premier interior design, and standard-setting amenities had made the ship an international legend in its own time. Life at sea could be as relaxed or as hectic as the traveler desired. Unlike today, there was no formally planned entertainment. In every class, conversation, letter writing, card playing, reading, and contemplating the next meal were the principal diversions.

In the general room in third class, far

Shipboard Activities

Those who have traveled aboard modern cruise ships probably recall their journey as being filled with nonstop activities ranging from bingo games to ice-sculpting demonstrations, from fitness lessons to trapshooting off the stern. Entertainment aboard *Titanic* was simpler. Passengers were largely left to while the time away on their own. *Titanic*'s orchestra gave daily concerts in first and second class, while the third-class general room featured a piano for passenger use. Libraries in first and second class were open from 8 A.M. until 11:30 P.M. and contained books provided by the *Times* of London's book service.

Physical fitness was as popular then as it is today. Turkish and electric baths on F deck were open to first-class women between 10 A.M. and 1 P.M., and from 2 to 6 P.M. for first-class men. Admission was $1, a considerable sum in 1912, and included use of the adjacent indoor swimming pool, among the first on the North Atlantic.

(Above) Olympic's pool. Few photographs were taken of Titanic. Images of her sister ship are often the best indication of Titanic's appointments.

(Right) A ticket to the Turkish bath.

The electric saddle (right) and the rowing machine (far right) were popular forms of exercise in the gym.

WHITE STAR LINE.

R.M.S. "TITANIC."

This ticket entitles bearer to use of Turkish or Electric Bath on one occasion.

Paid 4/- or 1 Dollar.

WHITE STAR LINE.

R.M.S. "TITANIC."

This ticket entitles bearer to use of Turkish or Electric Bath on one occasion.

Paid 4/- or 1 Dollar.

In the gymnasium on the boat deck, the latest in sports equipment was in almost constant use. Gym hours matched those of the Turkish baths; special hours for children were scheduled between 1 and 3 P.M.

For those more athletically inclined, G deck's squash court could be reserved for 50¢ an hour.

Informal card games in the smoking rooms, games on deck, a daily auction pool—all were components of *Titanic*'s on-board activities. By modern standards, however, the first four days of *Titanic*'s only voyage were quiet ones indeed.

From the ship's commander to the last scullion, company employees were strictly prohibited from gambling. Passengers, however, were free to participate in games of chance with casual or high stakes. Manufactured by the U.S. Playing Card Co., these cards display the "Steamboat 999" pattern.

The third-class general room (below left), with white enamelled walls and pine frames, featured a piano for passenger entertainment. This barber shop on *Olympic* (below) closely resembled *Titanic*'s. There were two on the liner, one for first class and one for second class. This would also be the place to buy souvenirs of the voyage.

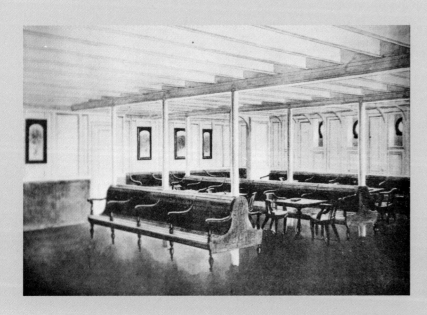

aft on C deck, women assembled with their children and engaged in conversation, sewing, and other social activities. For the men, there was a nearby smoking and card room with an adjacent bar, paneled in oak with teak furniture. Spittoons were strategically placed throughout the room.

Many of *Titanic*'s passengers would have brought their own forms of entertainment, including fiddles, musettes, accordions, and Irish pipes, resulting in long evening hours spent in impromptu sessions of singing and dancing.

Second-class passengers enjoyed a splendid library paneled in sycamore. Mahogany furniture upholstered in tapestry was placed throughout the room, and tall windows with silk curtains looked out onto the promenade. The dining saloon on D deck was decorated in early English style with oak paneling. Each table seated four to eight for a total of 394. Oak paneling and furniture upholstered in dark green leather dominated the smoking room on B deck aft. Cabins were light and airy, finished in white enamel with mahogany furniture. Some cabins had carpeted floors, others had linoleum tile. The overall effect was one of solid, middle-class comfort.

Electric heaters, individually controlled by the passenger, were a welcome feature of first-class staterooms. No detail was too small, no comfort was overlooked. The cabins had eight- to nine-foot-high ceilings, brass-framed windows, richly carved wood, thick carpeting, and magnificent chandeliers and light fixtures.

Perhaps no public area typifies *Titanic*'s dedication to superiority than the Verandah Café and Palm Court, located in rooms on the port and starboard sides of A deck, and the à la carte restaurant on B deck. Although not innovative, these elegant spaces represented the epitome of refinement and sophistication in North Atlantic travel in the Edwardian era. The port-side Verandah Café was connected to the smoking room by a revolving door. The starboard side of the café could be entered only from the promenade

Natural bristles are a feature of this painted wooden brush.

(Left) The profile of a youthful Queen Victoria adorns the lid to this toothpaste jar, its contents "fit for a queen."

An AutoStrop safety razor (far left), and a container of blades (left), both remarkably well-preserved.

A bottle of hair tonic (below, far left), the label still intact.

An assortment of bottles and stoppers (below) that may have come from the ship's dispensary.

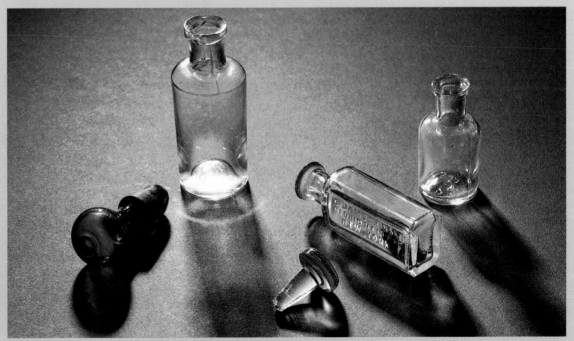

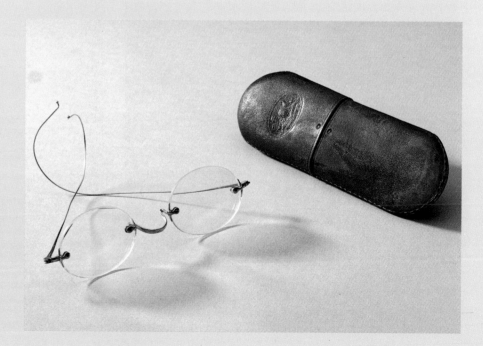

A pair of size 9 overshoes, (left) manufactured by the Old Colony Rubber Company of Boston.

(Far left) Stewards may have used this brush to polish passengers' shoes, left in the ship's corridors for cleaning.

Leather and metal coverings (far left) are all that remain of a common travel accessory in 1912, a flask typically used for alcohol.

These eyeglasses and their case (left), owner unknown, are among the most personal of the items retrieved from the wreck of Titanic.

deck. Each room opened to the promenade, but sliding doors could close them off in inclement weather. Twelve-foot-high windows, framed in intricately shaped bronze, provided an open vista of sea and sky.

Inside the café, ivy and other plants covered green-painted trellises between the windows. Small tables and wicker chairs upholstered in red and brown fabric dotted the room. Floors were covered with brown-and-buff tile in a checkerboard design. Here, one could relax and enjoy morning coffee or afternoon tea, a cup of bouillon, or hot chocolate served from a silver pot. At the adjacent bar, passengers sipped pre-dinner drinks or a final brandy before bed.

Perhaps the most comfortable and intimate space aboard *Titanic* was the à la carte restaurant on B deck aft of the fourth funnel. Open from 8 A.M. to 11 P.M., the restaurant offered

Perhaps a family gift, perhaps a souvenir, this ceramic figurine of a little Dutch boy and wooden shoe survived the destructive forces of Titanic's sinking.

meals at fixed prices shown on special menu cards issued each day. Reservations were made with the restaurant's manager, Luigi Gatti.

Augmenting the à la carte restaurant was the Café Parisien. Small-paned windows and ivy-covered trellises helped create a serene spot to enjoy food prepared and served out of a galley and pantry separate from the rest of the ship.

Before meals in the à la carte restaurant, diners gathered in a spacious reception room furnished with chairs and settees caned and upholstered in carmine silk and embroidered fabric. The restaurant itself measured approximately 50 by 70 feet and seated 141. It was decorated in the style of Louis XVI and paneled in fawn-colored French walnut. Rose-colored carpeting complemented the fifty-four walnut tables. Atop each table sat a pink-shaded lamp.

Dishes used in the à la carte restaurant featured a special design: wide, dark blue rims with a Greek key design in sparkling gold and white. In the dish's glazed, bone-white center was the gold, interwoven monogram *OSNC*, which stood for Oceanic Steam Navigation Company, White Star's corporate name.

Food was superb and cooked to order, accompanied by the finest wines and champagnes from the restaurant's own wine room. Fresh fruit and flowers from an adjacent cool room enhanced all meals. The staff was specially recruited from two famous London restaurants, Gatti's and Gatti's Adelphi. Although the staff was under White Star supervision, having signed ship's articles, they remained a separate working unit from the general crew.

Titanic departed Queenstown with, as near as can be determined, 337 first-class, 271 second-class, and 712 third-class passengers, and 908 crew, for a total of 2,228. Her fourteen lifeboats, two cutters, and four collapsibles could seat 1,178, an amount that exceeded archaic British Board of Trade requirements,

set in 1894, by more than 17 percent. Apart from the ship's officers, few people aboard, including most of the crew, were aware of the situation. And no one, including passenger J. Bruce Ismay, chairman of the White Star Line and thus *Titanic*'s nominal owner, seemed to care.

Between noon on Wednesday, April 10, and noon on April 11, during the ship's "inland voyage" from Southampton to Cherbourg to Queenstown, *Titanic* logged 404 miles. By noon on April 12, *Titanic* had traveled 386 more miles. Between noon on Saturday, April 13, and noon on Sunday, April 14, 546 miles had been logged. The mighty engines were being let out a bit more each day, and there was a rumor that all boilers would be lit for a speed run on Monday.

Wireless messages brought reports of icebergs and ice fields between 41° and 43° north and 49° to 51° west—directly in *Titanic*'s westbound path. As the messages were received, they were posted on the bridge: April 12, *Empress of Britain* and *La Tourraine*, both

The design on this cup (above) does not match any known White Star Line pattern. It may have been among a passenger's personal possessions.

This platter (left) bears a pattern also not found on White Star Line inventories for any period and is probably from the ship's cargo or a passenger's household property.

Like today, many passengers would have carried postcards from their travels abroad, kept as souvenirs or mailed on board. These two postcards (left) were among the many well-preserved paper artifacts found at the site. *Titanic* carried nearly 3,500 bags of mail. A large part of the profit made by White Star liners came from the mail they carried between continents.

(Above) In the age of transatlantic steamship travel, enterpeneurs from the great trusts and small businessmen alike used the social atmosphere of the voyage to make new contacts. Among the items recovered from the debris field were a number of business cards.

eastbound. April 14, *Noordam*, eastbound, and *Athinai*, westbound, the latter received via White Star's *Baltic*. This last warning was received at 1:42 P.M. Its posting on the bridge was delayed when Captain Smith handed the message to Ismay, who kept it to show to several friends until Smith requested its return around 7 P.M.

The weather had been clear and sunny but surprisingly cool. Few passengers braved the open decks, and even fewer reclined outdoors on the folding deck chairs. Almost all activities took place indoors. The libraries, smoking rooms, verandah cafés (closed to the chilly sea air), and the third-class general room became magnets. Businessmen and commercial travelers exchanged cards and discussed money, business conditions, and world affairs. The conviviality reached its zenith, and feelings of warmth, safety, anticipation, and general goodwill abounded.

Personal belongings began to take on new meaning. Such prosaic articles as fountain pens and cigarette cases, hair brushes and combs, hand mirrors, jewelry, travel clocks, pocket watches, datebooks, and postcards were a link to the lives and routines many passengers had left behind. Such mundane objects from the Old World might later be remembered nostalgically in the New.

As *Titanic* steamed ahead, her passengers, like all travelers, would have kept a close eye on these common but significant symbols of their identities.

Third Officer Herbert Pitman, who survived as the leader of lifeboat number 5, bought this sea chest in Bristol, England, in 1895. The chest was not aboard Titanic.

Profiles of Privilege

Archibald Butt was a military aide and dear friend to President Taft. Upon hearing of the tragedy, Taft sent a ship to contact Carpathia *regarding Butt's fate.*

Clad each night in elegant tuxedos and spectacular gowns, first-class passengers must have found the oak steps of *Titanic*'s resplendent grand stairs a natural showcase for the elite. Under the huge glass-and-wrought-iron dome, the world's wealthiest and most influential people made their entrances and exits. *Titanic*'s first-class passenger list read like a Who's Who of 1912. On board for what would be her only voyage were the following notables:

- Archibald W. Butt, President William Howard Taft's military aide-de-camp.
- George D. Widener, president of the Philadelphia streetcar system, his wife, Eleanor, and son, Harry.
- Benjamin Guggenheim, mining and smelting magnate.
- Dorothy Gibson, star of stage and silent movies.
- John Jacob Astor, New York real estate mogul, and his nineteen-year-old second wife, Madeleine.
- John B. Thayer, second vice president of the Pennsylvania Railroad, his wife, Marian, and seventeen-year-old son, Jack.
- Henry B. Harris, theater impresario, and his wife, René.
- Archibald Gracie, West Point graduate and military historian.
- William T. Stead, British spiritualist, evangelist, and editor.
- Francis Davis Millet, noted American painter.
- Albert A. Stewart, significant partner in the Barnum & Bailey Circus.
- Charles M. Hayes, president of the Grand Trunk Railroad of Canada.
- Jacques Futrelle, mystery writer, and his wife, May.
- Washington A. Roebling 2nd, son of the builder of the Brooklyn Bridge.
- Isidor Straus, a partner in Macy's Department Store, and his wife, Ida.
- R. Norris Williams II, winner of the Davis Cup in tennis.
- The Countess of Rothes, Scotland.
- Mrs. James Joseph ("Molly") Brown, wife of a Denver millionaire and philanthropist.

Their wealth and fame made these and other first-class passengers aboard *Titanic* instantly recognizable, but it did not guarantee their safety. Sixty percent of those in first class survived, the highest percentage for any group on board.

Colonel Archibald Gracie was able to save himself by swimming to overturned collapsible B. He later wrote a book about the disaster but died before it was published.

The Kitchen

A kitchen similar to this one on Olympic *provided service to both first- and second-class passengers aboard* Titanic.

This ribbed red tile is believed to have been found in Titanic's *galley areas, where the nonskid surface would have been useful. Each tile is labeled "Quality B" by its manufacturer, J. C. Edwards.*

The ravages of time, exposure, and acidity in the sediment on the ocean floor have taken their toll on this badly corroded cooking pot (right) made of nickel, copper alloy, and iron.

Olive jar (far right).

First-Class Dining

This breakfast mug and saucer were used in the first-class dining room. In many instances, the action of fine sediment in the ocean current has gently effaced White Star logos and decorative trim from dinnerware.

Crafted specifically for Olympic and Titanic, this silver chocolate pot was used in first class. Titanic's first-class service is also reflected in the fine silver sauce boat with vermeil interior at left.

(Above) The opulent first-class dining saloon.

A fine example of the silversmith's art, this serving dish (left) was made especially for use in first class aboard Olympic and Titanic. Of the many silver-plated items recovered from Titanic, this dish, along with a chocolate pot and sauce boat (previous page), were among those least corroded by chlorides.

Silver tray (above, far left).

This soup plate (upper right) came from the first-class dining saloon.

Vases such as this one (left), filled with flowers, were likely used to add a luxurious touch to Titanic's first-class public areas.

(Left) The only known photograph of Titanic's first-class dining room, taken during lunch, April 11, 1912.

À La Carte Dining

(Left) The popular and elegant à la carte restaurant where the ship's elite enjoyed such delicacies as oysters, squab, and chocolate éclairs.

This candy dish (far left) was used in first class.

Diners in Titanic's à la carte restaurant enjoyed coffee served in a delicate demitasse cup and saucer (left).

Passengers dining in the first-class à la carte restaurant were charged extra for their meals. Waiters recorded these charges on check forms like this one, expertly restored under carefully controlled conditions.

Second-Class Dining

Second-class meals came from the same kitchen as first-class and were nearly as elaborate. Olympic's second-class dining room is shown at right.

This shallow soup bowl (below left) and accompanying plate were used in the second-class dining saloon.

This cut crystal jam pot, or compote dish (right), would have been a common sight at the ship's breakfast tables.

Third-Class Dining

Third-class passengers enjoyed simple but hearty fare served in two dining rooms located amidship on F deck.

The pattern on this saucer is found on dinnerware aboard White Star Line vessels of an earlier vintage. Since basic dinnerware was typically reused from ship to ship, in 1912 it was probably a part of Titanic's third-class table service.

The utilitarian appearance of this carafe suggests that it was used in Titanic's third-class dining areas.

Food, Glorious Food

The handful of *Titanic* menus still in existence today reveals why strolls on the deck and visits to the gymnasium and the swimming pools were popular. The ship's four dining areas were open for much of the day: 8:30 to 10:30 A.M. for breakfast, 1 to 2:30 P.M. for luncheon, and 6 to 7:30 P.M. for dinner, followed by a late tea. Each class had its own restaurant, and meals were included in the fare.

The two third-class dining rooms were located amidships on F deck. For perhaps the first time in their lives, third-class passengers—themselves often the servants of others—enjoyed being waited on by attentive stewards. Food in third class was plain but ample. Typical menus included oatmeal porridge and smoked herring for breakfast; pea soup, fricassee rabbit, and bacon for dinner; and cod fish cakes, cheese, and pickles for tea.

In second class, the menu was more

This full jar of olives miraculously survived eight decades on the ocean floor.

extensive. Dinner might feature consommé tapioca; a choice of baked haddock, curried chicken, spring lamb, or roast turkey; a variety of vegetables; and plum pudding or ice cream for dessert. The second-class dining saloon, aft on D deck, was serviced by the same galley that supplied the first-class dining saloon on D deck amidships. The latter was a gastronome's paradise, with elaborate menu choices served by the most experienced stewards. One luncheon menu boasted no fewer than five entrées and a buffet with sixteen other dishes.

For those with even more exacting tastes and an ever-present appetite, both *Olympic* and *Titanic* offered an extra-tariff, à la carte restaurant on B deck aft, open from 8 A.M. to 11 P.M. Here, surrounded by fawn-colored walnut paneling and rose-colored carpeting, the ship's elite dined on such delicacies as oysters, filet mignon, roast duckling, squab, and chocolate eclairs.

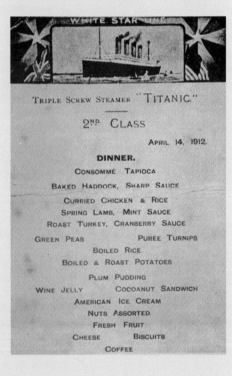

Just hours before disaster struck, diners in first and second class enjoyed selections from the menus above.

Café Dining

The Café Parisien (right) was a favorite meeting place for many of the ship's first-class passengers. It was designed to re-create the atmosphere of a Parisian boulevard café. Service was provided by French waiters. The enclosed Verandah Café and Palm Court (below)—actually two rooms on either side of the ship—featured ivy-covered trellises and large windows with a panoramic view of the sea.

First-Class Lounge

In the first-class lounge (right), passengers relaxed over a cup of tea or a game of cards.

Second-Class Lounge

The second-class lounge (right) featured sycamore panelling and upholstered mahogany furniture.

Cut crystal carafes like these (below) bearing the White Star logo could be found throughout first- and second-class areas.

(Left) A soda bottle.

(Right) A favorite after-dinner drink aboard Titanic was Benedictine liqueur.

(Above) Olympic's second-class
staircase and elevators.

Repeated in positive and negative
patterns, tiles like this one (right)
covered the floors of some second-
and third-class public areas.

Another of the remarkably well-
preserved textiles found at the site,
this men's tie (above) probably sig-
nified membership in a club or col-
lege association.

Smoking Rooms

Smoking rooms were found in each class aboard Titanic. Smoking in cabins and many other public rooms was prohibited. Men in first class gathered for a drink or a cigar in the Georgian smoking room (right), aft on A deck.

A pipe recovered from Titanic in 1987 (below center) still contained remnants of tobacco. Cigarette holders (below far right) were popular among smokers who wished to avoid staining their fingers with tobacco. The spittoon below, emblazoned with the White Star flag, is from the third-class smoking room.

Titanic's second-class accommodations were like first class on most other liners of the time. The second-class smoking room on Olympic (below), with its carved oak panelling, closely resembled that of Titanic.

On-board smoking was an activity almost exclusively enjoyed by males. While cigarettes were common, cigars were the tobacco of choice. Miraculously, after more than eight decades of submersion in corrosive conditions, J. Ackerhalt's "Turkish No. 1" tobacco in these cigarettes (right) still survives. Many smokers carried their own blend of tobacco in a leather tobacco pouch (far right).

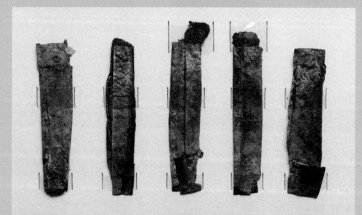

Marking Time at Sea

The centerpiece of *Titanic*'s sumptuous first-class accommodations was the grand staircase, and its focal point was a sculpture depicting Honor and Glory crowning Time. In the center of the sculpture, one of forty-eight electric clocks of various decorative styles and sizes aboard ship recorded the minutes' march. On a floating city like *Titanic*, accurate time keeping was of interest to all and a necessity to her officers and crew.

As *Titanic* steamed westward, her clocks were adjusted gradually to account for the five-hour time difference between the British Isles and New York. Upon arrival at her destination, all clocks would be synchronized with New York time. Indeed, the final 23-minute alteration occurred less than an hour after the ship collided with the iceberg.

Adjusting all forty-eight clocks every day might have been a daunting task for the stewards. But *Titanic*'s timepieces were regulated by two master clocks in the chart room near the bridge. The officer on duty simply set the master clocks, usually at noon or midnight, and within moments all clocks on board would show a uniform time.

On most ships, time's passage is marked by bells that sound at each half hour and are used to summon the crew to their watch posts. Starting at 12 midnight and noon, each half hour adds one bell until 4 o'clock, when eight bells are struck. The count then starts over with one bell at 4:30. Between 4 and 8 p.m., the method changes slightly. Six p.m. marks the end of the first dog watch, and the bell count stops at four. It is then reset to reach four bells again at 8 p.m., the end of the second dog watch.

Save for that of the central timepiece over the grand staircase, few photographs of *Titanic*'s clocks exist. The apparent remains of one clock were recovered during the 1993 *Titanic* Research and Recovery Expedition.

(Below left) Gears from one of Titanic's elaborate timepieces.

(Right) Detail of the grand staircase.

(Below) The height and position of the left arm of this bronze cherub make it possible that it once graced the aft first-class grand staircase entrance on A deck. The upraised arm supported a lamp. As was done for other metal objects, conservators used electrolysis to remove chemical deposits and corrosion from the cherub's surface.

chapter five

THE NIGHT OF APRIL 14, 1912

Cape Race wireless station, Newfoundland.

At 5:00 P.M. on Sunday, April 14, heading southwest, *Titanic* reached a navigational reference point at 42° N, 47° W, called "the Corner." Each spring, ships steamed further south than usual to avoid ice near the Grand Banks off Newfoundland. At the Corner, westbound liners typically turned toward due West, placing them on a path toward New York. Perhaps due to earlier ice warnings, after reaching the Corner Captain Smith ordered a delay of nearly 50 minutes before turning West, placing the ship several miles south of the usual route.

At that moment, *Titanic* entered upon the course that would take her into the ice field.

As the sun set, the air grew chilly. Passengers sought out the warmth of the library, the lounge, or their cabins. At 7 P.M., the air temperature was 43°. Second Officer Charles H.

At 10:55 P.M., an ice warning from the steamer Californian *blared loudly through to* Titanic *wireless operator Jack Phillips. "Shut up," Phillips cut in. "We are busy. We are working Cape Race." The warning was not repeated.*

Lightoller had the forward hatch secured so that its glow would not interfere with the lookouts' vision. By 7:30 P.M., the temperature had dropped four more degrees. A message from the freighter *Californian* to another ship warned of

ice near 42° N, 49° W. The message was picked up by *Titanic*'s wireless operator and taken to the bridge, where, almost at the same moment, Lightoller was taking a stellar observation. He gave the data to Fourth Officer Joseph Boxhall, who worked out the ship's position.

The air had become so frigid that Lightoller ordered the ship's carpenter to monitor the freshwater storage tanks lest they freeze over. The temperature was 33° by 9 P.M. Captain Smith appeared on the bridge and chatted with Lightoller. Before going to his quarters, the captain told his second officer that he was to be summoned immediately if there was any sign of haze.

Lightoller sent a message to the lookouts to stay alert. Another ice warning came at 9:40 P.M., when the liner *Mesaba* wired the following message to *Titanic:* "Much heavy pack ice and

Simon Fisher, Iceberg Right Ahead, *oil on canvas, 1996. Courtesy of the artist.*

Six Fateful Messages

Through wireless transmissions, *Titanic*'s officers received six ice warnings on her final day afloat, indications of the terrible danger that lay ahead.

• **9:00** A.M. From the Cunard liner *Caronia*: "Captain, *Titanic*—westbound steamers report bergs, growlers, and field ice in 42° N, from 49° to 51° W, April 14. Compliments, Barr."

• **1:42** P.M. From the White Star liner *Baltic*: "Greek steamer *Athinai* reports passing icebergs and large quantities of field ice today in latitude 41° 51′ N, longitude 49° 52′ W.... Wish you and *Titanic* all success. Commander."

• **1:45** P.M. A message from the liner *Amerika* to the Hydrographic Office in Washington, D.C., is relayed by *Titanic*'s wireless operator: "*Amerika* passed two large icebergs in 41° 27′ N, 50° 8′ W on April 14."

• **7:30** P.M. A message from the Leyland liner *Californian* to *Antillian* is overheard by *Titanic*: "To Captain, *Antillian*. Six-thirty P.M., apparent ship's time; latitude 42° 3′ N, longitude 49° 9′ W. Three large bergs 5 miles to the southward of us. Regards, Lord."

• **9:40** P.M. A message from the Atlantic Transport liner *Mesaba*: "From *Mesaba* to *Titanic*. In latitude 42° N to 41° 25′, longitude 49° W to 50° 30′ W, saw much heavy pack ice and great number large icebergs, also field ice, weather good, clear." This message never reached *Titanic*'s bridge.

• **10:55** P.M. A message from *Californian*, "We are stopped and surrounded by ice," is interrupted by *Titanic*'s wireless operator whose communication with Cape Race, Newfoundland, had been broken by *Californian*'s ice warning. The *Californian* operator ceased his transmission and did not repeat it.

Acting on the four messages of which he was made aware, Captain Edward J. Smith did order a course change, which took *Titanic* several miles to the south of her usual track.

View of Titanic *showing wireless cables.*

The Silent Menace

Icebergs form when pieces of ice calve, or break off, from a glacier and begin a months-long, 2,000-mile journey southward from Greenland to the Grand Banks of Newfoundland and beyond, carried by ocean currents. Sometimes they drift into the lanes traveled by ships. It is estimated that in a "normal" year approximately 350 bergs find their way south of Newfoundland; only six or eight find their way to the 40° latitude. Once a berg reaches the warm currents of the Gulf Stream, its life may be measured in days.

The winter of 1911–12 was exceptionally mild in the North Atlantic, resulting in a record number of iceberg sightings at latitudes much farther south than usual. According to established practice, the Atlantic steamship companies had already shifted the shipping lanes farther south when *Titanic* sailed. On his way to *Titanic*'s distress position, *Carpathia*'s captain, Arthur Rostron, ordered a junior crewman aloft to count the icebergs he could see. The crew-

man spotted twenty-five, each more than 200 feet high; he saw dozens more measuring between 50 and 150 feet high.

The height of the iceberg "season" runs from March through July, and in 1912 the Hydrographic Office in Washington, D.C., was kept busy publishing periodic reports of ice received from ships upon arrival in port or by wireless. Ships also shared this information directly. According to Sir James Bisset, second officer aboard the rescue ship *Carpathia*, "There are no sure signs of a vessel's approach to icebergs. The temperature of the water is no guide,... and as a rule no appreciable change in air tem-

perature can be detected near a berg."

On January 20, 1914, as a direct result of the *Titanic* disaster, the first International Conference on the Safety of Life at Sea established the International Ice Patrol, operated by the U.S. Coast Guard and funded by the nations whose ships ply North Atlantic waters. Except for interruptions of operations during the First and Second World Wars, the International Ice Patrol has maintained a continuous monitoring of ice conditions, and today employs satellite technology and shipboard facsimile units to do its vital work. To date, not a single vessel has been lost in the area monitored by the patrol.

SS Estonian *passed through the same ice field as* Titanic *two days earlier, when the ship's captain, W. F. Wood, took this photograph. He annotated this copy after the disaster. Only about one-ninth of an iceberg is visible from the surface.*

great number large icebergs . . . weather good, clear." The ice mentioned lay directly in *Titanic*'s path. Wireless traffic was extremely heavy that evening. Earlier, the ship had come within range of Cape Race, and many passengers were eager to send messages. Operator Jack Phillips, alone on duty, spiked *Mesaba*'s message. It never reached the bridge.

A watch change occurred at 10 P.M. Up in the crow's nest, lookouts Archie Jewell and George Symons were relieved by Fred Fleet and Reginald Lee. On the bridge, First Officer William Murdoch took over from Lightoller. The ship and her passengers were settling down for the night. Public rooms and corridors emptied, and late diners left the restaurants.

Shortly before 11 P.M., a flurry of activity erupted in the wireless room. *Californian*, stopped in ice some twenty miles north of *Titanic*, broke into operator Phillips's traffic, warning of ice. "Keep out," Phillips demanded, without listening to the complete message.

Time passed: 11:15 P.M., 11:30 P.M., seven bells. At the sound, on-duty crew and drowsy passengers alike gathered their coats or blankets, savoring the security of being aboard the world's greatest ship.

Several miles ahead, an awesome natural phenomenon lay in *Titanic*'s path, too dark

The pedestal for this aft steering wheel (far left) featured an indicator showing the rudder's position. Originally located on Titanic's *stern docking bridge, this telegraph mechanism (left) duplicated commands to the engine room issued from a similar instrument on the forward navigating bridge.*

Lookout Fred Fleet rang this warning bell (below) when he spotted the iceberg from the crow's nest.

Archie Jewell (below), one of Titanic's *lookouts, was the first to testify at the British inquiry, May 3, 1912.*

to be seen from more than a few hundred feet away as the faintly lit bulk approached. Lookouts Fleet and Lee stared ahead from the crow's nest, squinting. Suddenly they saw the berg. Fleet gave the warning bell's lanyard three sharp tugs, then snatched the telephone to the bridge from its cradle inside the mast. "Are you there?" he said into the mouthpiece.

"Yes. What do you see?"

"Iceberg right ahead."

From the bridge came the final amenity: "Thank you."

First Officer Murdoch took prompt action, ordering the wheel hard a' starboard (causing a turn to port), closing the watertight doors with a lever on the bridge, and having the engines reversed.

Thirty-seven seconds went by. The bow began its leftward swing. The men on the bridge and in the crow's nest sighed in relief as the berg passed along the starboard side of the ship. Suddenly they caught their breaths as they sensed, rather than felt, the faintest series of bumps, the strongest occurring as the berg

Harland and Wolff's Thomas Andrews was asked to assess damages after the ship struck the iceberg. Andrews advised that the ship would sink in less than two hours.

passed the bridge. Most passengers slept right through the jolts.

Captain Smith appeared immediately on the bridge. Murdoch made his report, and Smith dispatched Fourth Officer Boxhall to examine the ship and report back. In a series of bumps and scrapes, the berg had pierced the vessel's forward hull plating, opening the forepeak, holds 1 and 2, the mail room, number 6 boiler room, and, about six feet beyond the bulkhead, the number 5 boiler room.

Titanic could float with any two of her sixteen watertight compartments flooded. She could even float if four of the first five compartments—the ship's smallest—were flooded. But she could not float if all of the first five compartments were flooded. The watertight wall between the fifth and sixth compartments reached only as high as E deck. The weight of the water in the first five compartments would sink the bow so deeply that water would flow along non-watertight decks above the bulkheads, filling the sixth compartment, then the seventh, and so on. As Captain

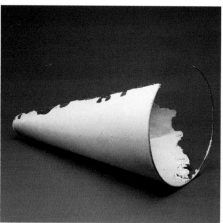

(Top) Captain Smith shouting, "Abandon ship!" in the last moments of Titanic's *sinking as portrayed in the* Daily Graphic *soon after the disaster. (Above) This aluminum megaphone from the wreck site may have been the one used by Smith.*

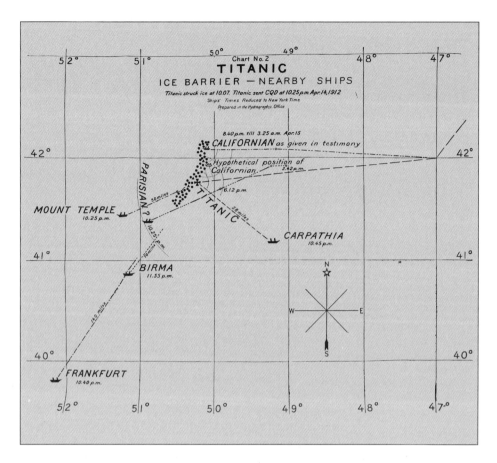

(Above) Titanic's relationship to other ships in the
North Atlantic on the night
of April 14 (U.S. Hydro-
graphic Office).

This porthole was probably from
the first-class dining saloon or its
adjacent galley.

Oil lamps, such as this one recovered from the wreck site, were
hung in passageways and at the
foot of each staircase.

A bronze-and-brass foremast lamp
used in combination with another
foremast lamp to indicate the direction the ship was traveling at night.

(Left) Simon Fisher, The Final
Blow, *oil on canvas, 1996.*
Courtesy of the artist.

(Right) James A. Flood, Titanic,
12:30 A.M., *acrylic on canvas,*
1997. Courtesy of the artist.

Smith learned after consulting with Harland and Wolff's Thomas Andrews, the great ship was doomed.

What happened aboard *Titanic* between 11:40 P.M. Sunday, April 14, and 2:20 A.M. Monday, April 15, has been told and retold many times and in many versions. Witnesses under stress observe and recall actions and events in different ways and are known to assign conflicting times to the same occur-

rences. Dim lights at sea become bright lights at hearings. Seconds become minutes, minutes become hours. Strong emotions cloud recall. Aversion turns into prejudice, and behavior is labeled bestial or heroic according to the dictates of personal recollection and public reaction.

As Walter Lord wrote so eloquently in his book *A Night to Remember*, "It is a rash man indeed who would set himself up as the

final arbiter of all that happened on that incredible night that the *Titanic* went down."

Many facts are known. At midnight, Captain Smith ordered the officers and boat crews mustered. A moment or two later, he ordered the lifeboats uncovered and the passengers assembled. Fourth Officer Boxhall worked out the ship's position; unfortunately, his lack of familiarity with the propellers' revolutions as an indication of speed resulted in a

Twenty Boats and a Dark Sea

Perhaps the greatest tragedy of that cold April night occurred during *Titanic*'s evacuation. The 90 minutes it took to fill, lower, and launch the ship's twenty lifeboats were marked by confusion, misunderstanding, and unpreparedness. Most passengers were convinced that the ship would not sink, and so did not rush to fill the boats. It was also difficult to count heads in the darkness. Some 472 seats—almost 40 percent of the 1,178 available—were sent away empty.

From 12:45 A.M. until the ship sank at 2:20, the boat deck was a scene of hurried activity. After removing covers and clearing away masts, the crew placed lanterns in several boats. To supplement the hard tack biscuits required by regulation, the ship's bakers distributed about 50 loaves of bread that had been intended for the next morning's breakfast. Now attention turned toward the davits, cranelike devices used to put boats over the side and lower them to the water. Most ships prior to *Titanic* had old-fashioned radial davits, which required plenty of crew and lots of strength to operate. About 1905, Danish engineer Axel Welin designed the "Welin quadrant davit," and

Titanic was among the first ships to use his time-saving innovation exclusively. Using a worm gear and a crank, the davits bearing the boat could be swung out together over the side; their long reach permitted a boat to be lowered even against a list.

Titanic's davits and boats were new, and some officers were concerned that an overloaded boat might crack in half. They were unaware that Harland and Wolff's shipyard tests had demonstrated ample strength. A plan to lower the boats half-filled, then board additional passengers from below, failed; by the time the boats were afloat, lower gangway doors were submerged. Some passengers preferred the illusory safety of the ship's decks to the harrowing uncertainty of the seven-storey descent. It is a tribute to *Titanic*'s crew that all of the boats were launched safely.

During the British inquiry, the total complement of the lifeboats was estimated at 826, the sum of the numbers given in the testimony of survivors. In reality, just 705 (Captain Rostron's count of "living souls" on *Carpathia*) of the 2,228 aboard were saved, including several who were pulled from the water.

PORT-SIDE LIFEBOATS

Number	Capacity	Number Aboard	Departure Time (A.M.)
6	65	28	12:55
8	65	28	1:10
10	65	55	1:20
12	65	43	1:25
14	65	60	1:30
16	65	56	1:35
2	40	25	1:45
4	65	40	1:55
Collapsible D	47	44	2:05
Collapsible B	47	14	2:20*
TOTAL	589	393	

STARBOARD-SIDE LIFEBOATS

Number	Capacity	Number Aboard	Departure Time (A.M.)
7	65	28	12:45
5	65	41	12:55
3	65	40	1:00
1	40	12	1:10
9	65	56	1:20
11	65	70	1:25
13	65	64	1:25
15	65	70	1:35
Collapsible C	47	39	1:40
Collapsible A	47	13	2:20*
TOTAL	589	433	

*Not launched, but floated off the ship as it sank.

All figures approximate.

A perilous moment for lifeboats 13 and 15:

"Stop lowering '15' our crew shouted, and the crew of No. 15, now only 20 feet above, cried out the same. The distance to the top, however, was some 70 feet, and the creaking of the pulleys must have deadened all sound to those above, for down she came—15 feet, 10 feet, 5 feet—and a stoker and I reached up and touched the bottom of the swinging boat above our heads. Just before she dropped, another stoker sprang to the ropes with his knife open in his hand. 'One,' I heard him say, and then 'Two,' as the knife cut through the pulley-ropes. The next moment the exhaust stream carried us clear."

—Passenger Lawrence Beesley's narrative. Illustration by Charles Dixon, published in the Daily Graphic, April 27, 1912. Courtesy the Mansell Collection.

After the Titanic disaster, controversy surrounded the behavior of Sir Cosmo and Lady Lucile Duff-Gordon (below), who managed to depart the sinking ship on a 40-capacity lifeboat with only 12 on board.

Montmagny, *a Canadian govern-ment fisheries vessel, was sent to retrieve bodies from the wreck site. Four were found, including one who died in this life jacket (left).*

(Right) F. Matania, Women and Children First, *lithograph, 1912. Courtesy the Mariners' Museum, Newport News, Virginia.*

calculation of 41°46` N, 50°14` W, which was actually several miles from *Titanic*'s true posi-tion and would later complicate the work of investigators.

Captain Smith personally brought the calculation to the wireless room and instructed the operators to stand by. Several minutes later, at 12:15 A.M., he gave the order, and the first distress call was sent out. An amended position was wired about ten minutes later.

Ships at sea responded quickly to the distressed *Titanic* with messages of inquiry and assurance. Within fifteen minutes of the 12:25 transmission, messages were received from *Ypiranga, Frankfurt, Baltic, Caronia, Prinz*

Friedrich Wilhelm, Mount Temple, and even *Titanic*'s sister *Olympic*, eastbound out of New York. Apparently, none was close enough to be of immediate assistance.

On the Cunard liner *Carpathia*, Harold Cottam, the vessel's sole radio operator, was getting ready to retire for the night. He was having difficulty unknotting a shoelace but finally worked it loose. Just before he got into bed, he placed a receiving earphone against his head. What he heard shocked him: It was *Titanic*'s 12:25 A.M. distress call. Two minutes later, Cottam would have been asleep. He immediately notified *Carpathia*'s captain, Arthur H. Rostron, who quickly calculated that

A Voice in the Ether

Some 35 minutes after the collision, Titanic's chief radio operator, John George Phillips, began the first of a long series of distress calls, asking any ship within wireless range for assistance. Titanic had the strongest and most modern wireless equipment available. It was powered by a five-kilowatt motor generator and an emergency generator or batteries. The set had a guaranteed range of 250 miles under any atmospheric condition, but usually could maintain communications over 400 miles. At night the receiving and transmitting range could reach 2,000 miles due to the "bounce" of the signal off of the ionosphere.

Two wireless sets were actually aboard, one for sending and one for receiving. The sending device was kept in a "silent room" so that the loud, buzzing rasp of its spark would not interfere with reception in

Senior wireless operator John "Jack" Phillips (top), age 25, and junior operator Harold Bride (above), 21, bravely remained at their post, transmitting until minutes before Titanic sank.

(Left) The only known photograph of Titanic's wireless room, with Bride at the key.

the main wireless cabin. Transmission was by means of a Morse key that required physical strength and finesse to operate. *Titanic*'s operators used the "continental" version of Morse code, a slight variation from the American version.

Phillips's first distress message consisted of six repetitions of "CQD MGY." Contrary to popular belief, CQD did not mean "Come Quick Danger." It simply denoted "all stations" (CQ) and "urgent" (D) in the wireless shorthand of the Marconi Company, the dominant provider of wireless equipment and operators. MGY were the call letters identifying *Titanic*. Many British vessels had call letters starting with M, including *Olympic* (MKC) and the rescue ship *Carpathia* (MPA). Later, Phillips switched to the new signal SOS. The letters of this famous call, selected by a 1908 international convention for ease of transmission and reception, likewise had no official meaning such as "Save Our Souls" or "Save Our Ship."

A ship's wireless station similar to Titanic's.

Phillips perished in the disaster, dying in a lifeboat after being pulled from the water following the sinking. Except for an exclusive April 28, 1912, newspaper story in the *New York Times*, and extensive testimony before the U.S. Senate and the British Board of Trade, junior radio operator Harold Bride rarely spoke of the disaster.

Profound difficulties in keeping a clear frequency for *Titanic*'s distress messages, confusion resulting from garbled messages, and the lack of 24-hour radio service aboard most ships led to the Federal Radio Act of 1912, which marked the first involvement of the U.S. government in the regulation of radio. The act required a separate frequency for and absolute priority to distress messages, the licensing of operators, the provision of wireless aboard passenger vessels, and at least two operators per ship for round-the-clock service. Guglielmo Marconi, inventor of wireless telegraphy, provided an automatic radio alarm that would awaken sleeping operators aboard cargo vessels, which were exempt from the 24-hour-service rule. In the advancement of communications technology and regulation, *Titanic*'s loss resulted in yet another legacy.

(Above) Isidor Straus, co-owner of Macy's Department Store, and his wife, Ida, were returning from a holiday on the French Riviera. Mrs. Straus refused to board a lifeboat, wanting to stay with her husband. "I will not be separated from my husband. As we have lived, so will we die. Together."

(Right, top) Madeleine Force Astor, 19, was returning from Paris with her husband of seven months, perhaps the most famous, and certainly the wealthiest, passenger on board, John Jacob Astor (right, bottom). She was five months pregnant.

(Left) Simon Fisher, The Final Plunge, oil on canvas, 1997. Courtesy of the artist.

his vessel was 58 miles southeast of *Titanic*. Rostron turned *Carpathia* from its course (Boston to the Mediterranean ports), ordered full steam, and had the entire crew mustered. *Carpathia* sped through the night. Would she arrive in time to rescue all aboard the sinking ship?

At 12:45 A.M. on *Titanic*, two events happened almost simultaneously: Boat number 7, with twenty-eight aboard, was lowered from the starboard side, and the first distress rocket was fired from the bridge. The rocket climbed 800 feet and exploded with a cannonlike roar and a burst of twelve brilliant white stars. Seven more rockets were fired over the next 55 minutes at five- to ten-minute intervals. Repeated efforts were made to signal a nearby vessel with *Titanic*'s powerful Morse lamp. The ship seemed to approach, then turned and left the vicinity.

As boat number 5 was loading on the starboard side at 12:55 A.M., Third Officer Herbert Pitman warned White Star chairman

J. Bruce Ismay not to interfere. He used mildly strong language, not realizing who the man was. Ismay meekly complied. As the boat containing thirty-eight was lowered, three men jumped from the deck and landed heavily inside the boat.

On the port side, boat number 6 was lowered without incident. Aboard and in charge was Quartermaster Robert Hichens, who was at the wheel when the collision with the iceberg occurred.

Captain Smith himself commanded the lowering of lifeboat 8 at 1:10 A.M. It carried twenty-four women passengers and four male crew members but had a capacity of sixty-five. Under First Officer Murdoch's direction, boat number 1, starboard, forward, was sent away. Aboard were five passengers, including Sir Cosmo and Lady Lucile Duff-Gordon, and seven crew. The boat had a capacity of forty. Suggestions of bribery and collusion would later arise, but nothing came of them.

While boat 8 was loading, Mr. and Mrs.

Isidor Straus encouraged Mrs. Straus's maid, Ellen Bird, to get into the boat; she did so. Mrs. Straus was urged to board as well. She turned to her husband, who said that he would not board until all the women were safe. Mrs. Straus replied that she would not be separated from her husband. Together, they remained on the ship to meet their fate.

At 1:20 A.M., on starboard boat number 9, famous mystery writer Jacques Futrelle bid farewell to his wife as he helped her into the boat. Port boat number 12 was sent away at 1:25 A.M., followed closely by starboard boat 11. Almost simultaneously, boat 13 was ordered lowered, a total of sixty-four aboard. It was almost hit by boat 15, which was being sent down from above. Those in boat 13 quickly cut the falls, and the boat drifted away with seconds to spare.

Titanic's bow was sinking deeper. The ship's lights still burned due to the heroic efforts of the engineering officers and their crew, who stayed below, manning the pumps and generators. In the wireless cabin, an ongoing exchange took place between the doomed liner and other vessels, some near, many far off. Music echoed across the water as the ship's orchestra, having played earlier at the forward first-class entrance, performed outside on the starboard deck, near the gymnasium.

By 1:35 A.M., with all but six of the boats lowered, panic set in. While loading boat 14, Fifth Officer Harold Lowe had to fire several shots from his revolver to prevent crowds from rushing the boat. By 1:40, most of the forward boats had been sent away and the crowd had moved aft. Collapsible C was attached to the davits used to lower boat 1. No women or children were in sight. As the boat was lowered, Bruce Ismay stepped in. His rationale, as he later reported, was that his testimony would be needed during the hearings. Though he was vilified by the American press for his actions, both the British press and the British people seemed to understand his motives.

Port-side boat number 2, a cutter, was lowered without incident at 1:45, with Fourth Officer Boxhall in charge. Aboard was an old third-class passenger, the only male, along with about twenty women and children and four crew.

Time was growing short. During the loading of port boat number 4, Colonel John Jacob Astor assisted his pregnant wife, Madeleine, into the boat and saw her safely seated. He then prepared to get in. Second Officer Lightoller, in charge of loading, reminded Astor that it was now "women and children

As Titanic *sank, Father Thomas R. Byles recited the rosary, heard confessions, and gave absolutions to more than a hundred passengers, mostly second and third class, on the aft end of the boat deck.*

The Navratil Brothers

(Far left) Marcelle Navratil with her sons.

(Left) The Navratil brothers, Michel and Edmond.

Among the survivors on Carpathia were two young French boys, the Navratil brothers, Michel, almost four, and Edmond, two. Unable to locate their parents, New Yorker Miss Margaret Hayes, fluent in French, volunteered to take care of them until a guardian was found. The story of the young survivors touched the hearts of many and was published in newspapers worldwide. A number of people wanted to adopt the boys.

Finally, Marcelle Navratil read the story in the Navratils' hometown of Nice and recognized them as her own sons. They had recently disappeared with her estranged husband, Michel, after he had them for an Easter weekend. Distraught over the separation from his wife, Michel had taken his sons to Monte Carlo and then sailed to England, where they boarded *Titanic* for New York. His belief was that his beloved wife would follow them, and they could start a new life in America.

On board, Michel went by the name Louis Hoffman and led fellow second-class passengers to believe that his wife was dead. As *Titanic* sank, he dressed his boys and handed them off to Second Officer Lightoller, who placed them in collapsible D, the last boat to leave the liner.

When Marcelle discovered the fate of her two sons, the White Star Line arranged passage for her to travel to New York. She was reunited with the boys on May 16. Two days later, they boarded *Oceanic* and returned to France.

only." Astor patted his wife's arm, stepped back on deck, and waved good-bye as the boat was sent away at 1:55 A.M. with forty aboard, including one stowaway.

At 2 A.M., only one boat, port collapsible D, remained in the davits waiting to be lowered. Lightoller ordered a group of crewmen to link arms and form a circle on deck around the boat. Only women and children were permitted to pass. A father, Michel Navratil, passed his two young sons through. New York theater producer Henry Harris escorted his wife, René, to the circle and stepped back. The boat, holding forty-four, was lowered at 2:05.

More than 1,500 souls were still aboard. *Titanic* sank lower and lower at the bow, and her stern began to rise out of the water.

Captain Smith went to the wireless cabin and released operators Phillips and Bride from duty. Walking forward to the bridge, he passed several crew. "It's every man for himself now," he told them.

The falls in the davits swung gently, remaining vertical as the decks sloped away from them. All was generally quiet, save for the distant sound of the still-playing orchestra and the cries of men as they dropped from the slanting decks and plunged into the frigid water.

Earlier, mining magnate Benjamin

Guggenheim and his valet, Victor Giglio, had returned to their cabins to dress in their evening clothes, for they wanted "to go down like gentlemen." After bidding farewell to his wife, Colonel Astor went below to F deck and the kennels, where he liberated his beloved Airedale, Kitty, along with other dogs. Those in the lifeboats later spotted Kitty scampering up and down the slanting decks.

The ship's orchestra had been performing popular songs, ragtime beats, and quick marches to keep spirits up. At bandmaster Wallace Hartley's murmured command, they began playing the beloved tune "Londonderry Air," known to most Americans as "Danny Boy." They played softly at first, then with increasing fervor as the deck slanted more and more steeply.

Aft on the boat deck, a hundred or more passengers of all faiths gathered in prayer, attended by two Roman Catholic priests, Father Thomas Roussel Byles of England and Father Joseph Permaschitz, a German Benedictine. The priests heard confessions and granted absolutions. Kneeling, they

---

(*Right*) Larry S. Anderson, Flooding of the Grand Staircase, *watercolor on board, 1997. Courtesy of the artist.*

joined in reciting the rosary before the churning waters washed over the deck and engulfed them all.

Thomas Andrews, his dream shattered, his mind likely numbed and overwhelmed by shock, was last seen in *Titanic*'s smoking room, standing near the fireplace over which hung Norman Wilkinson's painting *Plymouth Harbour*. His life jacket lay atop a nearby table.

The last minutes ticked by: 2:10 . . . 2:12 . . . 2:15. As *Titanic*'s stern rose higher out of the water, those aboard struggled to maintain their footing. Bandmaster Hartley released the musicians from duty. Alone, he began the first notes of a simple hymn—his personal favorite and the one played over the graves of brother musicians—"Nearer, My God, to Thee." One by one, the bandsmen, choosing not to leave,

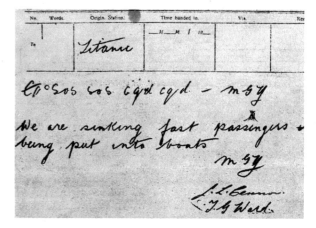

Mrs. Margaret Brown of Denver. Her behavior on lifeboat 6 earned her the nickname "the unsinkable Molly Brown."

joined in. It was the last song they would play, and it was the last sound heard by many survivors in the boats before the horrific crash of the sinking liner.

Titanic's end came at 2:20 A.M. The great vessel slipped beneath the sea's surface and disappeared from view, leaving surprisingly little surface turmoil. As the liner sank, collapsibles A and B floated off the boat deck. Boat B overturned as it reached the water, swept clear by the wash from the collapsing forward funnel. Swamped, boat A remained upright but half-submerged. Survivors in the water either clung to or climbed into the collapsibles.

Cries of freezing and drowning life-jacketed passengers filled the chill night air. Most of those in the lifeboats were reluctant to turn back for fear their boats would be inundated by panicked swimmers and overturned. Slowly, hauntingly, the voices diminished, then vanished into the stillness.

The last message from Titanic.

(Right) Simon Fisher, 2:15 A.M., oil on canvas, 1996. Courtesy of the artist.

chapter six

THE RESCUE

As *Titanic* met her watery fate, help was on the way in the form of the liner *Carpathia*. Every ounce of steam her boilers could generate was directed toward her throbbing engines. Hot water and cabin heaters were turned off to conserve energy. Captain Arthur Rostron issued orders for his crew to prepare to receive survivors. Slings were rigged, ladders were readied, hospital facilities were prepped, and blankets and pillows were distributed throughout public rooms. The nine-year-old vessel's speed was increased to 17-1/2 knots, 3-1/2 knots faster than her maximum.

At 3:30 A.M. on April 15, the ship encountered the ice field into which *Titanic* had traveled. Rostron ordered half-speed, then slow. *Carpathia* had to maneuver repeatedly to

Photographed on the morning of April 15, this was believed to have been the iceberg that caused Titanic *to sink. Red paint was observed near the iceberg's base.*

avoid striking the bergs. At 4:03 A.M., a green flare from one of *Titanic*'s lifeboats was spotted from *Carpathia*'s bridge.

With barely enough speed to sustain way, *Carpathia* swung around before taking in survivors through the shelter deck's open gangway. *Titanic*'s fourth officer, Joseph Boxhall, reported to Captain Rostron that the vessel had sunk at 2:20 A.M. The men, women, and children in the boats were her only survivors.

One by one, in the breaking light of dawn, *Titanic*'s boats came into view. At approximately 6 A.M., a slight breeze sprang up, making it more difficult to maneuver the boats. Aboard swamped collapsible B, footing and stability became nearly impossible. In response to shrill blasts from Second Officer Charles Lightoller's whistle, two boats rowed up to the submerging collapsible. Five survivors scrambled into boat 4, eight into boat 14. Lightoller was the last to board.

The lifeboats gathered at *Carpathia*'s side. Collapsible C was deboarded at 6:15 A.M.; boat 14, with collapsible D in tow, at 7 A.M., boat 4 at 7:30 A.M.; and boat 6 at 8 A.M. At 8:30, boat 12, which had departed the sinking liner with forty aboard, reached *Carpathia* with more than seventy survivors, including those

E. D. Walker, The Titanic Has Gone, Sir, *oil on canvas, 1997.*
Lifeboat no. 14 depicted in foreground. Courtesy of the artist.

(Above) At 28, Fifth Officer Harold Lowe was the youngest officer aboard. This was his first transatlantic crossing. Lowe left Titanic in charge of lifeboat 14 (left), seen here in the foreground approaching Carpathia with collapsible D in tow. Soon after the sinking, Lowe gathered five of the lifeboats together, redistributed those aboard, and went back to look for more survivors in the water, now thick with corpses. He was able to rescue three more.

(Right) Simon Fisher, Carpathia Picking Up Survivors, oil on canvas, 1995. Courtesy of the artist.

Lifeboat 9 (above) on the deck of Carpathia.

A crewman looks on as survivors are lifted aboard Carpathia.

transferred from collapsibles D and B.

Thirteen of *Titanic*'s boats were lifted to *Carpathia*'s deck. Boats 4, 14, and 15 and collapsibles B, C, and D were cast adrift, seacocks open, and quickly sank. Collapsible A, its passengers transferred to collapsible D, had been set adrift during the night by Fifth Officer Harold Lowe with three bodies aboard.

Rostron ordered a course set for New York. At 9 A.M., a service of remembrance and thanksgiving was held in the first-class dining saloon. Following the service, a roster of survivors was compiled, taken to *Carpathia*'s wireless room, and transmitted. In the afternoon, the bodies of four men who had died in the lifeboats were committed to the deep. At four o'clock in the morning on April 16, the body of William H. Lyons, a *Titanic* crewman who died from exposure during the night, was also committed.

An aura of depression and sorrow enveloped all aboard as the vessel, shrouded in fog, cut through the water. Driving rain kept most people indoors. On Tuesday morning, a collection was taken up for the survivors. It was early Wednesday morning before *Carpathia*'s

Lifeboat 9 (top left) approaching Carpathia. On board are Molly Brown, Quartermaster Robert Hichens, noted writer Helen Candee, and Major Arthur Peuchen. Peuchen was a first-class passenger and a yachtsman from Toronto. He was highly critical of the management and command of Titanic during the New York hearings.

Collapsible D (above), overloaded and flooded with frigid water, pulls alongside Carpathia. On board are the Navratil boys and René Harris, wife of well-known theatrical producer Henry B. Harris, who perished.

Life vests (left) have been discarded as passengers climb to safety aboard Carpathia.

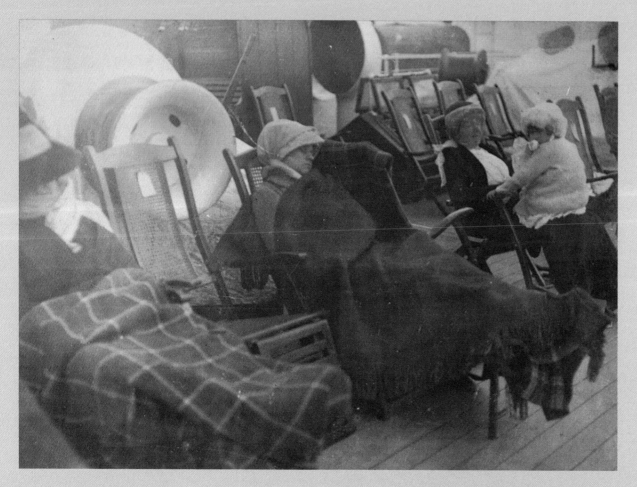

Many moving photographs, such as the one at left of Titanic survivors trying to stay warm on the deck of Carpathia, were taken by Carpathia passenger Mabel Fenwick, traveling on her honeymoon with husband James Fenwick (above).

Second-class passenger Lawrence Beesley (far left), a schoolteacher, with two other survivors. Beesley would later write a book about the experience, The Loss of the SS Titanic. Newlyweds Mr. and Mrs. George Harder (near left) talk with Sallie Beckwith. Beckwith's husband, Richard, her daughter, Helen Newsom, and Helen's fiancé, American tennis star Karl Behr, all survived.

A Gallant Liner

Captain Arthur Henry Rostron, on the deck of Carpathia, *leans against a* Titanic *lifeboat. Welcomed as a hero, he received numerous awards and was feted on both sides of the Atlantic.*

Captain Rostron (right) confers with Second Officer Charles H. Lightoller aboard Carpathia.

The Cunard liner *Carpathia* is forever recorded in the pages of history as the ship that rescued *Titanic*'s passengers and crew after a 58-mile, four-hour journey through treacherous, ice-filled waters.

Like all Cunard Line ships of the day, *Carpathia* was named for a Roman province. Launched on August 6, 1902, at the Wallsend-on-Tyne shipyard of C. S. Swan and Hunter, she completed trials on April 25, 1903, and made her maiden voyage from Liverpool to Boston via Queenstown, Ireland, on May 5 of that year. Later she was placed on the Liverpool–New York service.

The 558-foot-long *Carpathia* weighed 13,564 gross registered tons, making her about one third of *Titanic*'s size. When built, she had a capacity of 204 first-class passengers and 1,500 steerage. Of the latter, 486

were in cabins, the rest in austere dormitory-style accommodations. The liner's quadruple expansion engines gave her a cruising speed of 15 knots, though on her dash to *Titanic*'s distress position, it is believed she achieved 17-1/2 knots for brief periods.

In 1903, Cunard was appointed the official agent for Hungarian emigration to the United States, and the company moved its intermediate vessels *Aurania*, *Ultonia*, *Slavonia*, *Pavonia*, and *Carpathia* to its Mediterranean service soon thereafter. *Carpathia* returned to the Liverpool–New York route during the summer of 1904 and 1905. She was then expanded to carry 100 first class, 200 second class, and 2,250 third class, and assigned almost exclusively to the Mediterranean–New York run.

On that fateful night, *Carpathia*'s wire-

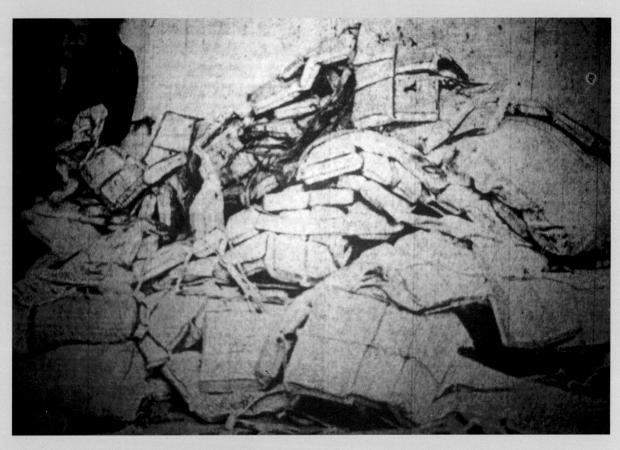

Captain Rostron and the officers of Carpathia *pose for a photograph on the ship's deck. All were praised as heroes.*

Titanic *life vests (above right) piled up in* Carpathia's *gangway.*

less operator, Harold Cottam, was about to go to bed when he heard *Titanic*'s distress call. The dramatic story of onboard preparations to receive the sinking vessel's passengers has been told repeatedly in books and on film. For their heroic efforts, *Carpathia*'s crew received medals from a *Titanic* survivors' committee that included Denver resident Margaret Tobin ("Molly") Brown. Captain (later Sir) Arthur Henry Rostron received a silver loving cup and later a gold medal from

the U.S. Congress, among many other honors.

Carpathia returned to service on the Liverpool–New York run in 1915. On July 17, 1918, she was torpedoed twice by German submarine U-55, 120 miles west of Fastnet, Ireland. The first torpedo struck just forward of the engine room, the second hit the engine room itself. *Carpathia* sank at 9:15 A.M. Five of her engineering staff were killed; some 215 passengers and crew survived.

wireless could send and receive messages without garbling. The ship was still a day and a half from New York.

The world anxiously awaited the rescue vessel's docking at New York on the evening of Thursday, April 18. At 6 P.M., *Carpathia* passed the Ambrose Light Vessel marking the entrance to New York Harbor. She hurried past a flotilla of small boats filled with reporters eager for stories from the survivors who silently crowded the liner's rails. *Carpathia* slowed only long enough to board the port physician from the quarantine boat.

Moving through heavy rain and strong winds, *Carpathia* steamed past the Battery at the southern tip of Manhattan and proceeded slowly up the North River, as the Hudson was known in the New York port. She went by her own dock at 14th Street and came to a stop opposite 20th Street—the White Star docks, piers 58 and 59. There, amid flashes of lightning and rain, *Titanic*'s lifeboats were lowered

There were many unconfirmed headlines such as this one (left) from New York's Evening Sun, *April 15, 1912, creating false hope for family and friends of Titanic victims.*

Crowds gather (top) in rain and cold at pier 54 in New York, anxiously awaiting the arrival of survivors. There were eventually 30,000 at the Cunard pier, with an additional 10,000 crowded along the Battery.

Californian (above left) approaches Carpathia on the morning of April 15, 1912, at about 8:30 A.M., well after the rescue had been completed. Stanley Lord (above) was the much maligned captain of Californian. Carpathia (right) approaching New York.

to the river, where they were picked up by the tug *Champion* and towed to the bulkhead between the two piers. That night, many items from the boats were carried off by souvenir hunters before company employees could remove them.

Carpathia docked at her own pier, number 54, and lowered her gangways at 9:30. Five minutes later, the 318 first- and second-class passengers exited onto the pier, where they were greeted by friends and family who had obtained special passes. It was about 11 P.M. when third-class passengers debarked from the aft gangway. They were met mostly by representatives from various relief agencies.

Half an hour later, the 214 surviving crew departed from the aft gangway. They crossed the pier, boarded the barge *George Starr*, and were towed upriver to pier 60, where they boarded the Red Star liner *Lapland*. (Red Star was part of IMM, which also owned the White Star Line.) Aboard *Lapland*, *Titanic*'s crew members, including eighteen surviving stewardesses, were assigned cabins: third class for crew, first class for the four surviving officers.

By midnight, pier 54 stood deserted, except for the guards. Nearly all the survivors had been taken to hotels or shelters.

(Top) Survivors at Carpathia's stern as it approaches New York. Passengers crowding Carpathia deck at New York (center). Dozens of reporters clamored for attention as survivors debarked (above).

Second wireless operator Harold Bride, whose feet were badly bruised and frozen, had to be carried off Carpathia.

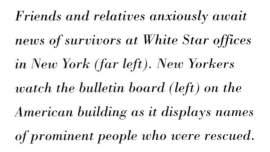

Friends and relatives anxiously await news of survivors at White Star offices in New York (far left). New Yorkers watch the bulletin board (left) on the American building as it displays names of prominent people who were rescued.

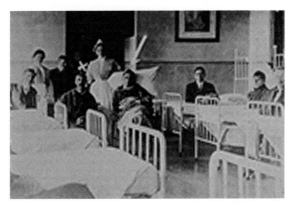

Survivors (left) at St. Vincent's Hospital, New York. Many hospitals donated services for those in need. Titanic's lifeboats are lowered from Carpathia (below left) at the White Star pier (below center). Workers removed company logos and nameplates from the lifeboats (below), which had been pillaged by souvenir hunters. The boats later disappeared.

The deaths of 624 of Titanic's 908-person crew widowed 289 women and left 727 children fatherless. Five orphaned boys of Titanic (left) with their House Matron at the Southampton Seaman's "At Home" soon after the disaster.

(Left) Third-class women and children survivors.

Surviving crew members of Titanic gathered on the steps of the Institute of the Seaman's Friend, New York (right).

City of Sorrow

Immediately following *Titanic*'s loss, the White Star Line asked its agents in Halifax, Nova Scotia (the major port nearest the sinking site), to oversee the recovery of victims of the disaster. Passing vessels had reported hundreds of bodies, buoyed by their white life jackets, floating generally northeastward in the Gulf Stream. Warnings to avoid the area were sent by wireless from one vessel to another.

Recovery efforts had begun with *Carpathia*'s arrival on April 15. Four bodies were removed from lifeboats and consigned to the sea after an onboard memorial service. Two days later, the first of four vessels chartered by White Star for the grim task arrived on the scene. The Commercial Cable Company's *Mackay-Bennett*, a cable-laying ship from Halifax, retrieved some 306 bodies and established a procedure that all subse-

First-class passengers' bodies were embalmed and put in coffins stored on Mackay-Bennett's stern (above), then placed on ice in the ship's hold and cable tanks. The vessel recovered 306 bodies, 116 of which were buried at sea.

Mackay-Bennett (left).

A Mackay-Bennett crew attempts to salvage collapsible B (right), which was subsequently abandoned.

A boat from Minia recovers a body (right). Photo taken from Mackay-Bennett.

Loading coffins aboard
Mackay-Bennett, Halifax.

Minia (below), was chartered by
White Star to assist Mackay-Bennett.

quent searchers would follow. Each victim was assigned a numbered page in a ledger book, and a piece of canvas stenciled with a corresponding number was attached to the body. On the ledger page, a full description was written, including hair color, height, weight, age, any scars or birthmarks, and a full inventory of the deceased's pockets. Addresses on letters, names on passports, and ticket numbers were all recorded to assist in identification. Personal property was placed in canvas bags also bearing the victim's number.

Of the 306 bodies found by *Mackay-Bennett*, 116 were too badly decomposed to be brought to port and were buried at sea. The cable ship returned to Halifax on Tuesday, April 30, with 190 victims aboard, some in caskets, others wrapped in canvas and placed in the ship's ice-filled cable tanks. Once ashore, some victims were photographed, and the photographs were apparently sent to White Star offices that had sold tickets for *Titanic*'s ill-fated voyage, in the hope that someone would recognize them.

The second vessel, the Anglo-American Telegraph Company's cable ship *Minia*, arrived at the site on April 26 and returned on May 6 after finding 17 bodies.

The Canadian government ship *Montmagny* left Sorel, Quebec, on May 3 and returned to Louisburg, Nova Scotia, on May 13, having recovered 4 victims. White Star's own *Oceanic* came across swamped collapsible A on May 13; its 3 dead occupants were buried at sea. The final chartered vessel, Bowring Brothers' *Algerine*, left St. John's, Newfoundland, on May 15 and recovered a single body, that of steward James McGrady. By now, sea life and ocean currents made further recoveries doubtful. Of the 336 recovered, 127 were buried at sea, 59 were claimed by loved ones, and the remaining

150 were interred at Halifax's Fairview, Mt. Olivet, and Baron de Hirsch cemeteries.

In 1991, members of Titanic International, a *Titanic* history group based in Freehold, New Jersey, used recovery records and information from other sources to identify 6 of the 42 previously unknown victims buried in Halifax. With appropriate ceremony, their headstones—supplied by White Star in 1912—were unveiled in September, finally bearing their names after almost eight decades.

Today, the city of Halifax has assumed responsibility for the graves' upkeep. A White Star trust fund established in 1912 and apparently once supplemented by Cunard, which merged with White Star in 1934, maintains the stones in perpetuity, aided by donations from around the world.

(Upper left) Fairview Cemetery, Halifax (detail, above).

Rabbi Jacob Walker and workers in Titanic section of Baron de Hirsch Jewish Cemetery in Halifax (left).

John Snow & Sons undertakers in Halifax (right) was able to enlist the help of virtually all undertakers in Canada's Maritime Provinces in the preparation of the bodies.

Hearses and extra coffins prepared for the arrival of Mackay-Bennett (far left).

A hearse carrying the body of John Jacob Astor leaves the dockyard (left).

chapter seven

THE AFTERMATH

It did not take long for the tragedy at sea to send shock waves rippling ashore. Michigan Senator William Alden Smith, a member of the U.S. Senate Committee on Commerce, introduced a resolution mandating an investigation into the loss of *Titanic*. His fellow senators appointed him chairman of a subcommittee to carry out the task. Although *Titanic* was a British ship, it was owned by the American conglomerate IMM. If Smith could prove there was negligence in the ship's operation, IMM could be sued in U.S. court for damages due to loss of life and property.

Smith's subcommittee convened first at New York's Waldorf-Astoria Hotel, then in Washington, D.C. Hearings took place over seventeen days between April 19 and May 25. Eighty-two witnesses were heard: fifty-three British subjects or residents, and twenty-nine residents or citizens of the United States. Thirty-four of the ship's crew testified, as did

Senator William Smith, chairman of the U.S. Senate committee investigating the Titanic *disaster.*

White Star Chairman J. Bruce Ismay, who, despite his efforts to return to England, was compelled to remain for the hearings.

The subcommittee's report, ordered printed on May 28, three days after the conclu-

sion of the hearings, was 19 pages long. Exhibits occupied another 44 pages, and testimony, affidavits, and depositions filled another 1,145 pages. The report's recommendations were few but far-reaching and formed the genesis of the topics discussed at the first international convention of Safety of Life at Sea (SOLAS), held in London in 1913. Among the recommendations were increased lifeboat capacity; adequate manning of boats and boat drills for passengers; and regulation of radiotelegraphy, including 24-hour wireless watches at sea. It was advised that the firing of colored "recognition signal" rockets be restricted to distress signals only. The subcommittee also called for a re-examination of existing maritime laws regarding navigation and the construction of all seagoing vessels.

Whereas American newspapers were almost unanimous in their approval of Smith's recommendations, the British press and gov-

J. Bruce Ismay being interrogated by the senatorial committee in a room at the Waldorf-Astoria, New York.

Jack Thayer dedicated his book, The Sinking of the S.S. Titanic, to the memory of his father, who went down with the ship. This leather-bound signed copy is a first edition, published in 1940.

Titanic *wireless operator Harold Bride and Guglielmo Marconi (below left), the inventor of the wireless telegraph and owner of the Marconi Company, at the U.S. hearing.*

American White Star Vice President P. A. S. Franklin (holding umbrella) and J. Bruce Ismay (below center) on their way to the U.S. inquiry at the Waldorf-Astoria.

Surviving crew members being questioned by a reporter (below right).

Crew members in Washington, D.C., waiting to testify (above). The men are now destitute, since White Star ceased payment of wages at the moment Titanic sank.

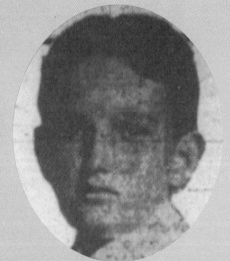

Carpathia passenger L. D. Skidmore made these drawings from a description of the sinking by 17-year-old survivor Jack Thayer (left). They show Titanic breaking in two before going under. Others claimed that the ship had remained intact. It was only when the ship was discovered in 1985 that the debate was laid to rest—Titanic had indeed broken in two while sinking.

J. Bruce Ismay testifies at the British inquiry.

ernment were not. The British Board of Trade (roughly comparable to the U.S. Department of Commerce) was particularly anxious to investigate *Titanic*'s loss on its own for fear its jurisdiction would be abruptly claimed by some other agency. The board itself had set the regulations under which the vessel had been constructed, operated, and lost.

Lord Mersey—Sir John Charles Bigham, Baron Mersey of Toxteth—was appointed wreck commissioner, receiving his warrant from Britain's Lord High Chancellor. His five assessors were duly authorized by the Home Secretary. Authority for the inquiry was granted by the Board of Trade itself.

The court sat for thirty-six days between May 2 and July 3. The resulting transcript contained 959 pages representing 25,622 questions asked of ninety-eight witnesses. Except for Monday, May 6, when the court visited Southampton to view *Olympic*, and the last two days of the hearing, July 1 and 3, when the court convened in London's Caxton Hall,

Lord Mersey, president of the Special Wreck Commission established to inquire into the disaster in England.

the entire inquiry was held at the drill hall of the Scottish Regiment, Buckingham Gate, Westminster, London.

Private deliberations took place from July 3 through July 8, and the commission's findings were published July 30. This report was more far-reaching than the U.S. Senate investigation. The commission found that the accident was caused by excessive speed, that there was an insufficient number of boats and trained men to handle them, and that a proper watch was not kept. The liner's construction was ruled inadequate, primarily in her watertight bulkhead design.

J. Bruce Ismay was exonerated, and one passenger, Sir Cosmo Duff-Gordon, was held blameless for his less-than-heroic behavior. The Board of Trade was chided for not updating its 1894 shipping rules, and Captain Rostron received praise for his rescue efforts. *Californian*'s captain, Stanley Lord, was deemed negligent in not coming to *Titanic*'s aid. Captain Lord, for his part,

Californian crew members (left) at the Scottish Drill Hall, the main site of the British inquiry. Second Officer Stone and apprentice James Gibson (fourth and fifth from right) were on watch when the rockets were sighted. Gibson testified against his captain, Stanley Lord. Wireless operator Cyril Evans is third from left. Archie Jewell (below left), Titanic crow's nest lookout, testifies.

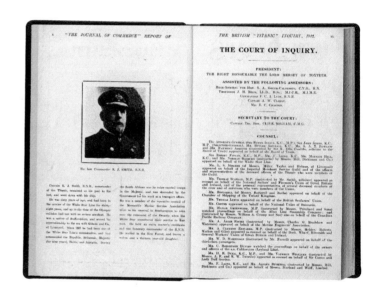

This bound Titanic inquiry book from the British investigation includes a verbatim record of each day's proceedings.

appeared only as a witness. His legal counsel was not given the opportunity to call witnesses who might have verified his statements, and attempts to exonerate Lord were denied in the months and years following the inquiry. It was not until 1992, some thirty years after Lord's death, that a formal investigation based on the location of the wreck site determined that *Californian* was indeed as much as twenty miles

from the sinking ship—too far to have made it through the ice field to reach *Titanic* in time.

Concurring with the American report, Mersey's recommendations included 24-hour wireless operation aboard oceangoing ships and frequent lifeboat drills for all crew members. He also called for an international conference

This seaman's discharge book (right) was owned by Edward Brown of Liverpool, a steward on Titanic. In it, each engagement and ship was entered. Unable to swim, Brown clung to a life ring for over an hour in the freezing water.

(Left) Front page of Britain's Daily Mirror, April 19, 1912. The photograph was taken on Titanic's second-class boat deck at Queenstown and shows some of the ship's few lifeboats.

(Right) Surviving crewmen Prentice, Brown, and Lucas.

(Above) Surviving stewardesses at Plymouth. Of 908 crew members aboard, some 23 were women, of whom three were lost; 22% of the male crew survived. Of 712 third-class passengers, 47% of the women and children survived, along with 14% of third-class men. Of 271 second-class passengers, 81% of the women and children survived, along with 10% of second-class men. Of 337 first-class passengers, 94% of the women and children survived, along with 31% of the men. (All figures approximate.)

Stewards gather for a homecoming portrait. Front row, left to right: Leo J. Hyland and C. J. Savage. Back row: Alfred Pugh and H. J. Prior.

(Right) Mrs. Marian Thayer and husband John B. Thayer. Mrs. Thayer and the couple's son, John "Jack" Thayer, Jr., survived; Thayer Sr. did not.

to consider adoption of regulations regarding safety at sea. "The importance of this Enquiry has to do with the future," Mersey commented. "No Enquiry can repair the past."

If the past could not be repaired, it could at least be remembered. The days following the tragedy were filled with memorial meetings and church services. At noon on Friday, April 19, a memorial service at St. Paul's Cathedral in London drew an overflow crowd. On the following Sunday, scarcely a church anywhere in the Western world did not memorialize *Titanic*'s dead, her heroes, and her heroines.

Fund-raising events to assist *Titanic* survivors were held at Covent Garden and Albert Hall in London and at Century Theatre in New York. Every Palace or Hippodrome in Britain and America gave benefit performances featuring local talent, or, in some instances, the most famous actors, singers, entertainers, and orchestras of the day. Thousands of dollars and pounds sterling poured into the relief funds of the American

Red Cross, the Salvation Army, and Britain's Mansion House.

Entrepreneurs moved quickly to exploit the disaster. The enormous output of memorabilia included dozens of postcards; a plethora of sheet music (more than 130 copyrighted compositions in America alone); so-called memorial editions hastily assembled from newspaper accounts and contemporary pictorial material; and books containing myths and rumors that must be refuted to this day. Newspapers published hundreds of poems that recounted and mourned the disaster.

Scholarly commentary was delivered in the press and in academic and technical journals, and a public debate ensued between novelist Joseph Conrad and author-critic George Bernard Shaw. In *The Titanic: End of a Dream*, author Wyn Craig Wade cited Conrad as an opponent of the "big ship" movement. Denouncing sentimental accounts of *Titanic*'s final moments as the band played on—"music to get drowned by," he called it—Conrad wrote: "It would have been

(Left) Titanic *memorial service at London's Westminster Cathedral, April 22, 1912.*

Titanic *crew (opposite) on the way to the memorial service in Southampton, where many of the lost crew had lived.*

(Below right) An advertisement for a traveling spectacle of eight tableaux depicting the Titanic disaster, one among many attempts to capitalize on the tragedy.

finer if the band of the *Titanic* had been quietly saved, instead of being drowned while playing . . . There is nothing more heroic in being drowned very much against your will, off a holed, helpless, big tank in which you bought your passage, than in quietly dying of colic caused by the imperfect salmon in the tin you bought from your grocer."

Titanic was in everyone's thoughts and on everyone's lips, and everyone, it seemed, had a theory, comment, or suggestion for keeping the seas safe. A mania had gripped the public. Memorials were dedicated to the heroic dead. Statues and plaques were unveiled saluting individuals such as Major Archibald Butt, journalist W. T. Stead, Mr. and Mrs. Isidor

TITANIC MEMORIAL.

Straus, and Captain Edward J. Smith. Slowly, the torrent began to ebb. Save for the occasional observance—a magazine article here, a reference on stage or screen there—*Titanic*'s story began to fade from the public imagination, its memory kept alive largely by devoted hobbyists, archivists, and historians.

Program cover for the Century Theatre's Woman's Titanic Memorial event.

Titanic memorial (left) outside City Hall in Belfast, the city of the liner's birth. Legend has it that tears shed by the figure caused moss to grow at her feet. Titanic monument in Southampton (right).

"GREATER LOVE HATH NO MAN THAN
THIS, THAT A MAN LAY DOWN HIS
LIFE FOR HIS FRIENDS."

JOSEPH BELL	JONATHAN SHEPHERD		ROBERT MILLAR	ALFRED P. MIDDLETON
WM. E. FARQUHARSON	CHARLES HODGE		WILLIAM Y. MOYES	ALBERT C. ERVINE
JNO. H. HESKETH	FRANCIS E. G. COY		WILLIAM McREYNOLDS	WILLIAM KELLY
NORMAN E. HARRISON	JAMES FRASER		HENRY P. CREESE	GEORGE A. CHISNALL
GEORGE F. HOSKING	HENRY R. DYER		THOMAS MILLAR	BUCK FITZPATRICK
EDWARD C. DODD	HERBY W. BROOKS		PETER SLOAN	ARTHUR A. ROUS
LEONARD HODGKINSON	ARTHUR WARD		ALFRED S. ALLSOP	WILLIAM L. DUFFY
JAMES M. SMITH	THOMAS B. KING		HERBERT JUPE	
BERT. WILSON	FRANK A. PARSONS			ALSO
HERBERT C. HARVEY	WILLIAM D. MACKIE		THOMAS ANDREWS	ARCHY FROST
			ROBERT KNIGHT	

TO THE MEMORY OF THE ENGINEER OFFICERS
OF THE R.M.S. "TITANIC" WHO SHOWED
THEIR HIGH CONCEPTION OF DUTY AND THEIR
HEROISM BY REMAINING AT THEIR POSTS
15TH APRIL 1912

THEIR FELLOW ENGINEERS AND FRIENDS
THROUGHOUT THE WORLD

THE LEGEND

Lobby card for Titanic *(1953), starring Barbara Stanwyck. The filmmakers built a twenty-foot model of the ship for the sinking sequence.*

Prior to 1953 and the 98-minute 20th Century-Fox film *Titanic*, the disaster at sea had been the subject of several motion pictures, none overwhelmingly popular or memorable, and most virtually forgotten today.

Among the procession of films that crossed the silver screen were *Saved from the Titanic* and *In Nacht und Eis*, both released in 1912. The former featured actress Dorothy Gibson, herself a survivor of *Titanic*, and the latter was purportedly based on the American and British hearings, yet neither was successful. As graphic dramatizations of a recent real-life disaster, perhaps the public felt they hit too close to home.

Atlantic, released in 1929, and *Titanic*, released in 1942, were verbose efforts and lacked dramatic impact, although the latter was rich in knowledge of the historical event and the people involved in it. Made in Germany, it was essentially an anti-British propaganda film.

In 1939, American producer David O. Selznick planned his own celluloid version, for which he hired a young British director named Alfred Hitchcock. It was to be Hitchcock's first American film. Selznick encountered a roadblock, however. The Mercantile Department of the British Board of Trade intervened, claiming that recounting the disaster would cast a negative light on British sailors and British shipping. Selznick's plans were abandoned, and the film was never made.

With the 1953 release of Fox's *Titanic* came a faithful, contemporary depiction of the tragic tale. Although somewhat weak in historical accuracy, the film's splendid production values and special effects made it one of the best on-screen portrayals.

Two years later, American historian Walter Lord published *A Night to Remember*. The book's lucid style, captivating realism, and historical accuracy made it the most influential single work about *Titanic* ever written. A bestseller translated into numerous languages, the book has been used in English and social studies courses throughout the United States. It was the basis for two celebrated docudramas about the disaster, Kraft Television Theater's live production on March

Poster for A Night to Remember, *based on Walter Lord's 1955 bestseller of the same title.*

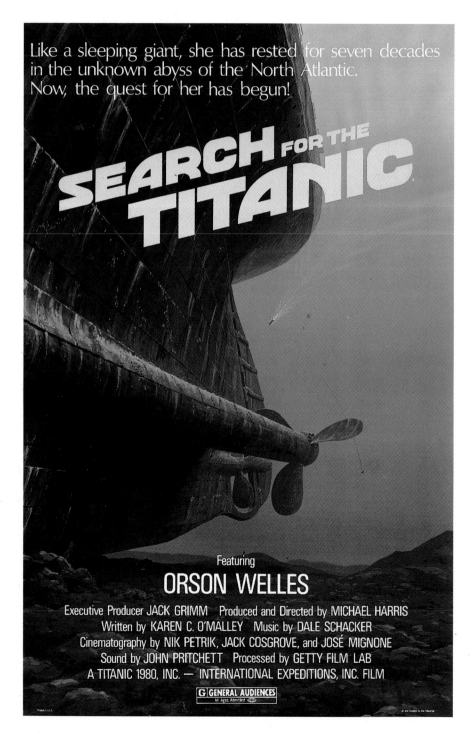

(Left) Poster for the 1981 documentary Search for the Titanic, *narrated by Orson Welles. The film was produced by Jack Grimm, sponsor of three searches for* Titanic's *wreck.*

28, 1956, and the 1958 British film of the same name, produced by William MacQuitty and starring Kenneth More.

The popular film version of Lord's *A Night to Remember* is the work to which nearly all subsequent films on the *Titanic* disaster have looked. *Raise the Titanic*, based on the book by Clive Cussler, made its screen debut in 1980.

Eighty-five years after the great vessel steamed into history, Hollywood's fascination with the legend continues. The special-effects extravaganza *Titanic*, directed by James Cameron, whose credits include the action-packed *Terminator*, *Aliens*, and *True Lies*, is scheduled to hit theaters in summer 1997. *Titanic* seems destined to make its mark into the twenty-first century and beyond.

(Right) The cover of Walter Lord's A Night to Remember; (far right) the cover of the Serbo-Croatian edition.

(Far left)
Advertisement for the
1980 film Raise the
Titanic, *based on Clive*
Cussler's best-selling
book of the same name.

(Left) French poster for
A Night to Remember.

(Bottom, far left)
Argentine poster for
SOS Titanic, *made in*
1979.

Enduring Fame

Titanic's story has long fascinated the world. Since the 1912 disaster, the liner's story has been told in many forms and in many languages.

- *Books:* 55 in print or planned, more than 150 known to have been published to date.
- *Sheet music:* more than 150 known titles.
- *Opera:* at least one, staged in Germany.
- *Broadway: Titanic,* a musical opening in New York in 1997 on the eighty-fifth anniversary of the start of her maiden voyage. Noël Coward's *Cavalcade,* which contained a *Titanic* sequence, was made into a film in the 1930s.
- Countless newspaper and magazine articles.
- *Films:* at least 11 feature films, some 20 documentaries, and many made-for-television movies and docudramas.
- *Art:* memorial handkerchiefs, postcards, reverse paintings on glass, and myriad other paintings and illustrations.
- *CD-ROMs:* at least three interactive CDs are available in Europe and the United States.
- *Audiotapes and CDs:* songs and music related to *Titanic.*
- *World Wide Web:* hundreds of sites and growing daily.
- *Memorials:* stained-glass windows, fountains, a cloistered garden, public statues, inscriptions on walls, a lighthouse, and many others.
- *Kitsch:* popular items, including towels, shower curtains, soap, key tags, belt buckles, so-called steward's badges, hats, lamps, posters, and prints.

William Parker, ship's carpenter on Minia, made this chess table from materials found floating at the wreck site. The picture frame below, also made by Parker, is a mosaic of wood from various Titanic staterooms, lounges, and corridors.

(left) The Spanish poster for A Night to Remember.

(Below) These period recordings enhanced the Titanic legend. "Nearer My God to Thee" was allegedly the final hymn played by the band played as the ship went down. "Be British," recorded after the disaster, was meant to convey the message that British passengers showed courage and did the right thing as the ship sank. "Stand to Your Post" referred to Captain Smith's orders to his crew to do their duty as the ship foundered.

(Right) Poster for A Night to Remember.

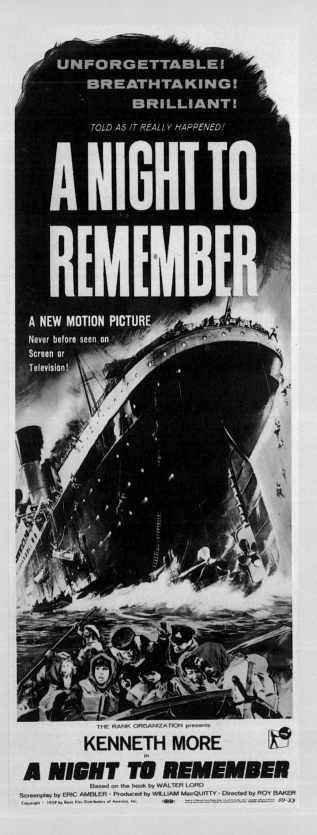

THE DISCOVERY

he first known plan to locate *Titanic* was conceived on April 20, 1912. From that point on, a series of attempts, both serious and crackpot, were made to locate the great ship's underwater grave. Yet the immense wreck would elude discovery until September 1, 1985.

Within five days of the sinking, a grief-stricken Vincent Astor, anxious to recover the body of his father, Colonel John Jacob Astor, met with a representative of the New York salvage firm Merritt-Chapman. Vincent wished to locate the sunken liner and blow it up with guncotton

---

The bow railing of Titanic *illuminated by Mir 2 submersible behind the forward anchor crane. Twin Russian submersibles,* Mir 1 *and* Mir 2, *photographed the wreck site extensively during a 1992 expedition that resulted in the IMAX feature film* Titanica.

The discovery of the Titanic *wreck in 1985 caused renewed public interest in Britain and around the world.*

to release the bodies trapped inside. The plan was scrapped when the colonel's body was found floating on the surface by *Mackay-Bennett* on April 22.

During World War II, materials and equipment were developed that could be used to explore ocean depths exceeding one and a half miles. It was not until after the war, when these tools became available to civilian engineers, that any serious plan to locate *Titanic* was considered. In the 1970s, with the advent of materials and electronic equipment able to withstand the extreme pressure at greater ocean depths, the monumental task began to attract skilled engineers and scientists.

In 1973, Dr. Robert D. Ballard, an underwater geologist from the Woods Hole Oceanographic Institution based in Cape Cod, Massachusetts, joined forces with the French agency IFREMER (*Institut Français de Recherche et Étude de la Mer*, the French Institute of Research and Study of the Sea) and became part of a two-year

As Titanic *sank, many passengers passed through these A-deck windows into lifeboats.*
This photograph was taken during the 1993 Titanic: Research and Recovery *expedition of*
RMS Titanic *and IFREMER.*

survey of the mid-Atlantic ridge. Although locating *Titanic* was not a goal of this expedition, Ballard and the IFREMER oceanographers would later become partners in a search for the wreck.

Equipment failure ended a 1977 expedition by Ballard to find and photograph *Titanic*, and during the late 1970s, he led or participated in several other deep-sea explorations around the world. In the early 1980s, he assisted in the design and

construction of a new type of unmanned submersible. Equipped with video and still cameras and elaborate lighting systems, these submersibles could be towed near the ocean bottom by a surface vessel. One such submersible, *Argo*, would eventually incorporate a remote-operated vehicle (ROV) and a system called ANGUS (Acoustically Navigated Geophysical Underwater Survey).

In 1980, 1981, and 1983, three

attempts to locate the wreck were made by a group consisting of Texas oil baron Jack Grimm, film producer Mike Harris, and Columbia University's Lamont-Doherty Geological Observatory, with limited participation from the Scripps Institute of Oceanography. Again, equipment failure, inadequate historical research, and uncooperative weather conditions brought a halt to each expedition.

Despite their lack of success, Grimm's expeditions proved that sidescan sonar was a valuable tool in exploring the sea's depths. IFREMER employed its version of the technology, *Sonar Acoustique Remorque* (SAR), in a 1985 joint French-American expedition to locate *Titanic*'s wreck. Under the direction of IFREMER project leader Jean Jarry, the expedition was conducted in two phases: The French research vessel *Le Suroit*, under Captain Jean-Louis Michel, was to systematically sweep the 150-square-mile area where *Titanic* was believed to lie. Once the wreck was located, the American research vessel *Knorr*, led by Ballard, would photograph it using *Argo* and ANGUS.

Armed with research and coordinates acquired by previous expeditions, *Le*

(Right) A view on Titanic's *starboard boat deck into windows to*
first-class cabins U and W, taken by Mir.

Suroit arrived in the area on July 9. For the next ten days, the vessel scanned the area south and east of *Titanic*'s distress position, but without success. On July 19, *Le Suroit* was forced to put in for supplies at St. Pierre, a small island off the coast of Newfoundland. Ballard joined the ship and was aboard when the French vessel's second cruise was conducted from July 26 through August 6. Again, no sign of the wreck was found.

After deboarding *Le Suroit* when it returned to St. Pierre, Ballard, Michel, and several French scientists flew to the Azores, where they joined *Knorr*. As the American vessel made its way into the area, Ballard and Michel re-evaluated *Titanic*'s

(Above) Titanic's *partially buried port-side propeller photographed with a wide-angle lens from a Mir porthole.*

Photographed during Robert Ballard's 1986 expedition, one of Titanic's *stern cranes (below left) lies dislodged from its base; below, "rusticles" trail from bollards on* Titanic's *forecastle.*

Titanic's *prow railing, photographed during the 1992 Mir expedition.*

(Opposite) Another propeller view, taken by Mir I, showing the immensity of Titanic's *propellers relative to the Mir II submersible.*

possible location based on data from *Le Suroit*'s two unsuccessful searches. They decided to search east and north of the earlier primary position.

Knorr's crew reached the site on August 24. *Argo*, with its newer imaging equipment, was chosen to make the initial searches, and the first dives were conducted on August 26 and 27. By August 31, eight east-west lines of the search's second phase had been completed, and the imaging equipment was well into its ninth pass. At midnight, the shipboard watch changed. Michel took over the scientific watch from Ballard, who retired to his cabin.

At approximately 12:48 A.M. on September 1, Woods Hole research specialist Stewart E. Harris was watching the video monitors when a piece of manmade debris suddenly came into view. He quickly alerted his fellow watch members, who crowded eagerly around the monitors as *Argo* transmitted the first images of *Titanic*'s wreck, more than two and a half miles down. Incredulity was followed by confirmation and shouts of joy and celebration. After seventy-three years, the search for *Titanic* was over.

At 2:30 A.M., a ceremony honoring

The force of the impact with the ocean floor is evident in this photo of a section of Titanic's *stern, which lies approximately 650 yards from the bow section. The ship's stern decks apparently collapsed onto one another upon impact. Torn electrical cables (above) crisscross the underside of a deck bent backwards over the rest of the stern.*

Titanic and her dead was held on *Knorr*'s fantail. When it was over, Ballard said quietly, "Thank you all. Now let's get back to work."

Over the next five days, in severe weather, equipment attached to ANGUS transmitted numerous images of the wreck and of articles surrounding it on the seabed. The first photographs and film footage of the wreck were broadcast on Canadian television and on the American television network CBS. After release by Woods Hole, photographs were published first in Canada, then throughout the world.

Knorr left the discovery site on September 6 and returned to Woods Hole to a hero's welcome.

No announcement had been made either by Ballard or Woods Hole regarding salvage of any artifacts from *Titanic*. As early as September 11, a bill was introduced in the U.S. House of Representatives "to designate

(Above) A close view of the forward port position where the last lifeboat, collapsible D, was launched. The tip of the toppled forward mast lies next to a fallen lifeboat davit.

the shipwreck of the *Titanic* as a maritime memorial and to provide for reasonable research, exploration and, if appropriate, salvage activities." Public hearings were held on October 29, 1985. An amended bill was introduced to the House on November 21 and again on December 2, when it was passed. The bill reached the U.S. Senate on January 27, 1986, and was passed on October 6. It was signed into law by President Ronald Reagan on October 21, 1986.

Ballard returned to the wreck in 1986, unaccompanied by the French, who reported a lack of government funding. Reaching the site aboard *Atlantis II* on July 1, he made his first dive on the following day. Aboard Atlantis II was *Alvin*, one of a half dozen manned submersibles capable of operating at *Titanic*'s depth. An electrical failure in *Alvin* forced Ballard and his two-man crew to surface hurriedly, but not before they caught a fleeting glimpse of *Titanic*'s bow.

After repairs, *Alvin* completed eleven dives over the next twelve days. The

small ROV *Jason Junior* allowed examination and televising of the wreck's interior. At night, while the manned diving equipment was undergoing maintenance and battery recharging, ANGUS was deployed to take still and moving images.

The dives were well documented in three issues of *National Geographic*, as well as in several books written by Ballard. National newsmagazines devoted special coverage to the discovery, and *Titanic* and her exploration were the subject of countless television and radio talk shows.

For the oceanographers at Woods Hole, the 1986 dives represented both a proud accomplishment and a challenging task, as scientists set out to catalog and identify thousands of images and thousands of feet of videotape and film brought back from the expedition.

Although not without controversy, many historians, scientists, and businessmen wished to recover objects from the site and restore them for display in a dignified manner as a way of preserving the story of *Titanic* for future generations. Efforts would soon be made toward further exploration of the wreck and retrieval objects from the debris field.

RECOVERY AND CONSERVATION

Since its discovery in 1985, fewer than 125 people have made the perilous 12,450-foot descent to *Titanic*'s wreck. Only six submersibles in the world—each requiring extensive technical support aboard a research vessel with a large crew—are capable of diving to the ship, which lies in one of the most inhospitable environments on Earth.

After the completion of the 1986 Woods Hole expedition, it was inevitable that others would seek the resources necessary to explore *Titanic*. Opinion became increasingly divided between those who felt that the site should be left untouched as a memorial, and those who believed that artifacts should be recovered from the site and preserved for public display.

In 1987, a group of businessmen willing to undertake the considerable risk and expense of an expedition to *Titanic* formed Oceanic Research and Exploration. Together with

The submersible Nautile *(above) being lowered into the water above the* Titanic *wreck site.*

cosponsor Titanic Ventures and others, the group secured the collaboration of IFREMER, which provided the research ship *Nadir*, the submersible *Nautile*, and the ROV *Robin*. The stated purpose of the expedition was to photograph remote areas of the ship not yet explored, to study the causes of the disaster, and to recover and conserve objects from the wreck. It was

agreed in advance that artifacts would be retrieved only from the debris field.

Nadir sailed from its home port of Toulon, France, on July 10, 1987, and arrived at the wreck site on the morning of July 22. Thirty-two dives to the wreck and debris field were completed between July 25 and September 10, and more than 1,800 objects were recovered and brought to France for restoration and conservation.

Late in the summer of 1987, fearful that the recovered objects would enter the world of international commerce, the U.S. Senate considered a bill prohibiting the importation to America of objects from RMS *Titanic*. The bill was passed, then tabled. The House of Representatives took no action.

In 1992, Titanic Ventures established its right to ownership of the wreck by successfully defeating a challenge by a group whose members included Jack Grimm, leader of three

A view of the French research vessel Nadir *(left), support ship for* Nautile, *which explored the wreck of* Titanic *during expeditions in 1987, 1993, 1994 and 1996.*

Falling by gravity with the aid of lead weights, Nautile (above) takes 90 minutes to reach the wreck site, two-and-a-half miles below the ocean's surface. The three-man submersible can reach a maximum depth of 20,000 feet.

(Above right) A diver assists the crew of Nautile as the submersible reaches the surface. Including slightly more than three hours of travel time, dives can last up to twelve hours.

earlier unsuccessful attempts to find *Titanic*. RMS Titanic, Inc. became successor to Titanic Ventures in May 1993; the new group reapplied for status as salvor-in-possession of the wreck, which was granted in the U.S. District Court in May 1993.

In June 1993, RMS Titanic, Inc. and IFREMER collaborated on an expedition called "*Titanic*: Research and Recovery." In fifteen dives in fifteen days, the group retrieved 800 artifacts to add to those recovered in 1987.

The wreck of *Titanic* lies at approximately 41.43°N, 49.56°W in the North Atlantic,

about 560 miles southeast of Newfoundland. As seventeen-year-old survivor Jack Thayer, Jr. had reported after the disaster, the ship broke in two as it sank, and now lies in one small and two large pieces of wreckage, the stern and bow sections separated by 650 yards. Most of the debris is scattered in a one-square-mile area around the main wreckage.

The descent to the wreck site is made in the twenty-eight-foot long by nine-foot wide battery-powered *Nautile*. Operated by a three-member crew, the submersible is built around a seven-foot-diameter, four-inch-thick titanium

(Above) *A robotic arm extending from* Nautile, *one of several methods for gently lifting artifacts from the ocean floor.*

Nautile *(left) is lifted from the ocean after a ten-hour exploration of* Titanic *and taken aboard* Nadir.

alloy sphere that can withstand the enormous pressure of dives up to 20,000 feet. The interior of the sphere is crowded but not cramped: Two metal foam-covered couches flank an upright seat in the middle. The pilot is positioned in the left couch, the observer occupies the right, and the co-pilot sits upright in the center chair. Prospective divers must pass a physical examination that includes assessment of heart condition and susceptibility to claustrophobia.

Each dive costs upwards of $150,000. A timeline and dive objectives are established and followed as closely as possible while accounting for unforeseen circumstances. With three tons of pressure on every square inch of *Nautile*, the environment allows no margin for error. All three crew members spend each dive watching attentively for obstructions, assisted by the submersible's powerful sonar and navigation systems. Everything is checked and rechecked by technicians, since failure of any on-board system could result in extreme danger.

There are no lavatory facilities aboard *Nautile*, and consumption of food and drink is not permitted for several hours prior to a dive. Descending at a rate of 120 feet per minute, it takes an hour and a half for *Nautile* to reach the site. The submersible's interior grows chilly from contact with the 32°F water, so the crew wears several layers of clothing. During the descent, *Nautile*'s interior is kept dark to conserve precious battery power. The only illumination comes from the electronic equipment that crowds the interior.

Apart from routine radio reports to the

surface every 10 minutes, the descent is silent. There is no hissing of air pressure, no creaking of the hull despite increasing pressure on *Nautile*'s outer surface. By the time the submersible reaches the ocean floor, its three occupants are already damp from the constant dripping of the condensed water vapor from their breaths. At dive's end, more than three gallons of "breathwater" will collect beneath them.

The crew peers into the depths through three portholes, each about 5 inches in diameter, made of conical plexiglas that flattens as the submersible descends and water pressure increases. Beyond the portholes, seawater gradually changes from bright blue-green to dark blue. At about 300 feet, all light has disappeared.

A "pinpoint" landing might damage the submersible or endanger the wreck, thus *Nautile* always touches down one-half to one mile from the ship. When the bottom is reached, the submersible's external lights are switched on. They illuminate a bubble of brilliance about 20 feet in diameter, extending above, below, and directly ahead of the submersible's path, revealing a sudden surprise: Incredibly, there is life here. Outside the ports, fish swim by. There are many, about three feet long, their thin bodies totally white, their large purple eyes apparently blind to *Nautile*'s lights.

Here and there tiny white starfish dot the sea floor.

Nautile moves slowly along its course, traveling about 15 feet above the seabed. The bottom is a pale, gray-tan undulating surface, not unlike a gently rolling sandy beach. Suddenly an object appears in the sand. *Nautile* travels past so quickly and the view is so limited that it is only recognizable as something out of place, something that doesn't belong there. Then there is another, and another. They are pieces of metal, some long and thin, others square and bulky. Their frequency increases. Then, beyond the porthole, a dark mass looms. Only ten feet away, it fills the port.

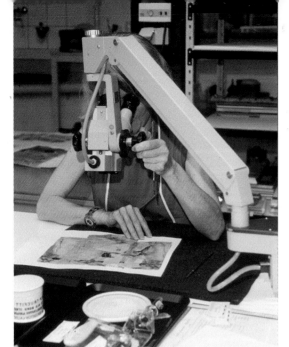

The first step in conservation and treatment consists of carefully observing the condition of the object. An LP3 conservator (above) looks at paper fragments under a special microscope. Using a tool made of bone (below), a conservator carefully opens the pages of a notebook. Once cleaned, these handwritten notations by a Titanic *passenger are perfectly legible after eight decades on the ocean floor.*

Rivet heads in straight rows. Demarcations of plating. A rusted surface, but here and there a hint of black paint. *Titanic*.

On a typical dive, *Nautile* moves upward in a large, slow arc along the hull, approaching a great tear in the ship's forward starboard side, opening onto G deck in a line directly below the ship's bridge and revealing the top of the number 6 boiler room's starboard forward coal bunker. Directly ahead through the breach is the post office. A sorting table can be seen against the room's aft bulkhead, surrounded by piles of mail sacks. Approaching the forward well deck from an altitude of 20 feet, moving directly across the bow, winches, bollards, fairleads, and hatches can all be seen clearly.

At the open number 1 hatch, *Nautile* stops, and the ROV *Robin* is sent down to inspect the condition of the lower decks. Maneuvering the tethered vehicle down the shaft and then retrieving it will take more than an hour. As it descends, *Robin* transmits remarkable pictures. Deck after deck can be seen receding into the ship's interior. At intervals, there are openings in the shaft's walls, closed off by barred gates that offer tantalizing glimpses of boxes, crates, and barrels.

A tour of the forward superstructure follows. The Marconi room reveals through its open skylight what appears to be equipment. A brief pass over the empty decks shows the spot where lifeboat number 2's davits now stand empty; the area on the boat deck's starboard side, outside the gymnasium, where the ship's musicians performed their final song; the sitting room, bedroom, and bathroom (tub still in place) of Captain Smith's quarters.

Then *Nautile* returns to a site above the forward grand staircase, where the glass-and-iron dome had once been. The pilot hovers above *Titanic*, and once again *Robin* emerges from its platform and is painstakingly guided inside the wreck, down the remnants of stairs on which the Wideners and Astors, Molly Brown and Benjamin Guggenheim once walked. The delicate metal tracery is now all but gone. Chandeliers hang askew from ceilings that once reverberated with conversation, laughter and music. *Robin* is carefully retrieved, and after nearly nine hours at the site, *Nautile*'s crew prepares for the ascent to the surface and *Nadir*.

Approximately 4,000 objects have made the trip from sea bed to ocean surface. The first group of artifacts, recovered in 1987, were conserved by Électricité de France in Paris.

An Uncertain Future

Long before *Titanic* was discovered, it was hypothesized that due to the extreme depth at which the wreck lies and the absence of dissolved oxygen in the water, the liner would be in excellent condition. While the assessment proved true for some organic materials in the debris field, to scientists' surprise *Titanic*'s undersea environment contained a variety of hostile elements that aroused concern for the future of both the wreck and its artifacts:

• Corrosion of the ship's metal structures—including decks, support beams and columns, and the hull itself—continues, a result of interaction between metal and salt water.

• Shipworm mollusks have devoured many wooden items, including the ship's wheel and her decks. Only steel underdecking remains, and in 1996 this was showing signs of corrosion perforation. The few wooden objects that remain probably have survived because their original heavy coats of varnish or shellac rendered them unpalatable to the mol-

lusks. This protection has dimished over time, however, and the objects are now almost invariably found in poor condition, posing special difficulties for conservators.

• Anaerobic bacteria from the seabed feed on metals, especially iron, causing degradation and staining of many artifacts. The so-called rusticles covering *Titanic* are outward signs that several different organisms are feeding on the iron and sulfur in the ship's steel. Based on a study during the 1996 expedition, colonies of these organisms already weigh an estimated 650 tons and have consumed approximately 15 percent of the hull's iron. Scientists are still trying to identify some of the organisms from samples obtained during this expedition. One has been confirmed as *Leptothrix*, a bacterium that consumes the inner surfaces of landside iron water pipes. The ship's hull and many objects in the debris field serve as natural magnets for bacteria colonies. According to a 1994 *Chemical and Engineering News* article, the organisms "multiply rapidly in anaerobic conditions" found at *Titanic*, which is a rich food source in comparison to the surrounding environment.

• Natural organic fibers such as paper, rope, and similar materials break down and sepa-

Safe door from Titanic's *Purser's office.*

rate in underwater conditions, causing them to become porous and fragile.

• Other objects absorb chlorides and sulfates from the sea water and become stained, weakened, and encrusted.

• The wreck site is swept by currents that frequently change in direction and intensity, picking up sand and depositing it over the objects in the debris field. Some items are becoming increasingly obscured by sediment, and many objects photographed in 1985 can no longer be located.

A view through the wreckage into the engine room (left). The formations resembling stalactites were dubbed "rusticles" by Titanic discoverer, Robert Ballard. This photograph was taken during the Mir expedition.

Realizing that further recoveries would take place over a long period of time, RMS Titanic, Inc., turned to LP3 Conservation, a private conservation laboratory located in the thirteenth-century village of Semur-en-Auxois in Burgundy, France. The professionals at LP3 Conservation are writing new chapters in the methodology of the restoration and conservation of artifacts recovered underwater. LP3's founders, Philippe Langot, Martine Plantec, Thierry Palanque, and Stéphane Pennec, and their staff bring a wide expertise to the task. Among their specialties are marine archaeology, and the conservation of ethnographic materials, metals, wood, textiles, paper, glass, ceramics, and modern materials such as plastic.

Using high-powered microscopes, a variety of chemicals, and tools ranging from simple household items to highly technical electrolytic processes, LP3 has cleaned, stabilized, and preserved hundreds of endangered artifacts from *Titanic*, many of which are initially so discolored and corroded through exposure to sea water, bacteriological action, oxidation, and other chemical reactions as to be almost unrecognizable. Although other objects appear to be almost new—glass and crystal, especially—they rapidly deteriorate if left untreated.

Paper items—correspondence, post cards, books, business cards, and currency—are black with decomposed sulfur compounds when recovered.

After objects are brought to *Nadir*'s deck from *Nautile*'s collecting basket or separately deployed lifting bags, they are immediately rinsed off with clear water inside an onboard laboratory. Surface debris is removed with a soft-bristled brush. They are then photographed and logged, each with its own number and brief description. This number is then cross-inventoried by an IFREMER staff member. The position on the seabed from which it

Mapping the Artifacts

Due to their fragility, *Titanic*'s artifacts must be recovered with the utmost care. Simultaneously, a precise record of their location must be kept so that future archaeologists and historians can learn from the arrangement of the artifacts on the ocean floor.

As is done at land-based archaeological sites, photographs of every object must be taken "in place" before any object is moved. Prior to the 1987, 1993, 1994, and 1996 recovery expeditions, such precision could be achieved only in relatively shallow waters. Divers would begin to work a site by establishing a grid system. Lines were strung across the ocean floor in a checkerboard pattern, and detailed records were made of every object at its grid location.

At *Titanic*'s depth, workers would have to use remote-controlled manipulator arms for even the simplest task. A new method had to be created that employed the latest high-tech equipment.

A support (above) from one of Titanic's *many deck benches lies on the ocean floor. Photograph taken during the* Mir *expedition.*

At the beginning of each *Titanic* expedition, underwater beacons, called transponders, are deposited on the ocean floor. The coordinates of the transponders are calculated to the nearest foot using signals from a network of global positioning system (GPS) satellites. Locking onto the transponders and GPS signals, the support ship *Nadir* and the submersible *Nautile* calibrate their on-board navigation systems. Once a dive begins, *Nautile* automatically sends its position to *Nadir* every 30 seconds. A computer plots the position on a site map, and displays it on a video monitor. The submersible's exact position is known at all times.

High-powered lights are switched on, and *Nautile*'s high-resolution still and video cameras document each object in situ. The submersible's position becomes part of the videotape, permanently recording the artifact's original location. Conversation between the crew and transmissions between the surface and *Nautile* are also recorded, providing a running account of the recovery process.

was recovered is carefully matched with an underwater videotape that bears the precise time and coordinates of the object's retrieval. This log becomes a permanent archaeological record.

Initial examination and cleansing are followed by the conservator's judgment as to whether the piece can be dry- or wet-stored. If dry, the objects generally are separated by material type, individually wrapped in protective plastic foam, and stored in shockproof containers. Wet-stored objects are immersed in fresh water, inside an appropriate container. Great care is taken to ensure that the descriptive labels match the conservator's log entries.

Large objects—bollards, ship's whistles, lifeboat davits—are lowered into huge deck-top baths, some of which have been constructed on board. Under constant observation from the moment they are retrieved, artifacts are housed in locked storage rooms until they can be off-loaded at a French port and delivered to a laboratory representative. Unopened, they are transported by truck to the LP3 Conservation laboratory.

Objects are stored in airtight vaults and cabinets in which temperature and humidity are carefully controlled. Before conservation can commence, each must be separated into its component pieces and cleaned. The materials are those that would have been found in any sizable English town in 1912: ceramics and table china, paper products, metallic objects, textiles, glass, leather, crystal, gold, silver, synthetic and real ivory, and an early plastic called Bakelite.

Corrosion products include surface salts and acidic silt, minor calcium incrustation, heavy chemical or galvanically induced stains, and deeply incursive metallic ions.

Many complex conservation techniques are required in the preservation of the varied objects. Objects of similar material are first desalinated in large trays, sometimes for long periods so that stability can be maintained. Corrosion is removed from metallic artifacts either chemically or electrolytically. After cleaning and stabilizing, these items receive a preservative coating to prevent further deterioration when exposed to air. Frequently, wax is also applied to further protect the object.

Organic materials such as paper and textiles must be fumigated to prevent mold damage, then freeze dried to remove moisture. Stains are identified and chemically removed. When necessary, paper is re-sized to bind its fibers.

Ceramics are bathed in ethanol to drive

Chefs in Titanic's *kitchen used these oven-ready porcelain dishes (above) for soufflés or casseroles. The reddish substance, which can also be observed in tiny fissures in the glazing of porcelain objects, is a residue of iron oxide. Concretions of iron oxide particles, emanating from the deteriorating hull and other debris on the seabed, cover all of the objects in the debris field.*

An extreme though common example (above) of salt water's corrosive effects stands in astonishing contrast to a similar silver plate that has been meticulously restored. The plate on the right, bearing the White Star Line logo, was made by Goldsmiths and Silversmiths Company of London.

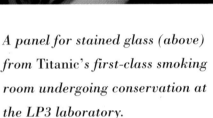

A panel for stained glass (above) from Titanic's *first-class smoking room undergoing conservation at the LP3 laboratory.*

(Above right) Titanic *departed Southampton with 6,000 tons of coal, much of which is scattered across the debris field. The ship burned 690 tons of coal a day.*

(Opposite) One of Titanic's *B deck portholes shrouded with rust.*

out moisture and corrosive, water-bearing salts. Leather is lubricated so it will not become brittle. After corrosion products have been identified and removed, a protective coating of polyethylene glycol is applied. Great care must be taken when desalinating crystal and glass so that the objects will not show signs of salt recrystallizing upon drying.

A growing abundance of sources awaits those interested in learning more about *Titanic*. New books on the subject are published every year, and library or online searches will yield hundreds of newspaper and magazine articles, many written since the ship's discovery in 1985. The *Halifax Star-Chronicle* offers a computer disk containing the text of more than a hundred

Titanic-related stories that have appeared in its pages over the years. Most libraries carry copies of 1912 newspapers on microfilm. Then, as now, newspapers varied widely in their accuracy. The *New York Times* and the *Times* of London are excellent sources, but it is perhaps in small-town newspapers that the best finds can be made. Unique interviews with survivors, especially those from second and third class, are often given space not found in big-city newspapers.

In the next several years, exhibitions throughout North America, Europe, and Asia will bring the objects recovered from *Titanic* to a wide public. Under an agreement between RMS Titanic, Inc., and the French government, whose ships and personnel made the recovery possible, the artifacts are to remain together as a collection. Ultimately, they will be placed in a permanent memorial museum, which will serve as a world center of *Titanic* research and remembrance.

As the number of living survivors dwindles, and as the once-beautiful liner continues to deteriorate, these artifacts will assume a new significance. One day, they will be the final tangible link to history's most famous ship, and to her passengers and crew, whose memory they honor.

Cargo Manifest

Wakem & McLaughlin	case wine		2 cases furniture	American Shipping Co	5 cases books
Thorer & Praetorius	bale skins	American Express Co	1 case elastics	Adams Express	35 cases books
Carter, W. E.	case auto		1 case gramophone	Lasker & Bernstein	117 cases sponges
Fuchs & Lang Mfg Co	cases printer's blankets		4 cases hosiery	Oelrichs & Co	2 cases pictures, etc
Spaulding A. G. & Bros.	34 cases athletic goods		5 cases books	Stechert, G .E. & Co	12 packages periodicals
Park & Tilford	1 case toothpaste		1 case canvas	Millbank, Leaman & Co	3 cases woollens
	5 cases drug sundries		1 case rubber goods	Vandegrift, F. B. & Co	63 cases champagne
	1 case brushware		3 cases prints	Downing, R. F. & Co	1 case felt
Maltus & Ware	8 cases orchids		6 cases films		1 case meal
Spencerian Pen Co	4 cases pens		1 case tweed		3 cases tennis balls
Sherman Sons & Co	7 cases cottons		1 case sero fittings		1 case engine packing
Claflin, H. B. & Co	12 cases cotton laces		[syringes?]	Dublin, Morris & Kornbluth	2 packages skins
Muser Bros	3 cases tissues		a quantity of old oak	International Trading Co	1 case surgical instruments
Isler & Guve	4 bales straw		beams		1 case ironware
Rydeman & Lassner	1 case tulle (netting for		1 case plants	Pitt & Scott	4 cases printed matter
	scarves or veils)		1 case speedometer		1 case cloth
Petry, P. H. & Co	1 case tulle		1 package effects	Davies, Turner & Co	4 cases printed matter
Metzger, A. S.	2 cases tulle		2 cases samples		1 case machinery
Mills & Gibb	20 cases cottons		8 cases paste		1 case pictures
	1 case gloves		3 cases camera and stand		1 case books
Field, Marshall & Co	1 case gloves		4 cases books		1 case merchandise
NY Motion Picture Co	1 case films	Sheldon, G. W. & Co	1 case machinery		1 case notions
Thorburn, J. M. & Co	3 cases bulbs	Maltus & Ware	15 cases alarm apparatus		1 case photo
Rawstick & H.Trading Co	28 bags sticks		11 cases orchids	Sheldon, G. W. & Co	1 case elastics
Dujardin & Ladnick	10 boxes melons	Hempstead & Sons	30 cases plants		2 cases books
American Express Co	25 cases merchandise	Brasch & Rothenstein	2 cases lace collars		1 box golf balls
Tiffany & Co	1 cask china		2 cases books		5 cases instruments
	1 case silver goods	Isler & Guve	53 packages straw	American Express Co	2 parcels merchandise
Lustig Bros	4 cases straw hats	Baring Bros & Co	68 cases rubber	Vandegrift, F. B. & Co	1 case merchandise
Kuyper, P. C. & Co	1 case elastic cords		100 bags gutta (percha)	Budd, S.	1 parcel merchandise
	1 case leather	Altman, B. & Sons	1 case cottons	Lemke & Buechner	1 parcel merchandise
Cohen, M. Bros	5 packages skins	Stern, S.	60 cases salt powder	Nicholas, G. S. & Co	1 case merchandise
Gross, Engle Co	1 case skins	Arnold, F. R. Co	6 cases soap	Walker, G. A.	1 case merchandise
Wilson, P. K. & Son	61 cases tulle	Shieffelin & Co	17 packages wool fat	Adams Express Co	4 rolls linoleum
Gallia Textile Co	1 case lace goods	American Motor Co	1 package candles		3 bales leather
Calhoun, Robbins & Co	1 case cotton laces	Strohmeyer & Arpe	75 bales fish		1 case hats
	1/2 case brushware	National City Bank of New York	11 bales rubber		6 cases confectionery
Victor & Achiles	1 case brushware	Kronfeld, Saunders & Co	5 cases shell		5 cases books
Baumgarten, Wm & Co	3 cases furniture	Richard, C. B.	1 case films		1 case tin tubes
Spielman Co	3 cases silk crepe	Corbett, M. J. & Co	2 cases hat leather, etc		2 cases soap
Nottingham Lace Works	2 cases cotton	Snow's Express Co	3 cases books		2 cases boots
Naday & Fleischer	1 case laces	Van Ingen, E. H. & Co	1 case woollens	Wells, Fargo Co	3 cases books
Rosenthal, Leo J. Co	4 cases cotton	Lippincott, J. B. & Co	10 cases books		2 cases furniture
Wakem & McLaughlin	25 cases biscuits	Lazard Freres	1 bale skins		1 case pamphlets
	42 cases wines	Aero Club of America	1 crate machinery		1 case plants
Leeming, T. & Co	7 cases biscuits		1 case printed matter		1 case eggs
Crown Perfume Co	3 cases soap perfume	Witcombe, McGrachlin & Co	856 rolls linoleum		1 case whiskey
Meadows, T. & Co	5 cases books	Wright & Graham Co	437 casks tea	International News Co	10 packages periodicals
	3 boxes samples	Gillman, J.	4 bales skins	Van Ingen, E. H. & Co	1 parcel
	1 case parchment	Arnold & Zeiss	134 cases rubber	Sterns, R. H. & Co	1 case cretonne [silk]
Thomas & Pierson	2 cases hardware	Brown Bros & Co	76 cases dragon's blood	Downing, R. F. & Co	1 case iron jacks
	2 cases books		3 cases gum		1 case bulbs

Cargo Manifest

Jacobson, James	1 case hosiery	Johnson, J. G. Co	2 cases ribbons		3 cases beans
Carbon Machinery Equipment Co	1 case clothing	Judkins & McCormick	2 cases flowers		10 cases mixed vegetables
Sanger, R. & Co	3 cases hair nets	Spielman Co	1 case gloves		13 cased peas
Flietmann & Co	1 case silk goods	American Express Co	18 cases merchandise		25 cases olives
Rush & Co	1 case hair nets	Wakem & McLaughlin	6 bales cork		12 bundles capers
Blum, J.A.	3 cases silk goods	Acker, Merrall & Condit	75 cases anchovies		10 bundles fish
Tiedeman, T. & Sons	3 cases silk goods		225 cases mussels		20 bundles merchandise
Costa, F.	1 case silk goods		1 case liquor	Austin, Nichols	25 cases olive oil
Tolson, A. M. & Co	1 case gloves	Engs, P. W. & Sons	190 cases liquor		14 cases mushrooms
Mathews, G. T. & Co	2 cases books and lace		25 cases syrups	Order	14 cases factice
Tice & Lynch	5 cases books	Schall & Co	25 cases preserves		13 cases gum
	1 bag frames	NY & Cuba SS Co	12 cases butter		14 casks gum
	1 case cotton		18 cases oil		285 casks gum
	2 cases stationery		2 hogsheads vinegar		8 bales skins
US Export Co	1 case scientific instruments		19 cases vinegar		4 cases opium
	1 case sundries		6 cases preserves		3 cases window frames
	3 cases test cords		8 cases dried fruit		8 bales skins
	1 case briar pipes		10 bundles of 2 cases wine		8 packages skins
	1 case sundries	DuBois, Geo C.	16 hogsheads wine		2 cases horsehair
	2 cases printed matter	Hollander, H.	185 cases wine		2 cases silk
Pape, Chas & Co	1,196 bags potatoes		110 cases brandy		8 bales raw silk
Sauer, J. P. & Co	318 bags potatoes	Van Renssaller, C. A.	10 hogsheads wine		4 packages hair nets
Rusch & Co	1 case velvets		15 cases cognac		200 packages tea
Mallouk, H.	1 case laces	Brown Bros & Co	100 cases shelled walnuts		246 cases sardines
Bardwill Bros	cases laces	Bernard, Judas & Co	70 bundles cheese		30 rolls jute bagging
Heyliger, A. V.	1 case velvet	American Express Co	30 bundles cheese		1962 bags potatoes
Peabody, H. W. & Co	13 bales straw goods		2 cases cognac		7 cases raw feathers
Simon, A. I. & Co	1 case raw feathers	Moquin Wine Co	case liquor		10 cases hatters' fur
Wilson, P. K. & Sons	2 cases linens		38 cases oil		3 cases tissue
Manhattan Shirt Co	3 cases tissues	Knauth, Nachod & Kuhne	107 cases mushrooms		1 case rabbit hair
Broadway Trust Co	3 cases coney skins [rabbit]		1 case pamphlets		31 packages crude rubber
Prost, G.	1 case auto parts	Lazard Freres	25 cases sardines		7 cases vegetables
Young Bros	1 case feathers		3 cases preserves		5 cases fish
Wimpfheimer, A. & Co	3 cases feathers	Acker, Merral & Condit	50 cases wine		10 cases syrups
Brown Bros & Co	15 cases rabbit hair	Dubois, Geo F.	6 cases vermouth		2 cases liquors
Goldster, Morris	11 cases feather		4 cases wine		150 cases shelled walnuts
Cobb, G. H.	1 case lace tissue	Heidelbach, Ickelheimer & Co	11 cases shelled walnuts		15 bundles cheese
Anderson Refrig Machinery Co	11 cases refrigeration	Brown Bros & Co	100 bales shelled walnuts		8 bales buchu
	apparatus	First National Bank of Chicago	300 cases shelled walnuts		2 cases grandfather clocks
Suter, Alfred	18 cases machinery	Blechoff, H. & Co	35 bags rough wood		2 cases leather
American Express Co	1 case packed packages	Baumert, F. X. & Co	50 bundles cheese	Holders of original bills	79 goat skins
	3 cases tissues	Rathenberger & Co	190 bundles cheese	of lading	16 cases calabashes
	2 barrels mercury	Haupt & Burgi	50 bundles cheese		5 bales buchu
	1 barrel earth	Sheldon & Co	40 bundles cheese		4 cases embroidery
	2 barrels glassware	Percival, C.	50 bundles cheese		3 barrels wine
	3 cases printed matter	Stone, C. D. & Co	50 bundles cheese		12 cases ostrich feathers
	1 case straw braids	Phoenix Cheese Co	30 bundles cheese		4 cases feathers
	1 case straw hats	Petry, P. H. & Co	10 bundles cheese		3 bales skins
	1 case cheese	Reynolds & Dronig	15 bundles cheese		33 bags argols
Meadows, Thomas & Co	3 cases hosiery	Fouger, E.	41 cases filter paper		3 bales sheep skins
Uchs & Hegnoer	3 cases silk goods	Munro, J. & Co	22 cases mushrooms		
Cauvigny Brush Co	1 case brushware		15 cases peas		

Passenger and Crew List

As *Carpathia* approached New York, the world waited anxiously for the names of survivors. Wireless transmissions from *Carpathia* were garbled by interference from other operators. When messages were received, many names were distorted by inventive spellings. Weeks passed before accurate lists of passengers and crew were made public. The passenger list below was compiled by *Titanic* historian Michael A. Findlay, © 1994. The crew list is presented as first published by the U.S. Senate committee that investigated the disaster.

PASSENGERS

Name	Residence	Age	Class
Abbing, Mr. Anthony		42	3rd
Abbott, Master Eugene Joseph	East Providence, RI	13	3rd
Abbott, Mr. Rossmore Edward	East Providence, RI	16	3rd
Abbott, Mrs. Stanton (Rosa)	East providence, RI	35	3rd
Abelseth, Miss Anna Karen	Norway to Los Angeles, CA	16	3rd
Abelseth, Mr. Olaus	Perkins County, SD	25	3rd
Abelson, Mr. Samuel	Russia to New York, NY	30	2nd
Abelson, Mrs. Samuel (Anna)	Russia to New York, NY	28	2nd
Abraham, Mrs. Joseph (Sophie Easu)	Greensburg, PA	18	3rd
Abrahamsson, Mr. August	Taalintehdas, Finland to Hoboken, NJ	20	3rd
Adahl, Mr. Mauritz Nils Martin	Asarum, Sweden to Brooklyn, NY	30	3rd
Adams, Mr. John	Bournemouth, England	26	3rd
Ahlin, Mrs. Johanna Persdotter	Sweden to Akeley, MN	40	3rd
Ahmed, Mr. Ali		24	3rd
Aijo-Nirva, Mr. Isak	Finland to Sundbury, ON	41	3rd
Aks, Mrs. Sam (Leah Rosen)	London to Norfolk, VA	18	3rd
Aks, Master Philip	London to Norfolk, VA	10m	3rd
Aldworth, Mr. Charles Augustus	Bryn Mawr, PA	30	2nd
Alexander, Mr. William	England to Albion, NY	23	3rd
Alhomaki, Mr. Ilmari Rudolf	Salo, Findland to Astoria, OR	20	3rd
Ali, Mr. William	Argentina	25	3rd
Allen, Miss Elisabeth Walton	St. Louis, MO	29	1st
Allen, Mr. William Henry	Lower Clapton, Middlesex, England	35	3rd
Allison, Miss Helen Loraine,	Montreal, PQ/Chesterville, ON	2	1st
Allison, Mr. Hudson Joshua Creighton	Montreal, PQ/Chesterville, ON	30	1st
Allison, Mrs. Hudson, J. C. (Bessie Waldo Daniels)	Montreal, PQ/Chesterville, ON	25	1st
Allison, Master Hudson Trevor	Montreal, PQ/Chesterville, ON	11m	1st
Allum, Mr. Owen George	Windsor, England to New York, NY	18	3rd
Andersen, Mr. Albert Karvin	Bergin, Norway	32	3rd
Andersen, Mr. Thor Olsvigen	Oslo, Norway to Cameron, WI	20	3rd
Anderson, Mr. Harry	New York, NY	47	1st
Andersson, Mr. Anders Johan	Sweden to Winnipeg, MB	39	3rd
Andersson, Mrs. Anders (Alfrida K. Brogren)	Sweden to Winnipeg, MB	39	3rd
Andersson, Miss Ebba Iris	Sweden to Winnipeg, MB	6	3rd
Andersson, Miss Ellis Anna Maria	Sweden to Winnipeg, MB	2	3rd
Andersson, Miss Erna	Ruotsinphyhtaa, Finland to New York, NY	17	3rd
Andersson, Miss Ida Augusta Margareta	Vadsbro, Sweden to Ministee, MI	38	3rd
Andersson, Miss Ingeborg Constancia	Sweden to Winnipeg, MB	9	3rd
Andersson, Mr. Johan Samuel	Hartford, CT	26	3rd
Andersson, Miss Sigrid Elizabeth	Sweden to Winnipeg, MB	11	3rd
Andersson, Master Sigvard Harald Elias	Sweden to Winnipeg, MB	4	3rd
Andersson, Mr. Paul Edvin	Sweden to Chicago, IL	20	3rd
Andrew, Mr. Edgar Samuel	Buenos Aires to New Jersey	18	2nd
Andrew, Mr. Frank	Cornwall, England to Hougton, MI		2nd
Andrews, Miss Kornelia Theodosia	Hudson, NY	63	1st
Andrews, Mr. Thomas, Jr.	Belfast, Northern Ireland	39	1st
Angheloff, Mr. Minko	Bulgaria to Chicago, IL	26	3rd
Angle, Mr. William A.	Warwick, England	32	2nd
Angle, Mrs. William A. (Florence)	Warwick, England	32	2nd
Appleton, Mrs. Edward Dale (Charlotte Lamson)	Bayside, Queens, NY	58	1st
Arnold, Mr. Josef	Altdorf, Switzerland	25	3rd
Arnold, Mrs. Josef (Josephine Frank)	Altdorf, Switzerland	18	3rd
Aronsson, Mr. Ernst Axel Algot	Sweden to Joliet, IL	24	3rd
Artagaveytia, Mr. Ramon	Montevideo, Uruguay		1st
Ashby, Mr. John	West Hoboken, NJ	57	2nd
Asim, Mr. Adola		35	3rd
Asplund, Mr. Carl Oscar Vilhelm Gustafsson	Sweden to Worcester, MA	40	3rd
Asplund, Mrs. Carl Oscar (Selma Augusta Johansson)	Sweden to Worcester, MA	38	3rd
Asplund, Master Carl Edgar	Sweden to Worcester, MA	5	3rd
Asplund, Master Clarence Gustaf Hugo	Sweden to Worcester, MA	9	3rd
Asplund, Master Edvin Rojj Felix	Sweden to Worcester, MA	3	3rd
Asplund, Master Filip Oscar	Sweden to Worcester, MA	13	3rd
Asplund, Mr. John Charles	Oskarshamn, Sweden to Minneapolis, MN	23	3rd
Asplund, Miss Lillian Gertrud	Sweden to Worcester, MA	5	3rd
Assaf, Mr. Gerios	Ottawa, ON		3rd
Assaf, Mrs. Mariana	Ottawa, ON	45	3rd
Assam, Mr. Ali		23	3rd
Astor, Col. John Jacob	New York, NY	47	1st
Astor, Mrs. John Jacob (Madeleine Talmadge Force)	New York, NY	19	1st
Attalah, Miss Malaka		17	3rd
Attala (Kalil), Mr. Solomon	Ottawa, ON	27	3rd
Aubert, Mrs. Leontine Pauline	Paris, France	23	3rd
Augustsson, Mr. Albert	Krakoryd, Sweden to Bloomington, Il	23	3rd
Baccos, Mr. Rafoul		20	3rd
Backstrom, Mr. Karl Alfred	Ruotsinphyhtaa, Finland to New York	32	3rd
Backstrom, Mrs. Karl Alfred (Maria Mathilda Gustafsson)	Ruotsinphyhtaa, Finland to New York	33	3rd
Baclini, Miss Eugenie	Syria to New York, NY	3	3rd
Baclini, Miss Helene	Syria to New York, NY		3rd
Baclini, Miss Maria	Syria to New York, NY		3rd
Baclini, Mrs. Solomon (Latifa)	Syria to New York, NY	24	3rd
Badman, Miss Emily Louisa	London to Skanteales, NY	18	3rd
Badt, Mr. Mohamed		40	3rd
Bailey, Mr. Percy Andrew	Penzance, Cornwall, England to Akron, OH	18	2nd
Baimbrigge, Mr. Charles R.	Guernsey	23	2nd
Balkic, Mr. Cerin		26	3rd
Balls, Mrs. Ada E. Hall	Bristol, England to Jacksonville, FL	36	2nd
Banfield, Mr. Frederick J.	Plymouth, England to Houghton, MI	28	2nd
Banoura, Miss Ayout	Syria to Youngstown, OH	15	3rd
Barbara, Mrs. Catherine	Syria to Ottawa, OH	45	3rd
Barbara, Miss Saude	Syria to Ottawa, ON	18	3rd
Barkworth, Mr. Algernon H.	Hessle, England		1st
Barry, Miss Julia	New York, NY	27	3rd
Barton, Mr. David	England to New York	22	3rd
Bateman, Rev. Robert James	Jacksonville, FL	51	2nd
Baumann, Mr. John D.	New York, NY		1st
Baxter, Mrs. James (Helene DeLaudeniere Chaput)	Montreal, PQ	50	1st
Baxter, Mr. Quigg Edmond	Montreal, PQ	24	1st
Beane, Mr. Edward	Norwich, England to New York, NY	32	2nd
Beane, Mrs. Edward (Ethel Clarke)	Norwich, England to New York, NY	19	2nd
Beattie, Mr. Thomson	Winnipeg, MB	36	1st
Beauchamp, Mr. Henry James	England	28	2nd
Beaven, Mr. William Thomas	England	19	3rd
Becker, Mrs. Allen Oliver (Nellie E. Baumgardner)	India to Benton Harbor, MI	36	2nd
Becker, Miss Marion Louise	India to Benton Harbor, MI	4	2nd
Becker, Master Richard F.	India to Benton Harbor, MI	1	2nd
Becker, Miss Ruth Elizabeth	India to Benton Harbor, MI	12	2nd
Beckwith, Mr. Richard Leonard	New York, NY	37	1st
Beckwith, Mrs. Richard Leonard (Sallie Monypeny)	New York, NY	47	1st
Beesley, Mr. Lawrence	London, England	34	2nd
Behr, Mr. Karl Howell	New York, NY	26	1st
Bengtsson, Mr. John Viktor	Krakudden, Sweden to Moune, IL	26	3rd

NOTE: *Survivors are noted in italics*

PASSENGERS continued

Name	Residence	Age	Class	Name	Residence	Age	Class
Bentham, Miss Lillian W.	Rochester, NY	19	2nd	*Caldwell, Master Alden Gates*	Bangkok, Thailand to Roseville, IL	10m	2nd
Berglund, Mr. Karl Ivar Sven	Tranvik, Finland to New York	22	3rd	Calic, Mr. Peter		17	3rd
Berriman, Mr. William S.	St. Ives, Cornwall, England to Calumet, MI	23	2nd	*Cameron, Miss Clear*	Mamaroneck, NY	31	2nd
Betros, Mr. Tannous	Syria	20	3rd	*Canavan, Miss Mary*		21	3rd
Bing, Mr. Lee	Hong Kong to New York, NY	32	3rd	Canavan, Mr. Patrick	Ireland to Philadelphia, PA	21	3rd
Birkeland, Mr. Hans	Brennes, Norway to New York	21	3rd	*Candee, Mrs. Edward*	Washington, DC	53	1st
Birnbaum, Mr. Jakob	San Francisco, CA	25	1st	(Helen Churchill Hungerford)			
Bishop, Mr. Dickinson H.	Dowagiac, MI	25	1st	Cann, Mr. Ernest		21	3rd
Bishop, Mrs. Dickinson H.	Dowagiac, MI	19	1st	*Caram (Kareem), Mr. Joseph*	Ottawa, ON		3rd
(Helen Walton)				*Caram (Kareem), Mrs. Joseph*	Ottawa, ON		3rd
Bjorklund, Mr. Ernst Herbert	Stockholm, Sweden to New York	18	3rd	(Maria Elias)			
Björnström-Steffansson,	Stockholm, Sweden/Washington, DC	28	1st	*Carbines, Mr. William*	St. Ives, Cornwall, England to Calumet, MI	19	2nd
Mr. Maurtiz Hakan				*Cardeza, Mrs. James Warburton*	Germantown, PA	58	1st
Blackwell, Mr. Stephen Weart	Trenton, NJ	45	1st	*Martinez, (Charlotte Wardle Drake)*			
Blank, Mr. Henry	Glen Ridge, NJ	39	1st	*Cardeza, Mr. Thomas Drake Martinez*	Austria-Hungary/Germantown, PA	36	1st
Bonnell, Miss Caroline	Youngstown, OH	29	1st	Carlsson, Mr. Carl Robert	Goteborg, Sweden to Huntley, Il	24	3rd
Bonnell, Miss Elizabeth	Birkdale, England	58	1st	Carlsson, Mr. Frans Olof	New York, NY	33	1st
Borebank, Mr. John James	London, England/Winnipeg, MB		1st	Carlsson, Mr. Julius		33	3rd
Bostandyeff, Mr. Guentcho	Bulgaria to Chicago, IL	26	3rd	Carlsson, Mr. August Sigfried	Dagsas, Sweden to Fower, MN	28	3rd
Botsford, Mr. William Hull	Elmira, NY/Orange, NJ	26	2nd	*Carr, Miss Helen*	Co Longford, Ireland to New York, NY	16	3rd
Boulos, Master Akar	Syria to Kent, ON	6	3rd	*Carr, Miss Jeannie*	Co Sligo, Ireland, to Hartford, CT	37	3rd
Boulos, Mr. Hanna	Syria		3rd	*Carrau, Mr. Francisco M.*	Montevideo, Uruguay		1st
Boulos, Mrs. Joseph (Sultana)	Syria to Kent, ON		3rd	Carrau, Mr. Jose Pedro	Montevideo, Uruguay		1st
Boulos, Miss Laura	Syria to Kent, ON	9	3rd	*Carter, Rev. Ernest Courtenay*	London, England	54	2nd
Bourke, Mr. John	Ireland to Chicago, IL	40	3rd	*Carter, Mrs. Ernest Courtenay*	London, England	44	2nd
Bourke, Mrs. John (Catherine)	Ireland to Chicago, IL	32	3rd	(Lilian Hughes)			
Bourke, Miss Mary	Ireland to Chicago, IL		3rd	*Carter, Mr. William Ernest*	Bryn Mawr, PA	36	1st
Bowen, Mr. David	Treherbert, Cardiff, Wales	26	3rd	*Carter, Mrs. William Ernest (Lucile Polk)*	Bryn Mawr, PA	36	1st
Bowen, Miss Grace Scott	Cooperstown, NY	45	1st	*Carter, Miss Lucile Polk*	Bryn Mawr, PA	14	1st
Bowenur, Mr. Soloman	London, England		2nd	*Carter, Master William Thornton II*	Bryn Mawr, PA	11	1st
Bowerman, Miss Elsie Edith	St. Leonards-on-Sea, England	22	1st	Carver, Mr. Alfred John	St. Denys, Southampton, England	28	3rd
Bracken, Mr. James H.	Lake Arthur, Chavez County, NM	27	2nd	*Case, Mr. Howard Brown*	Ascot, Berkshire, England/Rochester, NY	49	1st
Bradley, Miss Bridget Delia	Kingwilliamstown, Co Cork,	18	3rd	*Cassebeer, Mrs. Henry Arthur, Jr.*	New York, NY		1st
Ireland to Glens Falls, NY				(Genevieve Fosdick)			
Brady, Mr. James Bertram	Pomeroy, WA	40	1st	Cassem, Mr. Nassef Belmenly	Syria to Fredericksburg, VA		3rd
Braf, Mr. Elin Ester Maria	Medeltorp, Sweden to Chicago, IL	20	3rd	*Cavendish, Mr. Tyrell William*	Little Onn Hall, Staffordshire, England	36	1st
Brahim, Mr. Youssef			3rd	*Cavendish, Mrs. Tyrell William*	Little Onn Hall, Staffordshire, England		1st
Brandeis, Mr. Emil	Omaha, NE	48	1st	(Julia Florence Siegel)			
Braund, Mr. Lewis Richard	Bridgerule, Devon, England	29	3rd	Celotti, Mr. Francesco	London, England	24	3rd
Braund, Mr. Owen Harris	Bridgerule, Devon, England	22	3rd	*Chaffee, Mr. Herbert Fuller*	Amenia, ND	46	1st
Brayton, Mr. George Arthur	Los Angeles, CA		1st	*Chaffee, Mrs. Herbert Fuller*	Amenia, ND	47	1st
Brewe, Dr. Arthur Jackson	Philadelphia, PA		1st	(Carrie Toogood)			
Brobeck, Mr. Karl Rudolf	Sweden to Worcester, MA	22	3rd	*Chambers, Mr. Norman Campbell*	New York, NY/Ithaca, NY	27	1st
Brocklebank, Mr. William Alfred	Broomfield, Chelmsford, England	35	3rd	*Chambers, Mrs. Norman Campbell*	New York, NY/Ithaca, NY	31	1st
Brown, Miss Edith E.	Cape Town, South Africa to Seattle, WA	15	2nd	(Bertha Griggs)			
Brown, Mrs. James Joseph	Denver, Co	44	1st	Chapman, Mr. Charles H.	Bronx, NY	52	2nd
(Margaret Tobin)				Chapman, Mr. John Henry	Cornwall, England to Spokane, WA	30	2nd
Brown, Mrs. John Murray	Belmont, MA	59	1st	Chapman, Mrs. John Henry	Cornwall, England to Spokane, WA	28	2nd
(Caroline Lane Lamson)				(Elizabeth Lawry)			
Brown, Miss Mildred	London, England to Montreal, PQ	24	2nd	Chartens, Mr. David	Ireland to New York, NY	21	3rd
Brown, Mr. Thomas William Soloman	Cape Town, South Africa to Seattle, WA	45	2nd	Chebab, Mr. Emir Farres			3rd
Brown, Mrs. Thomas William	Cape Town, South Africa to Seattle, WA	40	2nd	*Cherry, Miss Gladys*	London, England		1st
Soloman (Elizabeth C.)				*Chevre, Mr. Paul*	Paris, France		1st
Brhyl, Miss Dagmar	Skara, Sweden to Rockford, IL	20	2nd	*Chibnall, Mrs. Edith Martha*	St. Leonards-on-Sea, England		1st
Bryhl, Mr. Kurt Arnold Gottfried	Skara, Sweden to Rockford, IL	25	2nd	Chip, Mr. Chang	Hong Kong to New York, NY	32	3rd
Buckley, Mr. Daniel	Kingwilliamstown, Co Cork, Ireland to New York, NY	21	3rd	*Chisholm, Mr. Roderick Robert*	Liverpool, England		1st
Buckley, Miss Katherine	Co Cork, Ireland to Roxbury, MA	20	3rd	Christmann, Mr. Emil		29	3rd
Bucknell, Mrs. William Robert	Philadelphia, PA	60	1st	*Christy, Mrs. Alice Frances*	London, England		2nd
(Emma Eliza Ward)				*Christy, Miss Julie*	London, England		2nd
Burke, Mr. Jeremiah	Co Cork, Ireland to Charlestown, MA	19	3rd	Chronopoulos, Mr. Apostolos	Greece	26	3rd
Burns, Miss Mary Delia	Co Sligo, Ireland to New York, NY	18	3rd	Chronopoulos, Mr. Demetrios	Greece	18	3rd
Buss, Miss Kate	Sittingbourne, England to San Diego, CA	36	2nd	*Clark, Mr. Walter Miller*	Los Angeles, CA	27	1st
Butler, Mr. Reginald Fenton	Southsea, Hampshire, England	25	2nd	*Clark, Mrs. Walter Miller*	Los Angeles, CA	26	1st
Butt, Major Archibald Willingham	Washington, DC	45	1st	(Virginia McDowell)			
Byles, Rev. Thomas Roussel D.	London, England		2nd	Clarke, Mr. Charles V.	England to San Francisco, CA	29	2nd
Bystrom, Mrs. Carolina	New York, NY	42	2nd	*Clarke, Mrs. Charles V. (Ada Maria)*	England to San Francisco, CA	28	2nd
Cacic, Mr. Grego	Croatia	18	3rd	*Clifford, Mr. George Quincy*	Stoughton, MA		1st
Cacic, Mr. Luka	Croatia	38	3rd	Coelho, Mr Domingos Fernandes	Portugal	20	3rd
Cacic, Mr. Manda	Croatia		3rd	*Cohen, Mr. Gurshon (Gus)*	London, England to Brooklyn, NY	19	3rd
Cacic, Mr. Maria	Croatia	30	3rd	Colbert, Mr. Patrick	Co Limerick, Ireland to Sherbrooke, PQ	24	3rd
Calderhead, Mr. Edward P.	New York, NY		1st	Coleff, Mr. Fotio		24	3rd
Caldwell, Mr. Albert Francis	Bangkok, Thailand to Roseville, IL	26	2nd	Coleff, Mr. Peyo	Bulgaria to Chicago, IL	36	3rd
Caldwell, Mrs. Albert Francis	Bangkok, Thialand to Roseville, IL	26	2nd	Coleridge, Mr. Reginald Charles	Hartford, Huntingdonshire, England	29	2nd
(Sylvia Mae Harbaugh)				Collander, Mr. Erik	Helsinki, Finland	27	2nd

NOTE: *Survivors are noted in italics*

Name	Residence	Age	Class	Name	Residence	Age	Class
Collett, Mr. Sidney C. Stuart	London to Fort Byron, NY	24	2nd	Dean, Mrs. Bertram (Eva)	Devon, England to Wichita, KS	33	3rd
Colley, Mr. Edward Pomeroy	Victoria, BC		1st	Dean, Master Bertram Vere	Devon, England to Wichita, KS	1	3rd
Collyer, Mr. Harvey	Bishopstoke, Hampshire, England to Fayette Valley, ID	35	2nd	Dean, Miss Elizabeth Gladys (Millvina)	Devon, England to Wichita, KS	2m	3rd
				de Brito, Mr. Jose Joaquim	Portugal to Sao Paolo, Brazil		2nd
Collyer, Mrs. Harvey (Charlotte Tate)	Bishopstoke, Hampshire, England to Fayette Valley, ID	31	2nd	Delalic, Mr. Regyo		25	3rd
				Del Carlo, Mr. Sebastiano	Lucca, Italy to California	28	2nd
Collyer, Miss Marjory	Bishopstoke, Hampshire, England to Fayette Valley, ID	8	2nd	Del Carlo, Mrs. Sebastiano (Argenia Genovese)	Lucca, Italy to California	22	2nd
Compton, Mrs. Alexander Taylor (Mary Eliza Ingersoll)	Lakewood, NJ	64	1st	De Messemaeker, Mr. William Joseph	Tampico, MT	36	3rd
				De Messemaeker, Mrs. William Joseph (Anna)	Tampico, MT	36	3rd
Compton, Mr. Alexander Taylor, Jr.	Lakewood, NJ	37	1st	De Mulder, Mr. Theo	Belgium to Detroit, MI	30	3rd
Compton, Miss Sara Rebecca	Lakewood, NJ	39	1st	Denbury, Mr. Herbert	Guernsey, England to Elizabeth, NJ	25	2nd
Conlin, Mr. Thomas Henry	Philadelphia, PA	31	3rd	Denkoff, Mr. Mito	Bulgaria to Coon Rapids, IA		3rd
Connaghton, Mr. Michael	Ireland to Brooklyn, NY	31	3rd	Dennis, Mr. Samuel		23	3rd
Connolly, Miss Kate	Ireland	30	3rd	Dennis, Mr. Willaim		26	3rd
Connolly, Miss Kate	Ireland	22	3rd	Devaney, Miss Margaret	Kilmacowen, Co Sligo, Ireland to New York, NY	19	3rd
Connors, Mr. Patrick			3rd	de Villiers, Madame Berthe	Belgium to Montreal, PQ		1st
Cook, Mr. Jacob		43	3rd	Dewan, Mr. Frank		65	3rd
Cook, Mrs. Selena Rogers	Pennsylvania	22	2nd	Dibden, Mr. Willaim	New Forest, England	18	2nd
Cor, Mr. Bartol	Austria	35`	3rd	Dibo, Mr. Elias			3rd
Cor, Mr. Ivan	Austria	27	3rd	Dick, Mr. Albert Adrian	Calgary, AB	31	1st
Cor, Mr. Ludovik	Austria	19	3rd	Dick, Mrs. Albert Adrian (Vera Gillespie)	Calgary, AB	17	1st
Corbett, Mrs. Walter H. (Irene Colvin)	Provo, UT	30	2nd	Dimic, Mr. Jovan		42	3rd
Corey, Mrs. Percy C. (Mary Phyllis Elizabeth Miller)	Pittsburgh, PA		2nd	Dintcheff, Mr. Valtcho		43	3rd
Corn, Mr. Harry	London, England	30	3rd	Dodge, Dr. Washington	San Francisco, CA		1st
Cornell, Mrs. Robert Clifford (Malvina Helen Lamson)	New York, NY	55	1st	Dodge, Mrs. Washington (Ruth Vidaver)	San Francisco, CA		1st
				Dodge, Master Washington	San Francisco, CA	4	1st
Cotterill, Mr. Harry	Penzance, Cornwall, England to Akron, OH	20	2nd	Doling, Mrs. Ada	Southampton, England	32	2nd
Coutts, Mrs. William (Minnie)	England to Brooklyn, NY	36	3rd	Doling, Miss Elsie	Southampton, England	18	2nd
Coutts, Master Neville	England to Brooklyn, NY	3	3rd	Dooley, Mr. Patrick	Ireland to New York, NY	32	3rd
Coutts, Master William Leslie	England to Brooklyn, NY	9	3rd	Dorkings, Mr. Edward Arthur	England to Oglesby, Il	19	3rd
Coxon, Mr. Daniel	Merrill, WI	59	3rd	Douglas, Mrs. Frederick Charles (Suzette Baxter)	Montreal, PQ	27	1st
Crafton, Mr. John Bertram	Roachdale, IN		1st				
Crease, Mr. Ernest James	Bristol, England to Cleveland, OH	19	3rd	Douglas, Mr. Walter Donald	Deephaven, MN	50	1st
Cribb, Mr. John Hatfield	Bournemouth, England to Newark, NJ	44	3rd	Douglas, Mrs. Walter Donald (Mahala Dutton)	Deephaven, MN	48	1st
Cribb, Miss Laura Alice	Bournemouth, England to Newark, NJ	17	3rd	Douton, Mr. William James	Holley, NY		2nd
Crosby, Capt. Edward Gifford	Milwaukee, WI	70	1st	Dowdell, Miss Elizabeth	Union Hill, NY	30	3rd
Crosby, Mrs. Edward Gifford (Catherine Elizabeth Halstead)	Milwaukee, WI	69	1st	Doyle, Miss Elizabeth	Ireland to New York, NY	24	3rd
				Drapkin, Miss Jennie	London to New York, NY	23	3rd
Crosby, Miss Harriet R.	Milwaukee, WI	36	1st	Drazonovic, Mr. Josef	Austria to Niagara Falls, NY		3rd
Cumings, Mr. John Bradley	New York, NY	39	1st	Drew, Mr. James Vivian	Greenport, NY	42	2nd
Cumings, Mrs. John Bradley, (Florence Briggs Thayer)	New York, NY	38	1st	Drew, Mrs. James Vivian (Lulu Thorne Christian)	Greenport, NY	34	2nd
Daher, Mr. Tannous			3rd	Drew, Master Marshall Brines	Greenport, NY	8	2nd
Dahl, Mr. Charles Edward	Australia to Fingal, ND	45	3rd	Driscoll, Miss Bridget	Ballydehob, Co Cork, Ireland to New York, NY	24	3rd
Dahlberg, Miss Gerda Ulrika	Norrlot, Sweden to Chicago, IL	22	3rd	Duff Gordon, Sir Cosmo Edmund	London England/Paris, France	49	1st
Dakic, Mr. Branko	Austria	19	3rd	Duff Gordon, Lady Lucille Wallace Sutherland	London, England/Paris, France	48	1st
Daly, Mr. Eugene	Co Athlone, Ireland, to New York, NY	29	3rd				
Daly, Miss Marcella	Co Athlone, Ireland, to New York, NY	30	3rd	Dulles, Mr. William Crothers	Philadelphia, PA	39	1st
Daly, Mr. Peter Denis	Lima, Peru		1st	Duquemin, Mr. Joseph	England to Albion, NY	24	3rd
Danbom, Mr. Ernst Gilbert	Stanton, IA	34	3rd	Duran y More, Miss Asuncion	Barcelona, Spain to Havana, Cuba		2nd
Danbom, Mrs. Ernst Gilbert (Anna Sigrid Maria Brogren)	Stanton, IA	28	3rd	Duran y More, Miss Florentina	Barcelona, Spain to Havana, Cuba		2nd
				Dyker, Mr. Adolf Fredrik	West Haven, CT	23	3rd
Danbom, Master Gilbert Sigvard Emanuel	Stanton, IA	4m	3rd	Dyker, Mrs. Adolf Fredrik (Anna Elizabeth Judith Anderson)	West Haven, CT	22	2nd
Daniel, Mr. Robert Williams	Philadelphia, PA	27	1st	Earnshaw, Mrs. Boulton (Olive Potter)	Mt. Airy, Philadelphia, PA	23	1st
Danoff, Mr. Yoto	Bulgaria to Chicago, IL	27	3rd	Econovic, Mr. Joso	Austria-Hungary		3rd
Dantcheff, Mr. Khristo	Bulgaria to Chicago, IL	25	3rd	Edvardsson, Mr. Gustaf Hjalmar	Tofta, Sweden to Joliet, IL	18	3rd
Davidson, Mr. Thornton	Montreal, PQ	31	1st	Eitemiller, Mr. George Floyd	England to Detroit, MI	23	2nd
Davidson, Mrs. Thornton (Orian Hays)	Montreal, PQ	27	1st	Eklund, Mr. Hans Linus	Karberg, Sweden to Jerome Junction, AZ	16	3rd
Davies, Mr. Alfred	West Bromwich, England to Pontaic, MI	24	3rd	Ekstrom, Mr. Johan	Effington Rut, SD	45	3rd
Davies, Mr. Charles Henry	Lyndhurst, England	21	2nd	Elias, Mr. Elias	Syria		3rd
Davies, Mr. Evan		22	3rd	Elias, Mr. John	Syria		3rd
Davies, Mr. John	West Bromwich, England to Pontiac, MI	21	3rd	Elias, Mr. Joseph	Syria to Ottawa, ON		3rd
Davies, Mr. Joseph	West Bromwich, England to Pontiac, MI	17	3rd	Elsbury, Mr. James	Illinois	47	3rd
Davis, Mrs. Agnes	St. Ives, Cornwall, England to Hancock, MI	49	2nd	Emanuel, Miss Virginia Ethel	New York, NY	5	3rd
Davis, Master John Morgan	St. Ives, Cornwall, England to Hancock, MI	8	2nd	Emmeth, Mr. Thomas			3rd
Davis, Miss Mary	London to Staten Island, NY	28	2nd	Enander, Mr. Ingvar	Goteborg, Sweden to Rockford, IL	21	2nd
Davison, Mr. Thomas Henry	Liverpool, England to Bedford, OH		3rd	Endres, Miss Carolina Louise	New York, NY		1st
Davison, Mrs. Thomas Henry (Mary Finck)	Liverpool, England to Bedford, OH			Eustis, Miss Elizabeth Mussey	Brookline, MA	53	1st
				Evans, Miss Edith Corse	New York, NY	36	1st
Deacon, Mr. Percy		18	2nd				
Dean, Mr. Bertram	Devon, England to Wichita, KS	26	3rd	Everett, Mr. Thomas James			3rd

NOTE: *Survivors are noted in italics*

PASSENGERS continued

Name	Residence	Age	Class
Fahlstrom, Mr. Arne Jonas	Oslo, Norway to Bayonne, NJ	19	3rd
Farrell, Mr. James	Aughnacliff, Co Longford, Ireland to New York, NY		3rd
Faunthorpe, Mr. Harry	England to Philadelphia, PA		2nd
Faunthorpe, Mrs. Lizzie (see Wilkinson)			2nd
Fillbrook, Mr. Charles	Cornwall, England to Houghton, MI		2nd
Finoli, Mr. Luigi	Italy to Philadelphia, PA		3rd
Fischer, Mr. Eberhard Telander			3rd
Flegenheim, Mrs. Alfred (Antionette)	New York, NY		1st
Flynn, Mr. James			3rd
Flynn, Mr. John			3rd
Flynn, Mr. John Irving	Brooklyn, NY		1st
Foley, Mr. Joseph	Ireland to Chicago, IL		3rd
Foley, Mr. William	Ireland		3rd
Foo, Mr. Choong	Hong Kong to New York, NY		3rd
Ford, Mr. Arthur	Bridgwater, Somerset, England		3rd
Ford, Miss Doolina Margaret	Rotherfield, Sussex, England to Essex Co, MA	21	3rd
Ford, Mr. Edward Watson	Rotherfield, Sussex, England to Essex Co, MA	18	3rd
Ford, Miss Maggie	Rotherfield, Sussex, England to Essex Co, MA	9	3rd
Ford, Mrs. Edward (Margaret Ann)	Rotherfield, Sussex, England to Essex Co, MA	48	3rd
Ford, Mr. Neil Watson	Rotherfield, Sussex, England to Essex Co, MA	16	3rd
Foreman, Mr. Benjamin Laventall	New York, NY	30	1st
Fortune, Miss Alice Elizabeth	Winnipeg, MB	24	1st
Fortune, Mr. Charles Alexander	Winnipeg, MB	19	1st
Fortune, Miss Ethel Flora	Winnipeg, MD	28	1st
Fortune, Miss Mabel	Winnipeg, MB	23	1st
Fortune, Mr. Mark	Winnipeg, MB	64	1st
Fortune, Mrs. Mark (Mary McDougald)	Winnipeg, MB	60	1st
Fox, Mr. Patrick	Ireland to New York, NY		3rd
Fox, Mr. Stanley H.	Rochester, NY		2nd
Franklin, Mr. Charles			3rd
Franklin, Mr. Thomas Parnham	Westcliff-on-Sea, Essex, England		1st
Frauenthal, Dr. Henry William	New York, NY	49	1st
Frauenthal, Mrs. Henry William (Clara Heinsheimer)	New York, NY		1st
Frauenthal, Mr. Isaac Gerald	New York, NY	44	
Frolicher, Miss Marguerite	Zurich, Switzerland	22	1st
Frolicher-Stehli, Mr. Maxmillian	Zurich, Switzerland	60	1st
Frolicher-Stehli, Mrs. Maxmillian (Margaretha Emerentia Stehli)	Zurich, Switzerland	48	1st
Funk, Miss Annie C.	Janjgir, India to Pennsylvania	38	2nd
Futrelle, Mr. Jacques	Scituate, MA	37	1st
Futrelle, Mrs. Jacques (May Peel)	Scituate, MA	35	1st
Fynney, Mr. Jospehy J.	Liverpool, England/Montreal, PQ	35	2nd
Gale, Mr. Harry	Cornwall, England to Clear Creek, CO	35	2nd
Gale, Mr. Shadrach	Cornwall, England to Clear Creek, CO	38	2nd
Gallagher, Mr. Martin	New York, NY	25	3rd
Garfirth, Mr. John			3rd
Garside, Miss Ethel	Brooklyn, NY	24	2nd
Gaskell, Mr. Alfred	Liverpool, England to Montreal, PQ	16	2nd
Gavey, Mr. Lawrence	Guernsey to Elizabeth, NJ	26	2nd
Gee, Mr. Arthur H.	St. Anne's on Sea, Lancashire, England	47	1st
Georges, Mrs. Shahini Weappi	Youngstown, OH		3rd
Gibson, Miss Dorothy	New York, NY	22	1st
Gibson, Mrs. Leonard (Pauline C. Boeson)	New York, NY	45	1st
Gilbert, Mr. William	Cornwall, England	45	2nd
Giles, Mr. Edgar	Cornwall, England to Camden, NJ	24	2nd
Giles, Mr. Frederick	Cornwall, England to Camden, NJ	21	2nd
Giles, Mr. Ralph	West Kensington, England	22	2nd
Gilinski, Mr. Leslie		22	3rd
Gill, Mr. John W.	Clevedon, England		2nd
Gillespie, Mr. William	Vancouver, BC	34	2nd
Gilnagh, Miss Katie	Co Longford, Ireland to New York, NY	16	3rd
Givard, Mr. Hans Christensen		30	2nd
Glynn, Miss Mary Agatha	Co Clare, Ireland to Washington, DC		3rd
Goldenberg, Mr. Samuel L.	New York, NY/Paris, France	49	1st
Goldenberg, Mrs. Samuel L. (Edwiga Grabowsko)	New York, NY/Paris, France		1st
Goldschmidt, Mr. George B.	New York, NY	71	1st
Goldsmith, Mr. Frank John	Strood, Kent, England to Detroit, MI	33	3rd
Goldsmith, Mrs. Frank John (Emily A. Brown)	Strood, Kent, England to Detroit, MI		3rd
Goldsmith, Master Frank John William	Strood, Kent, England to Detroit, MI	9	3rd
Goldsmith, Mr. Nathan	Philadelphia, PA	41	3rd
Goncalves, Mr. Manuel Estanslas	Portugal	38	3rd
Goodwin, Mr. Frederick	Wiltshire, England to Niagara Falls, NY	40	3rd
Goodwin, Mrs. Frederick (Augusta)	Wiltshire, England to Niagara Falls, NY	43	3rd
Goodwin, Mr. Charles E.	Wiltshire, England to Niagara Falls, NY	14	3rd
Goodwin, Miss Lillian A.	Wiltshire, England to Niagara Falls, NY	16	3rd
Goodwin, Master Harold V.	Wiltshire, England to Niagara Falls, NY	9	3rd
Goodwin, Miss Jessie A.	Wiltshire, England to Niagara Falls, NY	10	3rd
Goodwin, Master Sidney L.	Wiltshire, England to Niagara Falls, NY	6	3rd
Goodwin, Master William F.	Wiltshire, England to Niagara Falls, NY	11	3rd
Gracie, Colonel Archibald IV	Washington, DC	54	1st
Graham, Mr. George Edward	Winnipeg, MB	38	1st
Graham, Miss Margaret Edith	Greenwich, CT	19	1st
Graham, Mrs. William Thompson (Edith Junkins)	Greenwich, CT	58	1st
Green, Mr. George	Dorking, Surrey, England	40	3rd
Greenberg, Mr. Samuel	Bronx, NY		2nd
Greenfield, Mrs. Leo David (Blanche Strouse)	New York, NY	45	1st
Greenfield, Mr. William Bertran	New York, NY	23	1st
Gronnestad, Mr. Daniel Danielsen	Foresvik, Norway to Portland, ND	32	3rd
Guest, Mr. Robert			3rd
Guggenheim, Mr. Benjamin	New York, NY	46	1st
Gustafsson, Mr. Alfred Ossian	Waukegan, Chicago, Il	20	3rd
Gustafsson, Mr. Anders Vilhelm	Ruotsinphytaa, Finland to New York, NY	37	3rd
Gustafsson, Mr. Karl Gideon	Ruotsinphytaa, Finland to New York, NY	19	3rd
Gustafsson, Mr. Johan Birger	Ruotsinphytaa, Finland to New York, NY	28	3rd
Haas, Miss Aloisia	Altdorf, Switzerland	24	3rd
Hagardon, Miss Kare	Co Sligo, Ireland to New York, NY	17	3rd
Hagland, Mr. Ingvald Olsen	Norway to Belmar, NJ	28	3rd
Hagland, Mr. Konrad Mathias Reiersen	Norway to Belmar, NJ	19	3rd
Hakkarainen, Mr. Pekka Pietari	Helsinki, Finland to Monessen, PA	28	3rd
Hakkarainen, Mrs. Pekka Pietari (Elin Dolk)	Helsinki, Finland to Monessen, PA	24	3rd
Hale, Mr. Reginald	Auburn, NY	30	2nd
Hamalainen, Mrs. William (Anna)	Detroit, MI	23	2nd
Hamalainen, Master Viljo	Detroit, MI	1	2nd
Hansen, Mr. Peter Claus	Racine, WI	41	3rd
Hansen, Mrs. Peter Claus (Jennie L. Howard)	Racine, WI	45	3rd
Hansen, Mr. Henrik Juul	Denmark to Racine, WI	26	3rd
Hansen, Mr. Henry Damsgaard	Denmark to Racine, WI	21	3rd
Harbeck, Mr. William H.	Seattle, WA/Toledo, OH	44	2nd
Harder, Mr. George Achilles	Brooklyn, NY	25	1st
Harder, Mrs. George Achilles (Dorothy Annan)	Brooklyn, NY	21	1st
Harknett, Miss Alice		21	3rd
Harmer, Mr. Abraham		25	3rd
Harper, Mr. Henry Sleeper	New York, NY	48	1st
Harper, Mrs. Henry Sleeper (Myra Haxtun)	New York, NY	49	1st
Harper, Rev. John	Denmark Hill, Surrey, England to Chicago	29	2nd
Harper, Miss Nina	Denmark Hill, Surrey, England to Chicago	6	2nd
Harris, Mr. George	London, England	30	2nd
Harris, Mr. Henry Birkhardt	New York, NY	45	1st
Harris, Mrs. Henry Birkhardt (Irene Wallach)	New York, NY	36	1st
Harris, Mr. Walter	Walthamstow, England		2nd
Harrison, Mr. William Henry	Wallasey, Cheshire, England		1st
Hart, Mr. Benjamin	Ilford, Essex, England to Winnipeg, MB	43	2nd
Hart, Mrs. Benjamin (Esther)	Ilford, Essex, England to Winnipeg, MB	45	2nd
Hart, Miss Eva Miriam	Ilford, Essex, England to Winnipeg, MB	7	2nd
Hart, Mr. Henry	Ilford, Essex, England to Winnipeg, MB	28	2nd
Hassan, Mr. M. Houssein			3rd
Haven (Homer), Mr. Harry	Indianapolis, IN	35	1st
Hawksford, Mr. Walter James	Kingston, Surrey, England		1st
Hays, Mr. Charles Melville	Montreal, PQ	55	1st
Hays, Mrs. Charles Melville (Clara Jennings Gregg)	Montreal, PQ	52	1st
Hays, Miss Margaret Bechstein	New York, NY	24	1st
Head, Mr. Christopher	Middlesex, England/London, England		1st
Healy, Miss Nora	Co Galway, Ireland to New York, NY		3rd
Hedman, Mr. Oscar	Sioux Falls, SD	27	3rd
Hee, Mr. Ling	Hong Kong to New York, NY		3rd
Hegarty, Miss Nora	Co Cork, Ireland to Charlestown, MA	18	3rd
Heikkinen, Miss Laina	Helsinki, Finland to New York, NY	26	3rd

NOTE: *Survivors are noted in italics*

PASSENGERS continued

Name	Residence	Age	Class	Name	Residence	Age	Class
Heininen, Miss Wendla Maria	Laitila, Finland to New York, NY	23	3rd	Johansson, Mr. Erick	Frostensmala, Sweden	22	3rd
Hellstrom, Miss Hilda Maria	Stora Tuna, Sweden to Evanston, IL	22	3rd	Johansson, Mr. Gustaff Joel	Bockebo, Sweden to Sheyenne, ND	33	3rd
Hemming, Miss Nora		21	3rd	Johansson, Mr. Karl Johan	Duluth, MN	31	3rd
Hendekovic, Mr. Ignaz			3rd	Johansson, Mr. Nils	Chicago, IL	29	3rd
Henery, Miss Delia		23	3rd	Johansson, Mr. Oskar L.		26	3rd
Henriksson, Miss Jenny Lovisa	Stockholm, Sweden to Iron Mountain, MI	28	3rd	Johnson, Mr. Alfred		49	3rd
Herman, Miss Alice	Somerset, England to Bernardsville, NJ	24	2nd	Johnson, Miss Eleanor Ileen	St. Charles, IL	1	3rd
Herman, Miss Kate	Somerset, England to Bernardsville, NJ	24	2nd	Johnson, Mr. Malkolm Joackim	Minneapolis, MN	33	3rd
Herman, Mr. Samuel	Somerset, England to Bernardsville, NJ	49	2nd	Johnson, Master Harold Theodor	St. Charles, IL	4	3rd
Herman, Mrs. Samuel (Jane Laver)	Somerset, England to Bernardsville, NJ	48	2nd	Johnson, Mrs. Oscar W. (Alice Berg)	St. Charles, IL	27	3rd
Hewlett, Mrs. Mary D.	India to Rapid City, SD		2nd	Johnson, Mr. William Cahoone, Jr.	Hawthorne, NJ	19	3rd
Hickman, Mr. Leonard Mark	West Hampstead, London, England to Neepawa, MB	34	2nd	Johnston, Mr. Andrew G.	Thornton Heath, Surrey, England	34	3rd
Hickman, Mr. Lewis	West Hampstead, London, England to Neepawa, MB	32	2nd	Johnston, Mrs. Andrew G. (Elizabeth [Lily])	Thornton Heath, Surrey, England	34	3rd
Hickman, Mr. Stanley George	West Hampstead, London, England to Neepawa, MB	21	2nd	Johnston, Miss Catherine H. (Carrie)	Thornton Heath, Surrey, England	8	3rd
Hilliard, Mr. Herbert Henry	Brighton, MA		1st	Johnston, Master William A.	Thornton Heath, Surrey, England	9	3rd
Hiltunen, Miss Marta	Kontiolahti, Finland to Detroit, MI	18	2nd	Jones, Mr. Charles Cresson	Bennington, VT	46	1st
Hipkins, Mr. William Edward	London, England/Birmingham, England		1st	Jonkoff, Mr. Lazor			3rd
Hippach, Miss Jean Gertrude	Chicago, IL	16	1st	Jonsson, Mr. Carl	Huntley, IL	32	3rd
Hippach, Mrs. Louis Albert (Ida Sophia Fischer)	Chicago, IL	44	1st	Jonsson, Mr. Nils Hilding		27	3rd
Hirvonen, Mrs. Alexander (Helga E.)	Taalintehdas, Finland to Monessen, PA	22	3rd	Julian, Mr. Henry Forbes	London, England		1st
Hirvonen, Miss Hildur E.	Taalintehdas, Finland to Monessen, PA	2	3rd	Jussila, Miss Aina Maria	Paavola, Finland to New York, NY	21	3rd
Hocking, Mrs. Elizabeth	Cornwall, England to Akron, OH	53	2nd	Jussila, Mr. Erik	Helsinki, Finland to Monessen, PA	32	3rd
Hocking, Mr. George	Cornwall, England to Akron, OH	23	2nd	Jussila, Miss Katriina	Paavola, Finland to New York, NY	20	3rd
Hocking, Miss Ellen (Nellie)	Cornwall, England to Akron, OH	21	2nd	Kallio, Mr. Nikolai Erland	Finland to Sudbury, ON	17	3rd
Hocking, Mr. Samuel James	Devonport, England		2nd	Kalvig, Mr. Johannes K. Halverson	Bergen, Norway to IA	21	3rd
Hodges, Mr. Henry Price	Southampton, England		2nd	Kantor, Mr. Sinai	Moscow, Russia to Bronx, NY	34	2nd
Hogeboom, Mrs. John C. (Anna Andrews)	Hudson, NY	51	1st	Kantor, Mrs. Sinai (Miriam Sternim)	Moscow, Russia to Bronx, NY	30	2nd
Hold, Mr. Stephen	England to Sacramento, CA	42	2nd	Karajic, Mr. Milan			3rd
Hold, Mrs. Stephen (Annie Margaret)	England to Sacramento, CA	36	2nd	Karlsson, Mr. Einar Gervasius	Oskarshamn, Sweden to Brooklyn, NY	21	3rd
Holm, Mr. John Frederick Alexander	Karlshamn, Sweden to NY	43	3rd	Karlsson, Mr. Julius Konrad Eugen	Goteborg, Sweden	33	3rd
Holthen, Mr. Johan Martin		28	3rd	Karlsson, Mr. Nils August	Sweden to Palmer, MA	22	3rd
Holverson, Mr. Alexander Oskar	New York, NY	42	1st	Karnes, Mrs. J. Frank (Claire Bennett)	Pittsburgh, PA	22	3rd
Holverson, Mrs. Alexander Oskar (Mary Aline Towner)	New York, NY	35	1st	Karun, Miss Anna	Austria to Galesburg, IL	4	3rd
Honkanen, Miss Eluna	Finland to NY, NY	27	3rd	Karun, Mr. Franz	Galesburg, IL	39	3rd
Hood, Mr. Ambrose, Jr.	New Forest, England	21	2nd	Kassen, Mr. Fared			3rd
Horgan, Mr. John			3rd	Keane, Mr. Andrew	Ireland to Auburndale, MA	20	3rd
Hosono, Mr. Masafumi	Tokyo, Japan	41	2nd	Keane, Mr. Daniel			2nd
Howard, Mr. Benjamin	Swindon, England		2nd	Keane, Miss Nora A.	Harrisburg, PA		2nd
Howard, Mrs. Benjamin (Ellen Truelove)	Swindon, England		2nd	Keefe, Mr. Arthur	Rahway, NJ		3rd
Howard, Miss May	Southampton, England to Albion, NY		3rd	Kekic, Mr. Tido		38	3rd
Hoyt, Mr. Frederick Maxfield	New York, NY/Stamford, CT	38	1st	Kelly, Miss Annie Kate	Co Mayo, Ireland to Chicago, IL		3rd
Hoyt, Mrs. Frederick Maxfield (Jane Ann Forby)	New York, NY/Stamford, CT	35	1st	Kelley, Mrs. Florence (Fannie)	London to New York, NY	45	2nd
Hoyt, Mr. William F.	New York, NY		1st	Kelly, Mr. James			3rd
Humblen, Mr. Adolf Mathias Nikolai Olsen		42	3rd	Kelly, Mr. James			3rd
Hunt, Mr. George Henry	Epsom, England	33	2nd	Kelly, Miss Mary	Co Westmeath, Ireland to New York, NY	21	3rd
Hyman, Mr. Abraham	England to Springfield, MA	34	3rd	Kennedy, Mr. John	Co Limerick, Ireland to New York, NY	24	3rd
Ilett, Miss Bertha	Guernsey	17	2nd	Kent, Mr. Edward Austin	Buffalo, NY	58	1st
Ilieff, Mr. Ylio			3rd	Kenyon, Mr. Frederick R.	Southington/Noank, CT	41	1st
Ilmakangas, Miss Ida Livija	New York, NY	27	3rd	Kenyon, Mrs. Frederick R. (Marion)	Southington/Noank, CT		1st
Ilmakangas, Miss Pieta Sofia	Paavola, Finland to New York, NY	25	3rd	Khalil, Mr. Betros	Syria to Ottawa, ON	25	3rd
Isham, Miss Ann Eliza	Paris, France/New York, NY	50	1st	Khalil, Mrs. Betros (Zahie)	Syria to Ottawa, ON	20	3rd
Ismay, Mr. Joseph Bruce	Liverpool, England	49	1st	Khalil, Mr. Saad			3rd
Ivanoff, Mr. Konio	Bulgaria		3rd	Kiernan, Mr. John	Jersey City, NY	25	3rd
Jacobsohn, Mr. Sidney Samuel	London, England		2nd	Kiernan, Mr. Philip	Co Longford, Ireland to Jersey City, NJ	19	3rd
Jacobsohn, Mrs. Sidney Samuel (Amy Frances Christy)	London, England		2nd	Kilgannon, Mr. Thomas	Co Galway, Ireland to New York, NY	21	3rd
Jansson, Mr. Carl Olof	Orebro, Sweden to Swedeburg, NE	21	3rd	Kimball, Mr. Edwin Nelson, Jr.	Boston, MA	42	1st
Jardin, Mr. Jose Netto		21	3rd	Kimball, Mrs. Edwin Nelson, Jr. (Gertrude Parsons)	Boston, MA	40	1st
Jarvis, Mr. John Denzil	North Evington, England		2nd	Kink, Mr. Anton	Zurich, Switzerland to Milwaukee, WI	29	3rd
Jefferys, Mr. Clifford	Guernsey to Elizabeth, NJ		2nd	Kink, Mrs. Anton (Louise Heilmann)	Zurich, Switzerland to Milwaukee, WI	26	3rd
Jefferys, Mr. Ernest	Guernsey to Elizabeth, NJ		2nd	Kink, Miss Louise Gretchen	Zurich, Switzerland to Milwaukee, WI	4	3rd
Jenkin, Mr. Stephen Curnow	St. Ives, Cornwall, England to Houghton, MI		2nd	Kink, Miss Maria	Zurich, Switzerland to Milwaukee, WI	22	3rd
Jensen, Miss Carla Christine	Denmark to Portland, OR	19	3rd	Kink, Mr. Vincenz	Zurich, Switzerland to Milwaukee, WI	27	3rd
Jensen, Mr. Hans Peder		20	3rd	Kirkland, Rev. Charles Leonard	Glasgow, Scotland to Bangor, ME		2nd
Jensen, Mr. Niels Peder	Denmark to Portland, OR	48	3rd	Klaber, Mr. Herman			1st
Jensen, Mr. Svend Lauritz	Denmark to Portland, OR	17	3rd	Klasen, Miss Gertrud Emilia	Grimshult, Sweden to Los Angeles, CA	1	3rd
Jermyn, Miss Annie	Co Cork, Ireland to East Lynn, MA	22	3rd	Klasen, Mrs. Hulda Kristina	Grimshult, Sweden to Los Angeles, CA	36	3rd
Jerwan, Mrs. Amin S. (Marie Thuillard)	New York, NY	23	2nd	Klasen, Mr. Klas Albin	Grimshult, Sweden to Los Angeles, CA	18	3rd
Johannesen-Bratthammer, Mr Bernt	Eiko, Norway to New York	32	3rd	Kraeff, Mr. Theodor			3rd
Johanson, Mr. Jakob Alfred	Uusikaarlepyy, Finland to Vancouver, BC	34	3rd	Krekorian, Mr. Neshan	Turkey to Brantford, ON	25	3rd
				Kvillner, Mr. Johan Henrik Johannesson	Sweden to Arlington, NJ	31	2nd
				Lahowd, Mr. Sarkis	Turkey	30	3rd
				Lahtinen, Rev. William	Minneapolis, MN	30	2nd

NOTE: *Survivors are noted in italics*

Name	Residence	Age	Class	Name	Residence	Age	Class
Lahtinen, Mrs.. William (Anna Sylvan)	Minneapolis, MN	26	2nd	Maisner, Mr. Simon		34	3rd
Laitinen, Miss Kristina Sofia	Helsingfors, Finland to New York, NY	37	3rd	Makinen, Mr. Kalle Edvard	Ikalis, Finland to Glassport, PA	29	3rd
Laleff, Mr. Kristo	Bulgaria to Chicago, IL	23	3rd	Malachard, Mr. Noel	Paris, France		2nd
Lam, Mr. Ali	Hong Kong to New York, NY	38	3rd	Mallet, Mr. Albert	Paris to Montreal, PQ		2nd
Lam, Mr. Len	Hong Kong to New York, NY		2nd	*Mallet, Mrs. Albert (Antoinette)*	Paris to Montreal, PQ		2nd
Lamb, Mr. John James			2nd	*Mallet, Master Andre*	Paris to Montreal, PQ	2	2nd
Lamore, Mrs. Amelia	Chicago, IL	34	2nd	Mamee, Mr. Hanna			3rd
Landergren, Miss Aurora Adelia	Karlshamn, Sweden to New York, NY	22	3rd	Mampe, Mr. Leon	Belgium	20	3rd
Lane, Mr. Patrick	Co Limerick, Ireland to New York, NY		3rd	Mangan, Miss Mary	Co Mayo, Ireland to Chicago		3rd
Lang, Mr. Fang	Hong Kong to New York, NY	26	3rd	Mangiavacchi, Mr. Serafino Emilo	New York, NY		2nd
LaRoche, Mr. Joseph	Paris, France to Haiti	26	2nd	*Mannion, Miss Margaret*	Ireland to New York, NY	24	3rd
LaRoche, Mrs. Joseph (Juliette)	Paris, France to Haiti	22	2nd	Mansour, Mr. Hanna		22	3rd
LaRoche, Miss Louise	Paris, France to Haiti	1	2nd	Mantvila, Rev. Joseph	Worcester, MA	27	3rd
LaRoche, Miss Simonne	Paris, France to Haiti	3	2nd	Mardirosian, Mr. Sarkis	Turkey	25	3rd
Larsson, Mr. August Viktor	Stamford, CT	29	3rd	*Marechal, Mr. Pierre*	Paris, France		1st
Larsson, Mr. Bengt Edvin	Stockholm, Sweden to Hartford, CT	29	3rd	Marinko, Mr. Dmitri		23	3rd
Larsson-Rondberg, Mr. Edvard	Sweden to Missoula, MT	22	3rd	Markim, Mr. Johann			3rd
Leader, Dr. Alice Farnham	New York, NY		1st	Markoff, Mr. Marin	Bulgaria to Chicago, IL	35	3rd
Leeni, Mr. Fahim			3rd	*Marshall, Mrs. Kate Louise Phillips*	Worcester, England	19	2nd
Lefebre, Mrs. Frank (Frances)	France to Mystic, IA	39	3rd	Marvin, Mr. Daniel Warner	New York, NY		1st
Lefebre, Master Henry	France to Mystic, IA	4	3rd	*Marvin, Mrs. Daniel Warner (Mary Graham Carmichael Farquarson)*	New York, NY		1st
Lefebre, Miss Ida	France to Mystic, IA	2	3rd	*Masselmany, Mrs. Fatima*	Dearborn, MI	17	3rd
Lefebre, Miss Jeannie	France to Mystic, IA	6	3rd	Matinoff, Mr. Nicola			3rd
Lefebre, Miss Mathilde	France to Mystic, IA	11	3rd	Matthews, Mr. William John	St. Austeel, Cornwall, England	30	2nd
Lehmann, Miss Bertha	Berne, Switzerland to Central City, IA		2nd	Maybery, Mr. Frank H.	Weston-Super-Mare, England/Moose Jaw, SK	20	2nd
Leinonen, Mr. Antti Gustaf	Valitaipale, Finland to New York, NY	32	3rd	McCaffry, Mr. Thomas Francis	Vancouver, BC	46	1st
Leitch, Miss Jessie	London, England to Chicago, IL		2nd	*McCarthy, Miss Katie*	Co Tipperary, Ireland toGuttenberg, NJ	24	3rd
Lemberopolous, Mr. Peter L.	Greece to Stamford, CT	30	3rd	McCarthy, Mr. Timothy J.	Dorchester, MA	54	1st
Lemon, Mr. Denis	Ireland	21	3rd	*McCormack, Mr. Thomas J.*	Bayonne, NJ	19	3rd
Lemon, Miss Mary	Ireland	20	3rd	*McCoy, Miss Agnes*	Co Longford, Ireland to Brooklyn, NY	28	3rd
Leonard, Mr. Lionel		36	3rd	*McCoy, Miss Alice*	Co Longford, Ireland to Brooklyn, NY	22	3rd
Lester, Mr. James			3rd	*McCoy, Mr. Bernard*	Co Longford, Ireland to Brooklyn, NY	21	3rd
Levy, Mr. Rene Jacques	Montreal, PQ		2nd	McCrae, Mr. Arthur Gordon	Sydney, Australia		2nd
Lewy, Mr. Ervin G.	Chicago, IL		1st	McCrie, Mr. James Matthew	Sarnia, ON		2nd
Leyson, Mr. Robert William Norman			2nd	*McDermott, Miss Delia*	Ireland to St. Louis, MO		3rd
Lindahl, Miss Agda, V.	Stockholm, Sweden to Saranac Lake, NY	25	3rd	McElroy, Mr. Michael			3rd
Lindblom, Miss Augusta Charlotta	Stockholm, Sweden to Saranac Lake, NY	45	3rd	*McGough, Mr. James R.*	Philadelphia, PA	36	1st
Lindeberg-Lind, Mr. Erik Gustaf	Stockholm, Sweden	42	1st	*McGovern, Mrs. Hugh (Mary)*	New York, NY		3rd
Lindell, Mr. Edvard Bengtsson	Helsingborg, Sweden to Hartford, CT	36	3rd	*McGowan, Miss Annie*	Co Mayo, Ireland to Chicago, IL	15	3rd
Lindell, Mrs. Edvard Bengtsson (Elin Gerda)	Helsingborg, Sweden to Hartford, CT	30	3rd	McGowan, Miss Katherine	Chicago, IL	36	3rd
Lindquist, Mr. Eino William	Dals, Finland to Monessen, PA	20	3rd	McKane, Mr. Peter D.	Rochester, NY	46	2nd
Lindstrom, Mrs. Carl Johan (Sigrid Posse)	Stockholm, Sweden	55	1st	McMahon, Mr. Martin	Co Clare, Ireland to NYC	20	3rd
Linehan, Mr. Michael		21	3rd	McNamee, Mr. Neal	Ruskey, Co Donegal, Ireland/Salisbury, England	24	3rd
Lines, Mrs. Ernest H. (Elizabeth Lindsey James)	Paris, France	50	1st	NcNamee, Mrs. Neal (Eileen)	Ruskey, Co Donegal, Ireland/Salisbury, England	19	3rd
Lines, Miss Mary Conover	Paris, France	16	1st	Meanwell, Mrs. Marion Ogden			3rd
Ling, Mr. Lee	Hong Kong to New York, NY	28	3rd	Mechan, Mr. John	Paterson, NJ	22	3rd
Lingan, Mr. John			2nd	Meek, Mrs. Thomas (Annie L.)			3rd
Lithman, Mr. Simon		20	3rd	Melkebuk, Mr Philemon			3rd
Lobb, Mr. William Arthur	St. Austeel, England/Scranton, PA	30	3rd	*Mellenger, Mrs. Elizabeth Anne*	England to Bennington, VT	41	2nd
Lobb, Mrs. William Arthur (Cordelia Stanlicke)	St. Austell, England/Scranton, PA	26	3rd	*Mellenger, Miss Madeleine Violet*	England to Bennington, VT	13	2nd
Lockyer, Mr. Edward	London, England to Ontario, NY	21	3rd	*Mellor, Mr. William John*	Chelsea, England	19	2nd
Long, Mr. Milton Clyde	Springfield, MA	29	1st	Meo, Mr. Alfonso	Bournemouth, England	48	3rd
Longley, Miss Gretchen Fiske	Hudson, NY	21	1st	Meyer, Mr. August	Harrow on the Hill, Middlesex, England	30	2nd
Loring, Mr. Joseph Holland	London, England/New York, NY	30	1st	Meyer, Mr. Edgar Joseph	New York, NY	28	1st
Louch, Mr. Charles Alexander	Weston-Super-Mare, Somerset, England		2nd	*Meyer, Mrs. Edgar Joseph (Leila Saks)*	New York, NY		1st
Louch, Mrs. Charles Alexander (Alice Adelaide)	Weston-Super-Mare, Somerset, England		2nd	*Midtsjo, Mr. Karl Albert*	Oslo, Norway to Chicago, IL	21	3rd
Lovell, Mr. John		20	3rd	Mihoff, Mr. Stoytcho	Bulgaria	28	3rd
Lulich, Mr. Nicola	Austria to Minnesota	27	3rd	Miles, Mr. Frank			3rd
Lundahl, Mr. Johan	Fyrnan, Sweden to Spokane, WA	51	3rd	Millet, Mr. Francis Davis	East Bridgewater, MA	65	1st
Lundin, Miss Olga Elida	Meriden, CT	23	3rd	Milling, Mr. Jacob Christian	Copenhagen, Denmark	48	2nd
Lundstrom, Mr. Thure Edvin	Gislof, Sweden to Los Angeles, CA	32	3rd	*Minahan, Miss Daisy E.*	Green Bay, WI	33	1st
Lyntakoff, Mr. Stanko	Bulgaria to Coon Rapids, IA	44	3rd	Minahan, Dr. William Edward	Fond du Lac, WI	44	1st
Mack, Mrs. Mary	Southampton, England to New York, NY	57	2nd	*Minahan, Mrs. William Edward (Lillian E. Thorpe)*	Fond du Lac, WI	37	1st
MacKay, Mr. George William		20	3rd	Mineff, Mr. Ivan	Bulgaria to Coon Rapids, IA	24	3rd
Madigan, Miss Margaret	Co Limerick, Ireland to New York, NY	21	3rd	Minkoff, Mr. Lazar	Bulgaria to Coon Rapids, IA	21	3rd
Madill, Miss Georgette Alexandra	St. Louis, MO	15	1st	Mirko, Mr. Dika	Austria	17	3rd
Madsen, Mr. Frithiof	Trondheim, Norway to Brooklyn, NY	22	3rd	Mitchell, Mr. Henry	Guernsey to Montclair, NJ	71	2nd
Maenpaa, Mr. Matti Alexanteri	Finland to Sudbury, ON	22	3rd	Mitkoff, Mr. Mito	Bulgaria	23	3rd
Maguire, Mr. John Edward	Brockton, MA	30	1st	Mock, Mr. Philip E.	New York, NY		1st
Mahon, Miss Delia			3rd	*Mocklare, Miss Helen Mary*	Co Galway, Ireland to New York, NY	23	3rd
				Moen, Mr. Sigurd H.	Bergen, Norway to Minneapolis, MN	25	3rd
				Molson, Mr. Harry Markland	Montreal, PQ	55	1st

NOTE: *Survivors are noted in italics*

PASSENGERS continued

Name	Residence	Age	Class	Name	Residence	Age	Class
Moor, Mrs. Bella	Russia to New York, NY	27	3rd	O'Connor, Mr. Maurice	Co Limerick, Ireland to New York, NY		3rd
Moor, Master Meyer	Russia to New York, NY	6	3rd	O'Connor, Mr Patrick		24	3rd
Moore, Mr. Clarence Bloomfield	Washington, DC	47	1st	Odahl, Mr. Nils Martin	Orsjo, Sweden to Peoria, IL	23	3rd
Moore, Mr. Leonard Charles	Hoboken, NJ	19	3rd	*O'Dwyer, Miss Nellie*	Co Limerick, Ireland to New York, NY	23	3rd
Morawick, Dr. Ernest	Frankfort, KY		2nd	*Ohman, Miss Velin*	Mariestad, Sweden to Chicago, IL	22	3rd
Moran, Miss Bertha	Bronx, NY	28	3rd	O'Keefe, Mr. Patrick	Co Waterford, Ireland to New York, NY	22	3rd
Moran, Mr. Daniel J.	Bronx, NJ	27	3rd	*O'Leary, Miss Norah*	Kingwilliamstown, Co Cork Ireland to NY	17	3rd
Moran, Mr. James	Ireland	22	3rd	*Olsen, Master Arthur*	Trondheim, Norway to Brooklyn, NY	9	3rd
Morley, Mr. Henry Samuel	Worcester, England	39	3rd	Olsen, Mr. Charlie (Carl)	Brooklyn, NY	50	3rd
Morley, Mr. William	Petworth, Sussex, England		2nd	Olsen, Mr. Henry Margido	Bergen, Norway to New York, NY	28	3rd
Morrow, Mr. Thomas Rowan	Ireland to Gleichen, AB	30	3rd	Olsen, Mr. Ole M.	Skjarsvik, Norway to Longford, ND	31	3rd
Moubarek (Borak), Mr. Hanna (John)	Syria to Wilkes-Barre, PA		3rd	*Olsson, Miss Elida*	Sweden to St. Paul, MN	31	3rd
Moubarek, Mrs. George (Amenia)	Hardin, Lebanon to Clearfield Co, PA	26	3rd	Olsson, Mr. Nils Johan	Eslov, Sweden	28	3rd
Moubarek, Master George	Hardin, Lebanon to Clearfield Co, PA	7	3rd	Olsson, Mr. Oscar Johansson		32	3rd
Moubarek, Master William George	Hardin, Lebanon to Clearfield Co, PA	3	3rd	*Omont, Mr. A. Fernand*	Paris, France		1st
Moss, Mr. Albert Johan	Bergen, Norway to New York, NY	29	3rd	O'Neill, Miss Bridget			3rd
Moussa, Mrs. Mantoura Baloics	Syria to Troy, NY		3rd	Oreskovic, Mr. Jeko	Austria	23	3rd
Moutal, Mr. Rahamin		35	3rd	Oreskovic, Mr. Luka	Austria	20	3rd
Mudd, Mr. Thomas C.	Halesworth, England		2nd	Oreskovic, Mr. Maria	Austria	20	3rd
Mullins, Miss Katie	Co Longford, Ireland to New York, NY	19	3rd	Osen, Mr. Olof Elon	On, Sweden to Ethan, ND	16	3rd
Mulvihill, Miss Bertha E.	Providence, RI		3rd	*Osman, Miss Maria*	Austria to Steubenville, OH	31	3rd
Murdlin, Mr. Joseph			3rd	*Ostby, Mr. Engelhart Cornelius*	Providence, RI	64	1st
Murphy, Miss Katherine	Co Longford, Ireland to New York, NY		3rd	*Ostby, Miss Helen Raghnild*	Providence, RI	22	1st
Murphy, Miss Margaret	Co Longford, Ireland to New York, NY		3rd	O'Sullivan, Miss Bridget		22	3rd
Murphy, Miss Nora	Ireland to New York, NY	28	3rd	Ovies y Rodriguez, Mr. Servando			1st
Myhrman, Mr. Pehr Fabian Oliver Malkolm	Kristinehamn, Sweden to Chicago, IL	18	3rd	Otter, Mr. Richard	Middleburg Heights, OH	39	2nd
Myles, Mr. Thomas Francis	Cambridge, MA	64	2nd	*Oxenham, Mr. Percy Thomas*	Pondersend, England to New Durham, NJ	22	2nd
Nackid, Miss Maria	Syria to Waterbury, CT	1	3rd	*Padro y Manent, Mr. Julian*	Spain to Havana, Cuba		2nd
Nackid, Mr. Said	Syria to Waterbury, CT	20	3rd	Pain, Dr. Alfred	Hamilton, ON	24	2nd
Nackid, Mrs. Said (Mary Mowad)	Syria to Waterbury, CT	19	3rd	*Pallas y Castello, Mr. Emilio*	Spain to Havana, Cuba		2nd
Nahil, Mr. Toufik			3rd	Panula, Mr. Ernesti Arvid	Coal Center, PA	16	3rd
Naidenoff, Mr. Penko	Bulgaria to Chicago, IL	22	3rd	Panula, Mr. Jaakko Arnold	Coal Center, PA	14	3rd
Najib, Miss Adele Kiamie			3rd	Panula, Master Juha Niilo	Coal Center, PA	7	3rd
Nancarrow, Mr. William Henry	England to Yonkers, NY		3rd	Panula, Mrs. John (Maria Emilia)	Coal Center, PA	41	3rd
Nankoff, Mr. Minko	Bulgaria to Chicago, IL	32	3rd	Panula, Master Urho Abraham	Coal Center, PA	2	3rd
Nasr, Mr. Mustafa			3rd	Panula, Master William	Coal Center, PA	1	3rd
Nasser (Nasrallah), Mr. Nicholas	New York, NY		2nd	Parker, Mr. Clifford R.	St. Andrews, Guernsey	28	2nd
Nasser (Nasrallah), Mrs. Nicholas (Adele)	New York, NY	18	2nd	Parr, Mr. William Henry Marsh			1st
Nassr, Mr. Saade Jean			3rd	*Parrish, Mrs. Lutie Davis*	Woodford County, KY	50	2nd
Matsch, Mr. Charles H.	Brooklyn, NY	36	1st	Partner, Mr. Austin	Surbiton Hill, Surrey, England		1st
Naughton, Miss Hannah	Co Cork, Ireland to New York, NY	21	3rd	Pasic, Mr. Jakob	Bjuv, Sweden to Chicago, IL	21	3rd
Navratil, Master Edmond Roger	Nice, France	2	2nd	Paulner, Mr. Uscher			3rd
Navratil, Mr. Michel	Nice France	32	2nd	*Paulsson, Master Gosta Leonard*	Bjuv, Sweden to Chicago, IL	2	3rd
Navratil, Master Michel M.	Nice France	3	2nd	Paulsson, Mrs. Nils (Alma Cornelia Berglund)	Bjuv, Sweden to Chicago, IL	29	3rd
Nemaugh, Mr. Robert	Ireland to Chicago, IL	26	3rd	Paulsson, Master Paul Folke	Bjuv, Sweden to Chicago, IL	6	3rd
Nenkoff, Mr. Christo	Bulgaria to Coon Rapids, IA	22	3rd	Paulsson, Miss Stina Viola	Bjuv, Sweden to Chicago, IL	3	3rd
Nesson, Mr. Israel	Boston, MA	26	2nd	Paulsson, Miss Torborg Danira	Bjuv, Sweden to Chicago, IL	8	3rd
Newell, Mr. Arthur Webster	Lexington, MA	58	1st	Pavlovic, Mr. Stefo	Austria	32	3rd
Newell, Miss Madeleine	Lexington, MA	31	1st	*Payne, Mr. Vivian Ponsonby*	Montreal, PQ	22	1st
Newell, Miss Marjorie	Lexington, MA	23	1st	*Peacock, Master Alfred Edward*	Cornwall, England to Elizabeth, NJ	9m	3rd
Newsom, Miss Helen Moneypeny	New York, NY	19	1st	*Peacock, Mrs. Benjamin (Edith Nile)*	Cornwall, England to Elizabeth, NJ	26	3rd
Nicholls, Mr. Joseph Charles	Cornwall, England to Hancock, MI	19	2nd	*Peacock, Miss Treasteall*	Cornwall, England to Elizabeth, NJ	3	3rd
Nicholson, Mr. Arthur Ernest	Isle of Wight, England	64	1st	Pearce, Mr. Ernest		32	3rd
Nicola-Yarred, Master Elias	Hakoor, Lebanon to Jacksonville, FL	12	3rd	Pears, Mr. Thomas	Isleworth England		1st
Nicola-Yarred, Miss Jamila	Hakoor, Lebanon to Jacksonville, FL	14	3rd	*Pears, Mrs. Thomas (Edith)*	Isleworth England		1st
Nieminen, Miss Manta Josefina	Abo, Finland to Aberdeen, WA	29	3rd	Pecruic, Mr. Mate	Austria	17	3rd
Niklasson, Mr. Samuel	Orust, Sweden	28	3rd	Pecuric, Mr. Tome	Austria	24	3rd
Nilsson, Mr. August Ferdinand	Sweden to St. Paul, MN	21	3rd	Pedersen, Mr. Olaf	Seattle, WA	29	3rd
Nilsson, Miss Berta Oliva	Ransbysater, Sweden to Missoula, MT	18	3rd	Peduzzi, Mr. Joseph		24	3rd
Nilsson, Miss Helmina Josefina	Ramkvilla, Sweden to Joliet, IL	26	3rd	Pekoniemi, Mr. Edvard	Finland	21	3rd
Niskanen, Mr. Johan	Boston, MA	39	3rd	Peltomaki, Mr. Nikolai Johannes	Finland to New York, NY	25	3rd
Norman, Mr. Robert Douglas	Glasgow, Scotland		2nd	Penasco, Mr. Victor de Satode	Madrid, Spain	18	1st
Nosworthy, Mr. Richard Cater	Newton Abbott, Devon, England		3rd	*Penasco, Mrs. Victor de Satode (Josefa de Soto)*	Madrid, Spain	17	1st
Nourney, Mr. Alfred (Baron von Drachstedt)	Cologne, Germany	20	1/2	Pengelly, Mr. Frederick	Gunnislake, England to Butte, MT	20	2nd
Novel, Mr. Mansour	Sherbrooke, PQ		3rd	Perkin, Mr. John Henry		22	3rd
Nye, Mrs. Elizabeth Ramell	Folkestone, England/New York, NY	29	2nd	*Pernot, Mr. Rene*	Paris, France		2nd
Nysten, Miss Anna	Sweden to Passaic, NJ	22	3rd	Persson, Mr. Ernst Ulrik	Stockholm, Sweden to Indianapolis, IN	25	3rd
Nysveen, Mr. Johan H.	Oyer, Norway to Grand Forks, ND	61	3rd	Peruschitz, Rev. Joseph M.		40	2nd
O'Brien, Mr. Denis		21	3rd	Peter (Joseph), Miss Mary	Detroit, MI	1	3rd
O'Brien, Mr. Thomas	Co Limerick, Ireland to New York, NY	27	3rd	*Peter (Joseph), Mrs. Catherine*	Detroit, MI	24	3rd
O'Brien, Mrs. Thomas (Hannah Godfrey)	Co Limerick, Ireland to New York, NY	26	3rd	*Peter (Joseph), Master Michael J.*	Detroit, MI	4	3rd
O'Connell, Mr. Patrick D.		17	3rd	Peters, Miss Katie	Ireland to New York, NY	26	3rd

NOTE: *Survivors are noted in italics*

Name	Residence	Age	Class	Name	Residence	Age	Class
Peterson, Mr. Marius	Denmark to USA	24	3rd	Rouse, Mr. Richard Henry	Sittingbourne, England toCleveland, OH	50	3rd
Petranec, Miss Matilda	Austria	31	3rd	Rowe, Mr. Alfred, G.	Middlesex, England		1st
Petroff, Mr. Nedeca	Bulgaria to Chicago, IL	19	3rd	*Rugg, Miss Emily*	Guernsey to Wilmington, DE	21	2nd
Petroff, Mr. Pentcho	Bulgaria	29	3rd	*Rush, Mr. Alfred George John*	England to Detroit, MI	16	3rd
Pettersson Miss Ellen Natalia	Stockholm, Sweden to Iron Mountain, MI	18	3rd	*Ryan, Mr. Edward*	Co Limerick, Ireland to Troy, NY		3rd
Pettersson, Mr. John Emil	Vastermo, Sweden to Chicago, IL	25	3rd	Ryan, Mr. Patrick	Ireland to Bronx, NY		3rd
Peuchen, Major Arthur Godfrey	Toronto, ON	52	1st	Ryerson, Mr. Arthur Larned	Haverford, PA/Cooperstown, NY	61	1st
Phillips, Miss Alice	Ilfracombe, Devon, England	42	2nd	*Ryerson, Mrs. Arthur Larned*	Haverford, PA/Cooperstown, NY	48	1st
Phillips, Mr. Robert	Ilfracombe, Devon, England	21	2nd	(Emily Maria Borie)			
Pickard (Trembisky), Mr. Berk	London, England	32	3rd	*Ryerson, Miss Emily Borie*	Haverford, PA/Cooperstown, NY	18	1st
Pinsky, Miss Rosa	Russia	32	2nd	*Ryerson, Master John Borie*	Haverford, PA/Cooperstown, NY	13	1st
Plotcharsky, Mr. Vasil		27	3rd	*Ryerson, Miss Suzette Parker*	Haverford, PA/Cooperstown, NY	21	1st
Ponesell, Mr. Martin	Denmark to New York, NY	34		Saad, Mr. Amin			2nd
Portaluppi, Mr. Emilio	Milford, NH		2nd	*Saalfeld, Mr. Adolphe*	Manchester, England		1st
Porter, Mr. Walter Chamberlain	Worcester, MA	46	1st	Sadlier, Mr. Matthew	Ireland to Lakewood, NJ	20	3rd
Potchett, Mr. George		19	3rd	England to Providence, RI		17	3rd
Potter, Mrs. Thomas, Jr.	Mt. Airy, Philadelphia, PA	56	1st	Sadowitz, Mr. Harry			
(Lily Alexenia Wilson)				Sage, Miss Ada	Peterborough, England to Jacksonville, FL	9	3rd
Pulbaum, Mr. Frank	Paris, France		2nd	Sage, Miss Constance	Peterborough, England to Jacksonville, FL	7	
Quick, Mrs. Frederick C. (Jane Richards)	Plymouth, England to Detroit, MI	33	2nd	Sage, Miss Dorothy	Peterborough, England to Jacksonville, FL	13	3rd
Quick, Miss Phyllis May	Plymouth, England to Detroit, MI	2	2nd	Sage, Mr. Douglas	Peterborough, England to Jacksonville, FL	18	3rd
Quick, Miss Winifred Vera	Plymouth, England to Detroit, MI	8	2nd	Sage, Mr. Frederick	Peterborough, England toJacksonville, FL	16	3rd
2nRadeff, Mr. Alexander	Bulgaria to Chicago, IL	27	3rd	Sage, Mr. George	Peterborough, England to Jacksonville, FL	19	3rd
Raibid, Mr. Razi			3rd	Sage, Mr. John George	Peterborough, England to Jacksonville, FL	44	3rd
Reed, Mr. James George		19	3rd	Sage, Mrs. John George (Annie)	Peterborough, England toJacksonville, FL	44	3rd
Reeves, Mr. David	Brighton, England	36	2nd	Sage, Miss Stella	Peterborough, England to Jacksonville, FL	20	3rd
Renouff, Mr. Peter Henry	Elizabeth, NJ	34	2nd	Sage, Master Thomas	Peterborough, England to Jacksonville, FL	4	3rd
Renouff, Mrs. Peter Henry	Elizabeth, NJ	30	2nd	Sage, Master William	Peterborough, England to Jacksonville, FL	11	3rd
(Lillian Jefferys)				Salander, Mr. Karl Johan	Tjarby, Sweden, to Red Wing, MN	24	3rd
Reuchlin, Mr. John George	Rotterdam, Netherlands		1st	*Salkjelsvik, Miss Anna*	Alesund, Norway to Proctor, MN	23	3rd
Reynaldo, Mrs. Encarnacion	Spain	28	2nd	*Salomon, Mr. Abraham L.*	New York, NY		1st
Reynolds, Mr. Harold		21	3rd	*Salomen, Mr. Johan Werner*	Aberdeen, WA	39	3rd
Rheims, Mr. George Lucien	Paris, France/New York, NY		1st	Samaan, Mr. Elias			3rd
Rice, Master Albert	Co Athlone, Ireland to Spokane, WA	10	3rd	Samaan, Mr. Hanna			3rd
Rice, Master Arthur	Co Athlone, Ireland to Spokane, WA	4	3rd	Samaan, Mr Youssef			3rd
Rice, Master George	Co Athlone, Ireland to Spokane, WA	9	3rd	*Sandstrom, Mrs. Hjalmar*	Smaland, Sweden to San Francisco, CA	24	3rd
Rice, Master Eric	Co Athlone, Ireland to Spokane, WA	7	3rd	(Agnes Charlotta Bengtsson)			
Rice, Master Eugene	Co Athlone, Ireland to Spokane, WA	2	3rd	*Sandstrom, Miss Beatrice Irene*	Smaland, Sweden to San Francisco, CA	1	3rd
Rice, Mrs. William (Margaret Norton)	Co Athlone, Ireland to Spokane, WA	39	3rd	*Sandstrom, Miss Marguerite Rut*	Smaland, Sweden to San Francisco, CA	4	3rd
Richard, Mr. Emil	Paris, France to Montreal, PQ	23	2nd	Sather, Mr. Simon Sivertsen	Sydafrika, Norway		3rd
Richards, Master George Sideny	Cornwall, England to Akron, OH	10m	2nd	Saundercock, Mr. William Henry		20	3rd
Richards, Mrs. Sidney (Emily Hocking)	Cornwall, England to Akron, OH	25	2nd	Sawyer, Mr. Frederick	Basingstoke, Hants England to Halley, MI,	23	3rd
Richards, Master William Rowe	Cornwall, England to Akron, OH	3	2nd	Scanlan, Mr. James	Ireland to New York, NY		3rd
Ridsdale, Miss Lucy	Milwaukee, WI	50	2nd	*Schabert, Mrs. Paul (Emma Mock)*	New York, NY		1st
Riihivuori, Miss Sanni	Finland to Coal Center, PA	21	3rd	Sdycoff, Mr. Todor	Bulgaria to Chicago, IL	42	3rd
Rintamaki, Mr. Matti	Pantane, Finland to Sudbury, ON		3rd	Sedgwick, Mr. Charles	Liverpool, England		2nd
Riordan, Miss Hannah	Kingwilliamstown, Co Cork, Ireland to New York, NY	20	3rd	Frederick Waddington			
				Seman, Master Betros	Syria to Fredericksburg, VA	9	3rd
Risien, Mr. Samuel	Groesbeck, TX	68	3rd	Serota, Mr. Maurice			3rd
Risien, Mrs. Samuel (Emma)	Grosbeck, TVX	58	3rd	*Seward, Mr. Frederic Kimber*	New York, NY	34	1st
Robert, Mrs. Edward Scott	St. Louise, MO	43	1st	Sharp, Mr. Percival	Hornsey, England		2nd
(Elisabeth Walton McMillan)				Shaughnesay, Mr. Patrick	Ireland to New York, NY		3rd
Robins, Mr. Alexander A.	Yonkers, NY	50	3rd	Shedid (Sitik), Mr. Daher (Docart)	Kulpmont, PA	19	3rd
Robins, Mrs. Alexander A.	Yonkers, NY	47	3rd	*Sheerlinck, Mr. Jean*	Belgium to Detroit, MI	29	3rd
(Charity Laury)				Shellard, Mr. Frederick B.			3rd
Roebling, Mr. Washington	Trenton, NJ	31	1st	*Shelley, Mrs. William (Imanita)*	Deer Lodge, MT	25	2nd
Augustus 2nd				Shine, Miss Ellen	Co Cork, Ireland to New York, NY	20	3rd
Romaine, Mr. Charles Hallis	New York, NY		1st	Shorney, Mr. Charles		22	3rd
Rommetvedt, Mr. Karl Kristian Knut	Bergen, Norway to New York, NY	49	3rd	*Shutes, Miss Elizabeth W.*	New York, New York/Greenwich, CT	40	1st
Rogers, Mr. Harry			2nd	*Silven, Miss Lyyli*	Finland to Minneapolis, MN	18	2nd
Rogers, Mr. William John		29	3rd	*Silverthorne, Mr. Spencer Victor*	St. Louis, MO	36	1st
Rood, Mr. Hugh R.	Seattle, WA		1st	Silvey, Mr. William Baird	Duluth, MN	50	1st
Rosblom, Mrs. Viktor	Raumo, Finland to Astoria, OR	41	3rd	*Silvey, Mrs. William Baird*	Duluth, MN	39	1st
(Helena Wilhelmina)				(Alice Munger)			
Rosblom, Miss Salli Helena	Raumo, Finland to Astoria, OR	2	3rd	Simmons, Mr. John		39	3rd
Rosblom, Mr. Viktor Rickard	Raumo, Finland to Astoria, OR	18	3rd	*Simonius-Blumer, Col Alfons*	Basel, Switzerland	56	1st
Rosenbaum (Russell), Miss Edith Louise	Paris, France	33	1st	*Sincock, Miss Maude*	Cornwall, England to Hancock, MI	20	2nd
Ross, Mr. John Hugo	Winnipeg, MB		1st	Sirayanian, Mr. Arsun	Turkey to Brantford, OH		3rd
Roth, Miss Sarah	London to New York, NY	26	3rd	*Siukonnen, Miss Anna*	Finland to Washington, DC	30	2nd
Rothes, the Countess of (Noel	London to Vancouver, BC	27	1st	Sivic, Mr. Husen		40	3rd
Lucy Martha Dyer-Edwards)				Sivola, Mr. Antti	Mountain Home, Idaho	21	3rd
Rothschild, Mr. Martin	New York, NY	55	1st	*Sjoblom, Miss Anna Sofia*	Finland to Olympia, WA	18	3rd
Rothschild, Mrs. Martin	New York, NY	54	1st	Sjostedt, Mr. Ernst Adolf	Sault St. Marie, ON	59	2nd
(Elizabeth L. Barrett)				Skinner, Mr. Henry John		32	3rd
				Skoog, Master Harald	Hallekis, Sweden to Iron Mountain, MI	4	3rd

NOTE: *Survivors are noted in italics*

Name	Residence	Age	Class
Skoog, Master Karl	Hallekis, Sweden to Iron Mountain, MI	10	3rd
Skoog, Miss Mabel	Hallekis, Sweden to Iron Mountain, MI	9	3rd
Skoog, Miss Margit	Hallekis, Sweden to Iron Mountain, MI	2	3rd
Skoog, Mr. William	Hallekis, Sweden to Iron Mountain, MI	40	3rd
Skoog, Mrs. William (Anna Bernhardina Karlsson)	Hallekis, Sweden to Iron Mountain, MI	43	3rd
Slabenoff, Mr. Petco	Bulgaria	42	3rd
Slayter, Miss Hilda Mary	Halifax, NS	30	2nd
Slemen, Mr. Richard James	Cornwall, England	35	2nd
Slocovski, Mr. Selman		31	3rd
Sloper, Mr. William Thomson	New Britain, CT	28	1st
Smart, Mr. John Montgomery	New York, NY	56	1st
Smiljanovic, Mr. Mile	Austria to New York, NY	37	3rd
Smith (Schmidt), Mr. Augustus	Newark, NJ	22	2nd
Smith, Mr. James Clinch	St. James, Long Island, NY	56	1st
Smith, Mr. Lucien Philip	Huntington, WV	24	1st
Smith, Mrs. Lucien Philip (Mary Eloise Hughes)	Huntington, WV	18	1st
Smith, Miss Marion			2nd
Smith, Mr. Richard William	Streatham, Surrey, England		1st
Smyth, Miss Julia	Co Cavan, Ireland to New York, NY	20	3rd
Snyder, Mr. John Pillsbury	Minneapolis, MN	24	1st
Snyder, Mrs. John Pillsbury (Nelle Stevenson)	Minneapolis, MN	23	1st
Sobey, Mr. Hayden	Cornwall, England to Houghton, MI	25	2nd
Soholt, Mr. Peter Andreas Lauritz Andersen	Alesund, Norway to N. Minneapolis, MN	19	3rd
Solvang, Mrs. Lena Jacobsen	Haugesund, Norway to Centerville, SD	63	3rd
Somerton, Mr. Francis William	Great Field, Cheltenham, England	31	3rd
Sop, Mr. Jules	Belgium to Detroit, MI	25	3rd
Spector, Mr. Woolf		23	3rd
Spedden, Mr. Frederic Oakley	Tuxedo Park, NY	45	1st
Spedden, Mrs. Frederic Oakley (Margaretta Corning Stone)	Tuxedo Park, NY	40	1st
Spedden, Master Robert Douglas	Tuxedo Park, NY	6	1st
Spencer, Mr. William Augustus	Paris France	57	1st
Spencer, Mrs. William Augustus (Marie Eugenie)	Paris France		1st
Staehlin, Dr. Max	Basel, Switzerland	32	1st
Staneff, Mr. Ivan	Bulgaria to Chicago, IL	23	3rd
Stankovic, Mr. Jovan	Austria		3rd
Stanley, Miss Amy Elsie	England to New Haven, CT	24	3rd
Stanley, Mr. Edward Roland	Bristol, England to Cleveland, OH	21	3rd
Stanton, Mr. Samuel Ward	New York, NY	41	2nd
Stead, Mr. William Thomas	Westminster, Middlesex, England	62	1st
Stengel, Mr. Charles Emil Henry	Newark, NJ	54	1st
Stengel, Mrs. Charles Emil Henry (Annie May Morris)	Newark, NJ	43	1st
Stephenson, Mrs. Walter Bertram (Martha Eustis)	Haverford, PA	52	1st
Stewart, Mr. Albert A.	Paris France/New York, NY		1st
Stokes, Mr. Philip Joseph	Catford, Kent, England to Detroit, MI	25	2nd
Stone, Mrs. George Nelson (Martha E.)	Cincinatti, OH	63	1st
Storey, Mr. Thomas	Liverpool, England	51	3rd
Stoychoff, Mr. Ilia	Bulgaria	19	3rd
Strandberg, Miss Ida Sofia	Abo, Finland to New York, NY	22	3rd
Stranden, Mr. Juho	Kides, Finland to Duluth, MN	31	3rd
Straus, Mr. Isidor	New York, NY	67	1st
Straus, Mrs. Isidor (Ida Blun)	New York, NY	63	1st
Strilic, Mr. Ivan			3rd
Strom, Mrs. Wilhelm (Elna Matilda Persson)	Indiana Harbor, IN	29	3rd
Strom, Miss Selma Matilda	Indiana Harbor, IN	2	3rd
Sunderland, Mr. Victor Francis	England to Cleveland, OH	19	3rd
Sundman, Mr. Johan Julian	Munsala, Finland to Cheyenne, WY	44	3rd
Sutehall, Mr. Henry, Jr.		26	3rd
Sutton, Mr. Frederick	Haddonfield, NJ	61	1st
Svensson, Mr. Johan	Reftele, Sweden to Effington Rut, SD	74	3rd
Svensson, Mr. Johan Cervin	Knared, Sweden to Beresford, SD	14	3rd
Svensson, Mr. Olof	Osby, Sweden	24	3rd
Swane, Mr. George	England to Montreal, PQ	26	2nd
Sweet, Mr. George	Somerset, England to Bernardsville, NJ	14	2nd
Swift, Mrs. Frederick Joel (Margaret Welles Barron)	Brooklyn, NY	46	1st
Tannous, Mr. Thomas	Tripoli, Syria		3rd
Taussig, Mr. Emil	New York, NY	52	1st
Taussig, Mrs. Emil (Tillie Mandelbaum)	New York, NY	39	1st
Taussig, Miss Ruth	New York, NY	18	1st
Taylor, Mr. Elmer Zebley	London England/East Orange, NJ	48	1st
Taylor, Mrs. Elmer Zebley (Juliet Cummins Wright)	London England/East Orange, NJ		1st
Tenglin, Mr. Gunnar Isidor	Stockholm, Sweden to Burlington, IA	25	3rd
Thayer, Mr. John Borland	Haverford, PA	49	1st
Thayer, Mrs. John Borland (Marian Longstreth Morris)	Haverford, PA	39	1st
Thayer, Mr. John Borland, Jr.	Haverford, PA	17	1st
Theobald, Mr. Thomas Leonard	Kent, England to Detroit, MI	34	3rd
Thomas, Mrs. Alexander (Thelma)	Lebanon to Wilkes-Barre, PA	16	3rd
Thomas, Master Assed Alexander	Lebanon to Wilkes-Barre, PA	5m	3rd
Thomas, Mr. Charles	Wilkes-Barre, PA		3rd
Thomas, Mr. John Jr.		15	3rd
Thomas, Mr. John			
Thomson, Mr. Alexander		36	3rd
Thorne (Rosenshine), Mr. George	New York, NY	46	1st
Thorne, Mrs. Gertrude Maybelle	New York, NY		1st
Thorneycroft, Mr. Percival	England to Clinton, NY	36	3rd
Thorneycroft, Mrs. Percival (Florence Kate White)	England to Clinton, NY	32	3rd
Tikkanen, Mr. Juho	Finland to New York, NY	32	3rd
Tobin, Mr. Roger	Co Tipperary, Ireland to New York, NY		3rd
Todoroff, Mr. Lalio	Bulgaria to Chicago, IL	23	3rd
Toerber, Mr. Ernest William		41	3rd
Tomlin, Mr. Ernest Portage	Notting Hill, Middlesex, England	22	3rd
Toomey, Miss Ellen	Indianapolis, IN	50	2nd
Torfa, Mr. Assad		20	3rd
Tornquist, Mr. William Henry	Stockholm, Sweden to New York, NY	25	3rd
Touma (Thomas), Mrs. Darwin (Anna Razi)	Tibnin, Syria, to Dowagiac, MI	27	3rd
Touma (Thomas), Master George	Tibnin, Syria, to Dowagiac, MI	7	3rd
Touma (Thomas), Miss Hanna	Tibnin, Syria, to Dowagiac, MI	9	3rd
Troupiansky, Mr. Moses Aaron		22	2nd
Trout, Mrs. William H. (Jessie L.)	Columbus, OH		2nd
Troutt, Miss Edwina Celia	Bath, England to Massachusetts	27	2nd
Tucker, Mr. Gilbert Milligan, Jr.	Albany, NY	31	1st
Turcin, Mr. Stefan		36	3rd
Turja, Miss Anna Sofia	Oulainen, Sweden to Ashtabula, OH	18	3rd
Turkula, Mrs. Hedvig	Finland to Hibbing, MN	65	3rd
Turpin, Mr. William John	Plymouth, England	29	2nd
Turpin, Mrs. William John (Dorothy Ann Wonnacott)	Plymouth, England	27	2nd
Uruchurtu, Mr. Manuel E.	Mexico City, Mexico		1st
Uzelas, Mr. Joso	Austria	17	3rd
Van Billiard, Mr. Austin Blyler	Cape Town, South Africa to North Wales, PA	35	3rd
Van Billiard, Master James William	Cape Town, South Africa to North Wales, PA	10	3rd
Van Billiard, Master Walter John	Cape Town, South Africa to North Wales, PA	9	3rd
Van Derhoef, Mr. Wyckoff	Brooklyn, NY	61	1st
Van der Planke, Miss Augusta	Belgium to Freemantle, OH	18	3rd
Van der Planke, Mr. Jules	Belgium to Freemantle, OH	31	3rd
Van der Planke, Mrs. Jules (Emilie)	Belgium to Freemantle, OH	31	3rd
Van der Planke, Mr. Leon	Belgium to Freemantle, OH	16	3rd
Van der Steen, Mr. Leo Peter		28	3rd
Van de Velde, Mr. John Joseph	Belgium to Gladstone, MI	36	3rd
Van de Walle, Mr. Nestor	Belgium to New York, NY	28	3rd
Van Impe, Miss Catharine	Belgium	10	3rd
Van Impe, Mr. Jean Baptiste	Belgium	36	3rd
Van Impe, Mrs. Jean Baptiste (Rosalie Govaert)	Belgium	30	3rd
Vartunian, Mr. David	Turkey to Brantford, ON		3rd
Vassilios, Mr. Catevelas	Greece to Milwaukee, WI	18	3rd
Veale, Mr. James	Barre, Co Washington, VT	30	2nd
Vendel, Mr. Olof Edvin	Ostra Sallerup, Sweden to St. Paul, MN	20	3rd
Vereruysse, Mr. Victor	Swevezeale, Belgium to Fremont, OH	47	3rd
Vestrom, Miss Hulda Amanada Adolfina	Salmunds, Sweden to Los Angeles, CA	14	3rd
Vonk, Mr. Jenko	Austria to New York, NY	21	3rd
Waelens, Mr. Achille	Antwerp, Belgium to Stanton, OH	22	2/3rd
Walcroft, Miss Nellie	Mamaroneck, NY	35	2nd
Walker, Mr. William Anderson	East Orange, NJ	47	1st
Ware, Mr. Frederick		34	3rd

NOTE: *Survivors are noted in italics*

PASSENGERS continued

Name	Residence	Age	Class
Ware, Mr. John James	Bristol, England to New Britain, CT	30	2nd
Ware, Mrs. John James	Bristol, England to New Britain, CT	28	2nd
(Florence Louise Long)			
Ware, Mr. William, J.		23	2nd
Warren, Mr. Charles William		30	3rd
Warren, Mr. Frank Manley	Portland, OR	64	1st
Warren, Mrs. Frank Manley	Portland, OR	60	1st
(Anna S. Atkinson)			
Watt, Miss Bertha	Aberdeen, Scotland to Portland, OR	12	2nd
Watt, Mrs. James (Bessie Inglis Milne)	Aberdeen, Scotland to Portland, OR	40	2nd
Wazil, Mr. Yousif			3rd
Webber, Mr. James	San Francisco, CA	66	3rd
Webber, Miss Susan	England to Hartford, CT	36	2nd
Weir, Col. John	New York, NY	60	1st
Weisz, Mr. Leopold	Bromsgrove, England to Montreal, PQ	28	2nd
Weisz, Mrs. Leopold (Mathilde)	Bromsgrove, England to Montreal, PQ	32	2nd
Wells, Mrs. Arthur H. (Addie Trevaskis)	Cornwall, England to Akron, OH	29	2nd
Wells, Miss Joan	Cornwall, England to Akron, OH	4	2nd
Wells, Master Ralph Lester	Cornwall, England to Akron, OH	2	2nd
Wennerstrom, Mr. August Edvard	Malmo, Sweden to New York, Ny	27	3rd
Wenzel, Mr. Linhart			3rd
West, Miss Barbara J.	Bournemouth, England		2nd
West, Miss Constance Miriam	Bournemouth, England		2nd
West, Mr. Edwy Arthur	Bournemouth, England	36	2nd
West, Mrs. Edwy Arthur (Ada Mary)	Bournemouth, England	33	2nd
Wheadon, Mr. Edward	Guernsey to Edgewood, RI		2nd
Wheeler, Mr. Edwin			2nd
White, Mrs. J. Stuart (Ella Holmes)	New York, NY/Briarcliff Manor, NY	55	1st
White, Mr. Percival Wayland	Brunswick, ME	54	1st
White, Mr. Richard Frasar	Brunswick, ME	21	1st
Wick, Mr. George Dennick	Youngstown, OH	57	1st
Wick, Mrs. George Dennick	Youngstown, OH	45	1st
(Mary Hitchcock)			
Wick, Miss Mary Natalie	Youngstown, OH	31	1st
Wildegren, Mr. Charles Peter	Jamaica, Queens, NY	51	3rd
Widener, Mr. George Dunton	Elkins Park, Philadephia, PA	50	1st
Widener, Mrs. George Dunton	Elkins Park, Philadephia, PA	50	1st
(Eleanor Elkins)			
Widener, Mr. Harry Elkins	Elkins Park, Philadephia, PA	27	1st
Wiklund, Mr. Jacob Alfred	Nicolaistad, Finland to Montreal, PQ	18	3rd
Wiklund, Mr. Karl Johan	Nicolaistad, Finland to Montreal, PQ	21	3rd
Wilhelms, Mr. Charles	London, England	32	2nd
Wilkes, Mrs. Ellen	Cornwall, England to Akron, OH	45	3rd
Wilkinson, Mrs. Elizabeth Anne	Manchester, England		2nd
Willard, Miss Constance	Duluth, MN	20	1st
Willer, Mr. Aaron	Chicago, IL		3rd
Willey, Mr. Edward	Drayton, England to Schenectady, NY	18	3rd
Williams, Mr. Charles Duane	Geneva, Switzerland/Radnor, PA	51	1st
Williams, Mr. Charles Eugene	Harrow, England		2nd
Williams, Mr. Fletcher Lambert	London, England		1st
Williams, Mr. Howard Hugh		28	3rd
Williams, Mr. Leslie			3rd
Williams, Mr. Richard Norris II	Geneva, Switzerland/Radnor, PA	21	1st
Windelov, Mr. Einer		21	3rd
Wirz, Mr. Albert	Zurich, Switzerland to Beloit, WI	27	3rd
Wiseman, Mr. Phillippe	Quebec City, PQ	54	3rd
Wittenrongel, Mr. Camille	Westroosebeke, Belgium to Detroit, MI	36	3rd
Woolner, Mr. Hugh	London, England		1st
Wright, Mr. George	Halifax, NS		1st
Wright, Miss Marion	Yeovil, England to Cottage Grove, OR	26	2nd
Yalsevac, Mr. Ivan	Austria to Illinois		3rd
Yasbeck, Mr. Antoni	Lebanon to Wilkes-Barre, PA	27	3rd
Yasbeck, Mrs. Antoni	Lebanon to Wilkes-Barre, PA	15	3rd
(Celiney Alexander)			
Young, Miss Marie Grice	New York, NY/Washington, DC	36	1st
Youssef, Mr. Gerios			3rd
Yrois, Miss Henriette	Paris, France		2nd
Zabour, Miss Hileni			3rd
Zabour, Miss Tamini			3rd
Zakarian, Mr. Artun	Turkey to Brantford, ON		3rd
Zakarian, Mr. Maprieder			3rd
Zievens, Mr. Rene	Belgium to Detroit, MI	24	3rd
Zimmerman, Mr. Leo			3rd

CREW / DECK DEPARTMENT

Name	Rating
Archor, E.	A. B
Anderson, J.	
Brice, W.	A. B
Boxhall, J. G.	Fourth officer
Bailey, W.	Master at arms
Bright, A.	Quartermaster
Bradley, F.	A. B
Buley, E.	A. B
Couch, F.	A. B
Clench, G.	A. B
Clinch, F.	A. B
Davis, S. J.	A. B
Evans, F.	L. O
Evans, F. O.	A. B
Fleet, F.	L. O
Forward, J.	A. B
Foley, J.	Storekeeper
Hutchison, J. H.	Joiner
Haines, A.	Boatswain's mate
Hemmings, S.	Lamptrimmer
Humphreys, S.	Q. M
Hichens, R.	Q. M
Hogg, G. A.	L. O
Horswill, A. E.	A. B
Holman, H.	A. B
Hopkins, R.	A. B
Harder, W.	Window cleaner
Jewell, A.	L. O
Jones, T.	A. B
Johnson, A.[1]	[1] Not crew, American Line man, traveling as passenger
Johnson, W.[1]	[1] Not crew, American Line man, traveling as passenger
King, T.	Master-at-arms
Lightoller, C. H.	Second officer
Lowe, H. G.	Fifth officer
Lee, R. R.	L. O
Lucas, W.	A. B
Lyons, W. H.	A. B
Leonard, L.	Not Titanic crew, American Line man
Murdoch, W. M.	First officer
Moody, J. P.	Sixth officer
Maxwell, J.	Carpenter
Moore, G.	A. B
McCarthy, W.	A. B
Matherson, D.	A. B
McGough, J.	A. B
Mathias, M.	Mess-room steward
Nichol, A.	Boatswain
O'Loughlin, W. F. H.	Surgeon
Olliver, A.	Quartermaster
Osman, F.	A. B
Pitman, H. J.	Third officer
Perkis, W.	Quartermaster
Pascoe, C. H.	A. B
Peters, W. C.	A. B
Pigott, P.	A. B
Ponjdestae, J.	A. B
Rowe, G.	Quartermaster
Simpson, J. E.	Assistant surgeon
Symons, S.	L. O
Smith, W.	A. B
Scarrott, J.	A. B
Sawyer, R. F.	Window cleaner
Smith, E. J., Capt.	Commander
Taylor, C.	A. B
Terrell, D.	A. B
Tamlyn, F.	Mess-room steward
Turngust, W.	Not Titanic crew, American Line man
Wilde, H. T.	Chief officer
Winn, W.	Quartermaster
Weller, R.	A. B

CREW / ENGINE DEPARTMENT

Name	Rating
Allsop, A. S.	Junior Electrician
Adams, R.	Fireman
Allen, H.	Fireman
Allen, E.	Trimmer
Avery, J.	Trimmer
Abraham, C.	Fireman
Bell, J.	Chief engineer
Barlow, C.	Fireman
Beauchamp, G.	Fireman
Biggs, E.	Fireman
Baines, Rich	Greaser
Brown, J.	Fireman
Bendell, T.	Fierman
Bessant, W.	Fireman
Bennett, G.	Fireman
Bannon, J.	Greaser
Barrett, F.	Leading fireman
Blake, T.	Fireman
Bailey, G. W.	Fireman
Barrett, F. W.	Fireman
Ball, W.	Fireman
Brooks, J.	Trimmer
Bevis, J.	Trimmer
Brewer, H.	Trimmer
Bott, W.	Greaser
Burroughs, A.	Fierman
Benville, F.	Fireman
Blackman, H.	Fireman
Blake, P.	Trimmer
Black, D.	Fireman
Brown, J.	Fireman
Blancy, J.	Fireman
Barnes, J.	Fireman
Bradley, P.	Fireman
Billows, J.	Trimmer
Blake, S.	Mess steward
Burton, F.	Fireman
Binstead, W.	Trimmer
Briggs, W.	Fireman
Butt, W.	Fireman
Blann, E.	Fireman
Black, A.	Fireman
Biddlecombe, C.	Fireman
Beattie, F.	Greaser
Coy, F. E. G.	Junior third assistant engineer
Cunningham, B.	Fireman
Crimmins, J.	Fireman
Corcoran, D.	Fireman
Castleman, E.	Greaser
Cooper, H.	Fireman
Cherrett, W.	Fireman
Chorley, J.	Fireman
Carter, F.	Trimmer
Cavell, G.	Trimmer
Coe, H.	Trimmer
Couch, J.	Greaser
Cross, W.	Fireman
Clark, W.	Fireman
Curtis, A	Fireman
Collins, S.	Fireman
Camner, J.	Fireman
Crabb, H.	Trimmer
Cooper, J.	Trimmer
Carr, R.	Trimmer
Calderwood, H.	Trimmer
Coleman, J.	Mess steward
Cotton, A.	Fireman
Casey, T.	Trimmer
Creese, H.	Deck engineer
Chisnall, G.	Boilermaker
Coombs, G.	Fireman
Couper, R.	Fireman

NOTE: *Survivors are noted in italics*

Name	Rating
Copperthwaite, B.	Fireman
Dyer, H. R.	Senior fourth assistant engineer
Dodd, E. C.	Junior third assistant
Dodd, R.	Junior fourth assistant engineer
Duffy, William	Writer
Davies, T.	Leading fireman
Dilley, J.	Fireman
Dillon, T. P.	Trimmer
Dore, A.	Trimmer
Doel, F.	Fireman
Doyle, F.	Fireman
Dymond, F.	Fireman
Dawson, J.	Trimmer
Diaper, J.	Fireman
Dickson, W.	Trimmer
Ervine, A.	Assistant electrician
Evans, W.	Trimmer
Elliott, E.	Trimmer
Eagle, A. J.	Trimmer
Eastman, C.	Greaser
Farquharson, W.	Senior second engineer
Fraser, J.	Junior third assistant engineer
Fitzpatrick, H.	Junior boilermaker
Fitzpatrick, C. W.	Mess steward
Fredericks, W.	Trimmer
Ford, H.	Trimmer
Foster, A.	Storekeeper
Ford, T.	Ldg. fireman
Flarty, E.	Fireman
Ferris, W.	Ldg. fireman
Fraser, J.	Fireman
Fryer, A.	Trimmer
Ferrary, Auto	Trimmer
Fay, F.	Greaser
Golder, M. W.	Fireman
Gregory, D.	Greaser
Goree, F.	Greaser
Gosling, B.	Trimmer
Godley, G.	Fireman
Gosling, S.	Trimmer
Green, G.	Trimmer
Gear, A.	Fireman
Gordon, J.	Trimmer
Gunnery, G.	Mess steward
Gardner, F.	Greaser
Graham, T.	Fireman
Grodidge, F.	Fireman
Graves, S.	Fireman
Hesketh, J. H.	Second engineer
Harrison, N.	Junior second engineer
Harvey, H. G.	Junior second assistant engineer
Hosking, G. F.	Senior third engineer
Hodge, C.	Senior third assistant engineer
Hodgkinson, T.	Senior fourth engineer
Hands, B.	Fireman
Hurst, C. J.	Fireman
Hall, J.	Fireman
Hallett, G.	Fireman
Hurst, W.	Fireman
Hill, J.	Trimmer
Hart, T.	Fireman
Hunt, T.	Fireman
Harris, F.	Fireman
Hodges, W.	Fireman
Hinton, W.	Trimmer
Haslin, J.	Trimmer
Hasgood, B.	Fireman
Hunt, S.	Trimmer
Harris, F.	Trimmer
Hebb, A.	Trimmer
Head, A.	Fireman
Hendrickson, C.	Ldg. fireman
Haggan, J.	Fireman
Hannam, G.	Fireman
Harris, E.	Fireman
Hopgood, R.	Fireman
Instance, T.	Fireman
Ingram, C.	Trimmer
Jupe, H.	Assistant electrician
Joas, N.	Fireman
James, Thos.	Fireman
Judd, C.	Fireman
Jago, J.	Greaser
Jukos, J.	Greaser
Jacobson, John	Fireman
Jarvis, W.	Fireman
Kemp, Thos.	Executive fourth assistant engineer
Kelly, William	Assistant electrician
Kenchenten, Fredk.	Greaser
Kearl, C.	Greaser
Kirkham, J.	Greaser
Keegan, Jas.	Leading fireman
Kasper, F.	Fireman
Kerr, T.	Fireman
Kearl, G.	Trimmer
Kelly, Jas.	Greaser
Kemish, G.	Fireman
Kinsella, L.	Fireman
Kenzler, A.	Storekeeper
Knowles, Y.	Firemen's messman
Lindsay, W.	Fireman
Light, W.	Fireman
Long, F.	Trimmer
Lahy, T.	Fireman
Lee, H.	Trimmer
Light, C.	Fireman
Long, W.	Trimmer
Lloyd, W.	Fireman
Mackie, W. D.	Junior fifth assistant engineer
Millar, R.	Extra fifth assistant engineer
Magee, W.	Senior sixth assistant engineer
McReynolds, W.	Junior sixth assistant engineer
Millar, T.	Assistant deck engineer
Middleton, A.	Assistant electrician
McAndrew, Thos.	Fireman
Marrett, G.	Fireman
Mckae, Wm.	Fireman
Mintram, W.	Fireman
Major, W.	Fireman
Moores, R.	Greaser
Mason, J.	Leading fireman
McGregor, J.	Fireman
May, A.	Fireman
Maskell, L.	Trimmer
Morrell, R.	Trimmer
Morgan, A.	Trimmer
McInerney, T.	Greaser
McIntrye, W.	Trimmer
McGann, J.	Trimmer
Morris, W.	Trimmer
Moore, R.	Trimmer
Mitchell, B.	Trimmer
May, A. W.	Firemen's messman
Murdoch, W.	Fireman
Morgan, T.	Fireman
Moore, J.	Fireman
Mason, F.	Fireman
Morris, A.	Greaser
Mayo, W.	Leading fireman
McGaw, F.	Fireman
Mayzes, T.	Fireman
Marsh, F.	Fireman
Milford, Geo.	Fireman
McGarvey, E.	Fireman
McCastlen, W.	Fireman
McQuillan, W.	Fireman
McAndrews, W.	Fireman
Noon, John	Fireman
Noss, H.	Fireman
Nutbean, W.	Fireman
Newman, C.	Storekeeper
Norris, J.	Fireman
Nettleton, G.	Fireman
Noss, B.	Fireman
Olive, C.	Greaser
Othen, C.	Fireman
Oliver, H.	Fireman
O'Conner, J.	Trimmer
Parsons, F. A.	Senior fifth assistant engineer
Priest, J.	Fireman
Pand, G.	Fireman
Preston, T.	Trimmer
Pelham, G.	Trimmer
Pearce, J.	Fireman
Perry, E.	Trimmer
Podesta, J.	Fireman
Pregnall, G.	Greaser
Palles, T.	Greaser
Painter, C.	Fireman
Paice, R.	Fireman
Pusey, H.	Fireman
Phillips, G.	Greaser
Pitfield, W.	Greaser
Painter, F.	Fireman
Pugh, P.	Leading fireman
Proudfoot, R.	Trimmer
Perry, H.	Trimmer
Reed, R.	Trimmer
Read, J.	Trimmer
Richards, H.	Fireman
Rudd, H.	Storekeeper
Roils, A.	Plumber
Reeves, F.	Fireman
Rickman G.	Fireman
Roberts, G.	Fireman
Rice, C.	Fireman
Ranger, T.	Greaser
Smith, J. M.	Junior fourth engineer
Shepherd, J.	Junior second assistant engineer
Sloan, P.	Chief electrician
Stafford, M.	Greaser
Sparkman, H.	Fireman
Smither, H.	Fireman
Shiers, A.	Fireman
Senior, H.	Fireman
Saunders, W.	Fireman
Self, A.	Greaser
Stubbs, H.	Fireman
Snow, E.	Trimmer
Stanbrook, A.	Fireman
Self, E.	Fireman
Snooks, W.	Trimmer
Shillaber, C.	Trimmer
Stocker, H.	Trimmer
Skeats, W.	Trimmer
Sheath, F.	Trimmer
Steel, R.	Trimmer
Smith, F.	Trimmer
Shea, Thos.	Fireman
Saunders, T.	Fireman
Sullivan, S.	Fireman
Scott, Archd.	Fireman
Small, W.	Leading fireman
Sangster, C.	Fireman
Snellgrove, G.	Fireman
Scott, F.	Greaser
Street, A.	Fireman
Saunders, W	Trimmer
Turley, R.	Fireman
Triggs, R.	Fireman
Toung, F.	Fireman
Tizard, A.	Fireman
Thomas, J.	Fireman
Tozer, J.	Greaser
Threlfall, T.	Ldg. fireman
Thresher, G.	Fireman
Taylor, J.	Fireman
Taylor, W. H.	Fireman
Thompson, J.	Fireman
Taylor, J.	Fireman
Taylor, T.	Fireman
Veal, A.	Greaser
Vear, W.	Fireman
Vear, H.	Fireman
Wilson, B.	Senior second assistant engineer
Ward, A.	Junior fourth assistant engineer
Wardner, F.	Fireman
Woods, H.	Trimmer
Ward, J.	Ldg. fireman
Williams, E.	Fireman
White, F.	Trimmer
Wilton, Wm.	Trimmer
Webber, F.	Ldg. fireman
Witcher, A.	Fireman
White, W.	Trimmer
Witt, H.	Fireman
Webb, S.	Trimmer
Witt, F.	Trimmer
White, A.	Greaser
Woodford, H.	Greaser
Wateridge, E.	Fireman
Wyeth, J.	Fireman
Watson, W.	Fireman
Young, F.	Fireman

NOTE: *Survivors are noted in italics*

CREW / VICTUALING DEPARTMENT

Name	Rating	Name	Rating	Name	Rating	Name	Rating
Ayling, E.	Assistant vegetable cook	Basilico, G.	(R) Waiter	Ede, G. B.	Steward	Henry, W.	Assistant boots
Allen, F.	Scullion	Banfi	(R) Waiter	*Ellis, J.*	Assistant vegetable cook	Ings, W.	Scullion
Andrews, C.	Assistant stewaed	Beaux, D.	(R) Assistant waiter	Fairall, H .	Saloon steward	Ingrouville, H.	Steward
Akermann, A.	Steward	Bernardi, B.	(R) Assistant waiter	Freeman, E.	Deck steward	Ide, H.	Bedroom steward
Ashcroft, A.	Clerk	Bolhens, H.	(R) Larder cook	Fletcher, P.	Bugler	*Jessop, Miss*	Stewardess
Allsop, F.	Saloon steward	Bietrix, G.	(R) Sauce cook	*Faulkner, R.*	Bedroom steward	Johnston, J.	Saloon steward
Ashe, H.	G. H. steward	Blumet, J.	(R) Plateman	Fellows, A.	Assistant boots	Jones, R. V.	Saloon steward
Ahler, P.	Saloon steward	Berthold, Florentini	(R) Assistant scullery man	Fenton, F.	Saloon steward	Jenner, H.	Saloon steward
Abbott, E.	Pantryman	Bazzi, L.	(R) Waiter	*Fropper, R.*	Saloon steward	Jones, H.	Roast cook
Allan, F.	Lift attendant	Charman, L.	Saloon steward	Ford, F.	B. R. steward	Johnston, H.	Assistant ship's cook
Allan, R.	Bedroom steward	Christmas, H.	Assistant steward	Ford, E.	Steward	*Joughin, J.*	Chief baker
Allaria, B.	(R) Assistant waiter	*Chapmn, J.*	Boots	Foley, W. C.	Steward	Junaway, W.	Bedroom steward
Aspelagi, G.	(R) Assistant plateman	Chitty, G.	Steward	Finch, H.	Steward	Jackson, H.	Assistant boots
Anderson, W.	Bedroom steward	Cox, W.	Steward	Fox, W.T.	Steward	Jones, A.	Saloon steward
Akerman, J.	Assistant pantryman	Cecil, C.	Steward	Farrendon, E.	Confectioner	Jenson, C. V.	Saloon steward
Bennett, Mrs.	Stewardess	Crispin, W.	G. H. steward	Franklin, A.	Saloon steward	Jones, A.	Plates
Bliss, Miss	Stewardess	Campbell, D. S.	Clerk	Feltham, G.	Vienna	Jeffrey, W.	(R) Controller
Burke, W.	Saloon steward	Crow, G. F.	Saloon steward	Fanette, M.	(R) Assistant waiter	Janin, C.	(R) Soup cook
Brown, E.	Saloon steward	Carney, W.	Lift attendant	Fei, Carlo,	(R) Sculleryman	Jaillet, H.	(R) Pastry cook
Best, E.	Saloon steward	Corben, E.	Assistant printer	*Gibbons, J. W.*	Saloon Steward	Jouanmault, G.	(R) Assistant sauce
Boyes, H.	Saloon steward	Clark, T.	Bedroom steward	Gunn, J.	Assistant steward	Kingscote, W. F.	Saloon steward
Bristowe, H.	Saloon steward	*Cunningham, A.*	Bedroom steward	*Gold, Mrs.*	Stewardess	King, A.	Lift attendant
Boughton, E.	Saloon steward	*Crawford, A.*	Bedroom steward	*Gregson, Miss*	Stewardess	Kieran, M.	Assistant storekeeper
Barker, E.	Saloon steward	Cullen, C.	Bedroom steward	Goshawk, A.	Saloon steward	Ketchley, H.	Saloon steward
Barrows, W.	Saloon steward	Crumplin, C.	Bedroom steward	Gollop, C.	Assistant cook	*Knight, Geo.*	Saloon steward
Burr, E.	Saloon steward	*Caton, Miss*	T. B. attendant	Gill, P.	Ship's cook	Kitching, A.	Saloon steward
Barringer, A.	Saloon steward	Crosbie, J. R.	T. B. attendant	Giles, J.	Second baker	*Keene, P.*	Saloon steward
Brown, W.	Saloon steward	Cave, H.	Saloon steward	Geddes, R.	Bedroom steward	Kelland, T.	Library
Baggott, A.	Saloon steward	*Crafter, F.*	Saloon steward	Gill, S.	Bedroom steward	Klein, H.	Barber
Benham, T.	Saloon steward	Cartwright, J.	Saloon steward	Guy, J.	Assistant boots	Kieran, J.	Chief third-class steward
Bully, H.	Boots	Cook, George	Saloon steward	Gatti, L.	(R) Manager	Knight, L.	Steward
Barlow, G.	B. R. steward	Coleman, A.	Saloon steward	Guilo, Casali	(R) Waiter	King, F. W.	Clerk
Boothby, W.	B. R. steward	Cheverton, A.	Saloon steward	Gilardino, V.	(R) Waiter	Kerley, W. T.	Assistant steward
Byrne, J.	B. R. steward	Crisp, H.	saloon steward	Gros, Claude G.	(R) Assistant coffee man	King, G.	Scullion
Beedman, G.	B. R. steward	Casswill, C.	Saloon steward	Hughes, H.	Assistant second steward	Kennell, C.	Cook
Bogie, L.	B. R. steward	Conway, P.	Saloon steward	Howell, A.	Saloon steward	Lane, A. E.	Saloon steward
Brookman, J.	Steward	Caunt, W.	Grill cook	House, W.	Saloon steward	Lydiatt, C.	Saloon steward
Bristow, R.	Steward	Coombs, C.	Assistant cook	Hoare, Leo	Saloon steward	Lefever, G.	Saloon steward
Barton, S.	Steward	*Colgan, J.*	Scullion	Handy, C.	Saloon steward	Levett, G.	Assistant pantryman
Burrage, A.	Plates	*Collins, John*	Scullion	Harris, C. W.	Saloon steward	Light, C.	Plate washer
Baxter, H. R.	Steward	Chitty, G.	Assistant baker	Heinen, J.	Saloon steward	Lovell, J.	Grill cook
Barker, R.	Second purser	Crovella, L.	(R) Assistant waiter	Hawkesworth, John	Saloon steward	Lock, A.	Assistant cook
Bailey, G.	Saloon steward	Coutin, A.	(R) Entree cook	Humphreys, H.	Assistant steward	Leader, A.	Assistant confectioner
Bochetez, J.	Assistant chef	Charboison, A.	(R) Roast cook	Hinckley, G.	Baths	*Lavington, Miss*	Stewardess
Bedford, W.	Assitant cook	Cornaire, M.	(R) Assistant roast	Hamblyn, E.	B. R. steward	*Leather, Mrs.*	Stewardess
Bull, W.	Scullion	Deeble, A.	Saloon steward	Harding, A.	Assistant B. R. steward	Latimer, A.	Chief steward
Beere, W.	Kitchen porter	Dyer, W.	Saloon steward	Humby, F.	Plates	Lloyd, H.	Saloon steward
Buckley, H.	Assistant vegetable cook	Derrett, A.	Saloon steward	*Hart, J.*	Steward	*Littlejohn, A.*	Saloon steward
Burgess, C.	Extra third baker	Dodd, Geo.	Second steward	*Hylands, L.*	Steward	Lake, W.	Saloon steward
Barnes, W.	Assistant baker	Deslands, P.	Saloon steward	Hill, R.	Steward	*Lucas, W.*	Saloon steward
Barker, A.	Assistant baker	Davies, R. J.	Saloon steward	*Halford, R.*	Steward	Lawrence, A.	Saloon steward
Barker, T.	Assistant butcher	Davies, J.	Extra second baker	*Hartnell, F.*	Saloon steward	Lacey, Bert. W.	Assistant steward
Bride, H. S.	Second Marconi	Dinenage, J.	Saloon steward	Harrison, A.	Saloon steward	Lougmuir, J.	Assistant B. R. steward
Barrow, H.	Assistant butcher	Dolby, J.	Reception-room attendant	Holland, T.	Assistant reception room attendant	Leonard, M.	Steward
Butt, R.	Saloon steward	Davies, Gordon	Bedroom steward			*Lewis, A.*	Steward
Bagley, E.	Saloon steward	Donogbue, F.	Bedroom steward	Hawksworth, W.	Assistant deck steward	Middleton, M. V.	Saloon steward
Boyd, J.	Saloon steward	Dashwood, W.	Saloon steward	Hamilton, E.	Assistant S. R. steward	Muller, T.	Interpreter
Butterworth, J.	Saloon steward	Doughty, W.	Saloon steward	Halloway, S.	Assistant clothes pressor	Mabey, J.	Steward
Boston, W.	Assistant deck steward	Dean, J.	Assistant steward	Harris, C. H.	Bell boy	Mantle, R.	Steward
Burke, R.	Lounge attendant	*Daniels, S.*	Steward	Hayter, A.	Bedroom steward	Mullen, T.	Steward
Back, C.	Assistant attendant	Dunford, W.	Hospital steward	Hill, J.	Bedroom steward	McElroy, H. W.	Purser
Broome, Athol.	Assistant veranda cafe	Dennarsico	(R) Assistant waiter	Hewett, T.	Bedroom steward	MacGrady, J.	Saloon steward
Bessant, E.	Baggage master	De Breucq, M.	(R) Assistant waiter	Hogg, C.	Bedroom steward	Mellor, A.	Saloon steward
Barrett, A.	Bell boy	Donati, Italio	(R) Assistant waiter	*Hardy, John*	Chief second-class steward	McCrawley, T. W.	Gymnasium
Broom, H.	Bath steward	Dornier, S.	(R) Assistant fish	Hall, F.	Scullion	Mishellany, A.	Printer
Baxter, F.	Linen keeper	Desvernini, L.	(R) Assistant pastry	Hutchison, J.	Vegetable cook	McMurray, W.	Bedroom steward
Bishop, W.	Bedroom steward	Ennis, W.	T. B. attendant	*Hardwick, R.*	Kitchen porter	Marks, J.	Assistant pantryman
Bond, W.	Bedroom steward	Evans, Geo.	Saloon steward	Hatch, H.	Scullion	Marriott, J. W.	Assistant pantryman
Brewster, G. H.	Bedroom steward	*Etches, H. S.*	Bedroom steward	Hines, G.	Third baker	*Morris, F.*	Bath steward
Bunmell, F.	Plate washer	Edwards, C.	Assistant pantryman	Hensford, J.	Assistant butcher	Major, E.	Bath steward
Bradshaw, J.	Plate washer	Edge, F.	Deck steward	Harris, A.	Assistant pantryman	Moore, A.	Saloon steward
Ball, Percy	Plate washer	Egg, W. H.	Steward	Hiscock, S.	Plate washer	*Martin, A.*	Scullion
Bowker, Miss	(R) Cashier	Evans, Geo.	Steward	Hogue, E.	Plate washer	*Mills, C.*	Assistant butcher
Bochot, G.	(R) Second waiter	Edbrooke, F.	Steward	Hopkins, F.	Plate washer	*Maynard, J.*	Entrée cook

NOTE: *Survivors are noted in italics*

CREW / VICTUALING DEPARTMENT continued

Name	Rating	Name	Rating	Name	Rating	Name	Rating
Maytum, A.	Chief butcher	Paintin, A.	Captain's steward	Stroud, E. A.	Saloon steward	Turner, L.	Saloon steward
Morgan, W.	Assistant storekeeper	Pennell, F.	Bath steward	Samuels, W.	Saloon steward	Turvey, C.	(R) Page boy
Marsden, Miss	Stewardess	Penrose, J.	Bedroom steward	Smith, C.	B.R. steward	Tietz, C.	(R) Kitchen porter
McLaren, Mrs.	Stewardess	Price, E.	(R) Barman	Stone, E	B. R. steward	Testoni, E.	(R) Assistant glass man
Martin, Mrs.	Stewardess	Piazza, P.	(R) Waiter	*Seward, H.*	Pantryman	Urbini, R.	(R) Waiter
Moss, H.	Saloon steward	Phillips, J.	(R) Storeman	Sedunary, S.	Steward	Veal, T.	Saloon steward
MacKay, C.	Saloon steward	Piatti, L.	(R) Assistant waiter	Slight, H. J.	Steward	Vine, H.	(R) Assistant controller
McMicken, A.	Saloon steward	Perotti, A.	(R) Assistant waiter	Sevier, W.	Steward	Valvarsori, E.	(R) Waiter
McMullen, J.	Saloon steward	Poggi, E.	(R) Waiter	Savage, C.	Steward	Vioni, R.	(R) Waiter
Martin, Miss	(R) Second Cashier	Petrachio, A.	(R) Assistant waiter	Saunders, W. E.	Saloon steward	Vicat, J.	(R) Fish cook
Monores, J.	(R) Assistant waiter	Petrachio, S.	(R) Assistant waiter	Simmons, F. C.	Saloon steward	Vilvarlarge, P.	(R) Assistant soup
Monteverde, J.	(R) Assistant entrée	Pedrini, Alex	(R) Assistant waiter	*Stewart, J.*	Veranda café	Voegelin, H.	(R) Coffeeman
Mattman, A.	(R) Ice man	Pacherat, J.	(R) Assistant larder	Swan, W.	Bedroom steward	Warwick, F.	Saloon steward
Manga, Paul	(R) Kitchen clerk	Ricks, C.	Assistant storekeeper	Siebert, J.	Bedroom steward	Webb, B.	Smoke-room steward
McCarty, F.	Bedroom steward	Rogers, E. J.	Assistant storekeeper	Stone, E.	Bedroom steward	Wright, F.	Racquet-court attendant
MacKie, G.	Bedroom steward	*Roberts, Mrs.*	Stewardess	Stebbing, S.	Chief boots	Watson, W.	Bell boy
Nichols, A.	Steward	*Robinson, Mrs.*	Stewardess	Scott	Assistant boots	Wareham, R.	Bedroom steward
Nichols, W. K.	Assistant steward	Rovoll, W.	Saloon steward	Smith, F.	Assistant pantryman	Wittman, H.	Bedroom steward
Neale, H.	Assistant baker	*Ray, F.*	Saloon steward	Shea, J.	Saloon steward	Ward, P.	Bedroom steward
Nicholls, T.	Saloon steward	Rowe, M.	Saloon steward	Smith, R. G.	Saloon steward	Ward, E.	Bedroom steward
Nannini, F.	(R) Head waiter	Ranson, Jas.	Saloon steward	Symonds, J.	Saloon steward	Walpole, J.	Chief pantryman
Orr, J.	Assistant vegetable cook	Rummer, G.	Saloon steward	Stagg, J. H.	Saloon steward	Wrapson, H.	Assistant pantryman
Osborne, W.	Saloon steward	Robinson, J.	Saloon steward	Stroud, H.	Saloon steward	*Williams, W.*	Assistant steward
Orpet, W.	Saloon steward	*Rule, S.*	Bath steward	Stubbings, H.	Cook and mess	Wood, J. T.	Assistant steward
Owens, L	Assistant steward	Roberts, H.	Bedroom steward	Slight, W.	Larder cook	*Witter, J.*	Smoke-room steward
Olive, E. R.	Clothes presser	Rogers, M.	Saloon steward	Simmons, W.	Pass cook	*Widgery, J.*	Baths
O'Connor, T.	Bedroom steward	Russell. R.	Saloon steward	Simmonds, A.	Scullion	Willis, W.	Steward
Phillamore, H.	Saloon steward	Ridout, W.	Saloon steward	Smith, C.	Scullion	White, J.	G. B. steward
Parsons, R.	Saloon steward	Randall, F.	Saloon steward	Shaw, H.	Scullion	Wright, W.	G. B. steward
Proctor, C.	Chef	Ross. R.	Scullion	Smith. J	Assistant baker	*Windebank, J.*	Sauce cook
Platt, W.	Scullion	Roberts, F.	Third butcher	Scovell, R.	Saloon steward	Welch, W. H.	Assistant cook
Phillips, J.T.	First Marconi	*Ryerson, W. E.*	Saloon steward	Sesca, Gino	(R) Waiter	Whitford, A.	Saloon steward
Penny, W.	Assistant steward	Robertson, G.	Assistant steward	Scavino, C.	(R) Carver	Wiltshire, W.	Assistant butcher
Pacey, R.	Lift attendant	Reed, C.	Bedroom steward	Saccaggi, G.	(R) Assistant waiter	Wake, S.	Assistant baker
Perrin, W.	Boots	Rice, P.	Steward	Salussolla, G.	(R) Glass man	Williams, A.	Assistant storekeeper
Potty, E.	Bedroom steward	Ryan, R.	Steward	Taylor, W.	Saloon steward	*Whiteman, A. H.*	Barber
Pearcey, A.	Pantry	Rice, J. R.	Clerk	*Thomas, A. C.*	Saloon steward	White, A.	Assistant barber
Pook, R.	Assistant bedroom steward	Rotta, A.	(R) Waiter	*Thessinger, A.*	Bedroom steward	Walsh, Miss	Stewardess
Prideaux, J. A.	Steward	Ratti, E.	(R) Waiter	Tucker, B.	Second pantryman	Wallis, Mrs.	Matron
Port, F.	Steward	Ricardona, R.	(R) Assistant waiter	Terrill, F.	Assistant steward	*Wheat, J.*	Assistant second steward
Pearce, A.	Steward	Rousseau, P.	(R) Chef	Talbot, G. F. C.	Steward	*Wheelton, E.*	Saloon steward
Prior, H. J.	Steward	Rigozzi, A.	(R) Waiter	Thayler, M.	Steward	Weatherstone, T.	Saloon steward
Pugh, A.	Steward	*Stap, Miss*	Stewardess	Taylor, C.	Steward	White, L.	Saloon steward
Parsons, E.	Chief storekepper	*Sloan, Miss*	Stewardess	Turner, G. F.	Stenographer	*Ward, W.*	Saloon steward
Prentice, F.	Assistant storekeeper	*Smith, Miss*	Stewardess	Topp, T.	Second butcher	*Whiteley, T.*	Saloon steward
Pritchard, Mrs.	Stewardess	*Snape, Mrs.*	Stewardess	Thorley, W.	Assistant cook	Worinald, T.	Saloon steward
Puzey, Jno	Saloon steward	*Slocombe, Mrs.*	T. B. attendant	Thompson, H.	Second storekeeper	Yoshack. J.	Saloon steward
Pryce, W.	Saloon steward	Strugnell, Jno	Saloon steward	Taylor, L.	T. B. attendant	*Yearsley, H.*	Saloon steward
Perriton, H.	Saloon steward	Smillie, J.	Saloon steward	Toms, F.	Saloon steward	Zarracchi, L.	(R) Wine butler
Perkins, J.	Telephone operator	Skinner, E.	Saloon steward	*Thomas, B.*	Saloon steward		

NOTE: *Survivors are noted in italics*

Glossary

aft–toward or in the rear, or stern, of a ship.

bow–the front section of a ship.

bridge–a crosswise platform above the main deck, where the ship's controls are located.

bulkheads–the upright partitions dividing a ship into compartments to prevent the spread of fire or water. *Titanic*'s bulkheads did not extend all the way to the highest deck. As a result, when the pumps were unable to stem the flow, water flooded over the top of each bulkhead from one compartment to the next.

CQD–a distress signal used by ships prior to the adoption of SOS as the international distress call. When *Titanic* sailed, SOS had just been introduced. After the liner struck the iceberg, her Marconi operator sent out the more established signal of CQD, repeated six times followed by the ship's call letters. He then switched to SOS.

crow's nest–a small, partially enclosed lookout platform, usually situated high on the foremast of a ship.

davit–a small crane that projects over the side of a ship. Davits are used to raise and lower cargo or anchors as well as to lower lifeboats from the top deck to the ocean surface.

displacement–the amount of water pushed aside while a ship is afloat. Displacement is measured in tons.

forward–toward the bow or in the front of a vessel.

greasers–workers whose duty was to keep the ship's engines lubricated.

great circle route–a navigational route calculated by following an arc along a circle formed by the intersection of a plane that passes through the center of the earth. An arc along such a circle is the shortest distance between two points.

growler–a small iceberg.

knot–a unit of speed, one nautical mile per hour, which is equivalent to 1-1/6 statute miles per hour. "Per hour" is implied in the term; thus, a ship is said to travel at 10 knots, never at 10 knots per hour.

latitude–the distance north or south of the equator, measured in degrees along a meridian, as on a map or globe.

longitude–the distance, east or west, between the prime meridian at Greenwich, England, to the point on the earth's surface for which the longitude is being determined. Longitude is expressed either in degrees or in hours, minutes, and seconds.

port–the left side of a ship when facing the bow.

promenade deck–one of the main decks on a ship. *Titanic*'s promenade deck was enclosed for passenger comfort in all kinds of weather.

propeller–a rotating screw with two, three, or four blades. As the angled blades turn in the water, they move in a "screwing" motion, pushing the ship forward.

purser–the ship's officer in charge of financial matters. The purser also handles passengers' money and valuables.

rudder–a large, flat piece of metal, located beneath the stern of a ship, used for steering.

SOS–the international distress signal, represented by the Morse code signal • • • — — — • • •.

starboard–the right side of a ship when facing the bow.

stern–the rear part of a ship.

stokers–workers whose responsibility was to tend to the boilers.

waterline–the line on the hull of a ship to which the surface of the water rises. The waterline varies depending on the weight of the ship's cargo.

watertight doors–doors placed between bulkheads that could be shut automatically to prevent flooding between compartments in case the ship was damaged.

Sponsors

PATRONS
Mertie Buckman
Edward W. Cook

PRINCIPAL SPONSORS

City of Memphis
Coca Cola Enterprises
International Paper
Memphis-Shelby County Port Commission

Federal Express Corporation
ICI Acrylics, Inc.
The Kroger Company
Universal Outdoor, Inc.

OFFICIAL AIRLINE
Delta Air Lines, Inc.

Lenders

WONDERS: The Memphis International Cultural Series
expresses its profound gratitude to the following individuals and institutions
for the loan of objects for this unprecedented exhibition:

RMS TITANIC, Inc.
New York, New York

Ocean Liner Memorabilia
Denis Cochrane
London, England

John Eaton
Cold Springs, New York

W. K. and Rita Haines
North Canton, Ohio

Contributors

MAJOR SPONSORS

Grand Rental Station
Seessel's Supermarkets
The Peabody
Tennessee Department of Tourist Development
University of Memphis
World Spice Technologies

CONTRIBUTORS

Alexander International
American Society of Training and
Development, Memphis Chapter
Borders Books and Music
Center City Commission
The Commercial Appeal
Empire Express, Inc.
FOX - 13
Graceland
Crowne Plaza
Hospitality Sales and Marketing Association
Hunt-Phelan Home
Key Magazine
Lithograph Printing Company
Memphis Area Transit Authority
Memphis Brooks Museum of Art
Memphis Business Journal
Memphis Convention and Visitors Bureau
Memphis Eye & Cataract Associates

Memphis Flyer
Memphis Hotel Managers Association
Memphis Magazine
Memphis Park Commission
Memphis Queen Line
Metro Memphis Attractions Association
Nolans, Inc.
National Council of Jewish Women, Memphis Section
The Ridgeway Inn
The Spaghetti Warehouse
The Sleep Inn, Court Square
Travel Host Magazine
Tri - State Defender
Visitors Information Channel
Volunteer Center of Memphis
WMC Family of Stations
WPTY-WLMT
WREG-TV

WONDERS
The Memphis International Cultural Series

EXECUTIVE STAFF
Jon K. Thompson, *Executive Director*
Helen "Peachie" Bailey, *Administrative Assistant*

OPERATIONS AND FINANCE
Glen A. Campbell, *Director*
Vernetta Anderson, *Volunteer/Operations Manager*
Rebecca Cook, *Cash Control/Finance Manager*
Velma Johnson, *Gift Shop Manager*
Barbara Gales, *Receptionist*

MARKETING AND PUBLIC RELATIONS
Twyla Dixon, *Director*
Erin Kuzmiak, *Admissions Manager*
Tracy Paden, *Public Relations Manager*
Paige Perkins, *Group Sales/Special Events Manager*

SECURITY
Major Michael E. Lee, Sr., *Director*
Lieutenant Jimmie Kelly, *Assistant Director*

CURATORIAL AND EDUCATIONAL SERVICE
Steve Masler, *Chief Curator*
Louella Weaver, *Assistant Curator*

CORPORATE AND COMMUNITY DEVELOPMENT
Narquenta Sims, *Director*

OPERATIONS AND FINANCE

Glen A. Campbell, *Director*

Volunteer Administration
Vernetta Anderson, *Manager*
Cindy Leigh, *Supervisor*

Exhibition Operations
Vernetta Anderson, *Manager*
Peggie Edgmon, *Floor Manager*
Robin Stone, *Floor Manager*
Timothy Urbanowicz, *Floor Manager*

Recorded Tour
Beverly Oliver, *Manager*
Ronnie Biggs, *Assistant Manager*
Michael Kiggens, *Assistant Manager*
Geraldine Montgomery, *Assistant Manager*
Robert Niederhauser, *Assistant Manager*
Patrick Perry, *Assistant Manager*

Antenna Theatre
Chris Tellis, *Director of Audio Tours*
Harriet Moss, *Executive Director*
Kathy Baldwin, *Project Manager*
David Helvarg, *Writer*
Sally Rudich, *Writer*

Catalogue Production
John P. Eaton, *Text*
Charles A Haas, *Text*

Lithograph Publishing Company, a division
  of Lithograph Printing Company
  Russ Gordon, *Project Manager*
  Connie Reeves, *Production Coordinator*

Alan Stevens, *Project Manager*
  for International Paper

Curatorial Assistance, Inc., Los Angeles
  Graham Howe, *Director*
  Garrett White, *Editor*
  Karen Bowers, *Graphic Design*
  Philip Goldwhite, *Digital Imaging & Design*
  Karen Hansgen, *Editorial Staff*
  Diane Woo, *Editorial Staff*
  Philipp Scholz Rittermann, *Artifact
  Photographer*

Insurance
Sedgwick James of Tennessee, Inc.
George Moreland
Skip Moreland

Cash Control
Rebecca Cook, *Manager*
Dorothy McEwen, *Assistant Manager*

Video Tour Presentation
Carcon Productions
Dan Conaway, *Executive Producer*
William Carrier III, *Director*

**Art Handling, Transportation and
  Installation**
Alexander International
  Special Projects/Fine Arts Division
  LeRoy Pettijohn, *Director*
  Wayne O'Steen
  Bill Ramia
  Mel Strough
  Melzie Wilson

Federal Express Corporation
  Larry Smith
  Larry Ashkenaz
  Carolyn Freeman
  Walter McLaughlin

Martinspeed, Ltd.
  Ian Rogers

Food Services
Fine Host Corporation
Eric Bayne, *General Manager*

MARKETING AND PUBLIC RELATIONS

Twyla Dixon, *Director*

Group Sales and Special Events
Paige Perkins, *Manager*

Admissions
Erin Kuzmiak, *Manager*
Patrick McDevitt, *Assistant Manager*
Rich Kuzmiak, *Mail Services*

Ticketmaster
  Charles Ryan, *President*

Public Relations
Tracy Paden, *Manager*
Kay McDowell, *Consultant*
Andrea Arentsen, *Assistant*

Advertising and Marketing
Archer/Malmo
  Ward Archer, *President, CEO*
  Greer Simonton, *Executive Vice President*
  Mike Villanueva, *Account Manager*
  Gary Backaus, *Creative Director*
  Teri Rhodes-White, *Associate Creative Director*
  Robin McCuddy, *Senior Copywriter*
  Jessica Dheere, *Copywriter*
  Anthony Biggers, *Art Director*
  Wayne Hastings, *Designer*
  Tonda Thomas, *Production Manager*
  Wil High, *Media Services*
  Dana McElyea, *Archer/Malmo Direct*

Speakers Bureau
Marjorie Gerald, *Coordinator*
The Ridgeway Inn

Memphis Convention and Visitors Bureau
  Kevin Kane, *President*
  John Oros, *Vice President Convention Development*
  Regena Bearden, *Director Tourist Development*
  Denise DuBois Taylor, *Director Communications*
  Patricia Morgan, *Director Visitor Information Center*

Tennessee State Department of Tourist Development
The Honorable John Wade, *Commissioner*

Unique Planning Network
Maudie Kite-Powell, *President*

Titanic Media Tour
Delta Air Lines, Inc.
  Nikki Taylor, *District Marketing Supervisor*
  Anne Plumlee, *Sales Representative*

Unique Planning Network
  Jay Kirkpatrick, *Vice President*

Media Preview Day
The Peabody Hotel

Special Events Florals
Piano's Flowers & Gifts
David Strong, AIFD

Grand Inaugural Gala
Mary Schmitz, *Coordinator*
Heartbeat Productions
Fine Host Catering

Eighty-Fifth Anniversary Commemoration
Heartbeat Productions
Jon Anderson, *President*
Melinda Grable, *Vice-President*

DESIGN AND CONSTRUCTION

Exhibition Design/Architectural Design
Williamson Haizlip and Pounders, Inc.
  Louis Pounders, *Architect*
  Clayton Rogers, *Project Leader*
  Scott Carter
  Dawn Owens

Exhibition Design Consultant
Charles Mack Design
  Charles Mack, *Chief Designer*

Graphic Design
Designsmith
  Allyson Smith

Graphic Productions
White Graphics and Signs
  Tony White

Engineering Design
Mangam Thompson and Associates
  Samual Turner, III
  Shannon G. Gilliam
  Beverly A. Marmon
  Christopher B. Murray
  Dr. Vivek S. Savar
  Ronald Brown
  Eugenia Spence
  Gerald W. Rogers

Mountmaking
Robert Fugelstadt

Titanic Model
Curatorial Assistance, Inc.
Maritime Replicas International, Inc.
Warren Samut, *Project Coordinator*

DESIGN AND CONSTRUCTION
(continued)

Titanic Seabed Model
Curatorial Assistance, Inc.

Studio 1030
  Craig Burdick, *Principal*
  Hanne Bøing, *Principal*
  Daniel Koch, *Project Team*
  Christy Burdick, *Project Team*
  Todd Burdick, *Project Team*
  Eugene Rizzardi, *Consultant*

Photographic Collections and Services
RMS Titanic, Inc.
Archive Photos
John Eaton
Charles Haas
Michael Findlay
Chromelab
Smithsonian Institution
Vance Color Lab

Exhibition Construction
Wooldridge Construction Company
  Jim Wooldridge, *President*
  Jeffery J. Emerson, *Senior Project Manager*
  Robert Casper, *Job Superintendent*

Advance Manufacturing Company
  David Craig, *President*

Precision Plastics, Inc.
  Chris Marshall

Introductory Multimedia
Todd Gipstein, *Producer*

Object Conservation and Preparation
LP3 Conservation, Semur-en-Auxois, France
  Stéphane Pennec
Electricité de France
Larry Anderson

GIFT SHOP
Velma Johnson, *Manager*
Jason Carr, *Associate Manager*
Cassandra Howard, *Assistant Manager*

STS, Inc., Gift Shop Product Development
and Production
  Francis Cianciola, *President*
  Jim Hyatt III, *Assistant to the President*
  Shirlee Montgomery, *Market Trade Associate*

SECURITY
Major Michael W. Lee, Sr., *Director*
Lieutenant Jimmie Kelly, *Assistant Director*
Frank Tarrance, *Communications*
Tim Morrow, *Communications*

City of Memphis Police Services

CURATORIAL AND
EDUCATIONAL SERVICE

Steve Masler, *Chief Curator*
Louella Weaver, *Assistant Curator*
Regina Rastall, *Curatorial Assistant*

Docent Training
University of Memphis
  Division of Short Courses
  Maryann Macdonald, *Director*

Memphis Brooks Museum of Art
  Dave Garst

The Fogleman Center
  University of Memphis

COMMUNITY AND
CORPORATE DEVELOPMENT

Narquenta Sims, *Director*

WONDERS For Children
State of Tennessee
Senator John Ford
Betty Goff Cartwright
Federal Express Corporation
Ann and Mason Hawkins
International Business Machines
Memphis Area Transit Authority
Memphis City School System
Dr. Theron Northcross
Tuesday Study Club
Dr. Skip Watson
Ann Wallace

CITY OF MEMPHIS

Office of the Chief Administrative Officer
Rick Masson, *Chief Administrative Officer*
Darrell Eldred, *Assistant to the CAO*
Lillian Hite, *City Auditor*
Diane Brown, *Administrative Assistant*

Division of Police Services
Walter J. Winfrey, *Director*
William P. Oldham, *Deputy Director*

Division of Finance and Administration
Roland McElrath, *Director*
Mark Brown, *Deputy Director*
Danny Wray, *Comptroller*
David Crum, *Deputy Comptroller*
Vicki Lewis, *Senior Fund Accountant*
Don Morris, *Manager Accounts Payable*
Jerome Smith, *Supervisor*
Sherry Whitt Miller, *Technician*
Joan Washington, *Technician*
Lenzie Thomas, *Purchasing Agent*
Lisa Yarbrough, *Buyer Analyst*

Division of Public Works
Benny Lendermon, *Director*
John Conroy, *City Engineer*
Ron Griffin, *CIP Coordinator*
Paul Cheema, *Supervisor Traffic Operations*
Larry Johnson, *Manager City Sign Shop*

Division of Legal Services
Monice Hagler, *City Attorney*
Kenneth L. McCown, Jr., *Deputy City Attorney*
Patti C. Bowlan, *Assistant City Attorney*
Russell Hensley, *Assistant City Attorney*
Dorothy Osradker, Senior Assistant City
  Attorney

Division of Information Services
John F. Hourican, *Director*
Claudia C. Shumpert, *Deputy Director*
Jerry M. Carr, *Communications Manager*
Celeste J. Bursi, *Systems Analyst*
Cassandra D. Ray, *Systems Analyst*

Division of General Services
Rodney "Butch" Eder, *Director*

Division of Personnel Services
Westelle Florez, *Director*
Bob Bishop, *Manager Compensation*
Diane Minton, *Manager Employment*

CITY OF MEMPHIS CITY COUNCIL

Chairman
Jerome Rubin

John Bobango
Joe Ford
Barbara Swearengen Holt
Janet Hooks
E. C. Jones
Myron Lowery
Tom Marshall
Dr. Talib-Karim Muhammad
Rickey Peete
Patricia Vander Schaaf
Brent Taylor
John Vergos

MEMPHIS-SHELBY COUNTY PORT COMMISSION

Chairman
Thomas E. Fisher

Commissioners
Pete Aviotti, Jr.
Humphrey E. Folk, Jr.
Theodore C. Fox, III
Henry H. Hancock
Rick Masson
Archie Willis, III

Executive Director
Donald C. McCrory

Legal Council
E. Brady Bartusch

Further Reading

BOOKS

Armstrong, Warren. *Last Voyage*. New York: John Day, 1958.

Baarslag, Karl. *SOS to the Rescue*. New York: Oxford University Press, 1935.

Ballard, Robert D. *How We Found the Titanic*. Vol. 168, No. 6. Washington, D.C.: National Geographic Society, 1985.

————. *The Discovery of the Titanic*. New York: Warner Books, 1987.

————. *Epilogue for Titanic*. Vol. 172, No. 4. Washington, D.C.: National Geographic Society, 1987.

————. *Exploring the Titanic*. New York: Madison Press, 1988.

————. *The Bismarck Found*. Vol. 176, No. 5. Washington, D.C.: National Geographic Society, 1989.

————. *A Long Last Look at Titanic*. Vol. 170, No. 9. Washington, D.C.: National Geographic Society, 1989.

————. *The Discovery of the Bismarck*. Toronto, Ontario: Madison Press Books, 1990.

Beesley, Lawrence. *The Loss of the SS Titanic*. Boston: Houghton Mifflin, 1912.

Behe, George. *Titanic: Psychic Forewarnings of a Tragedy*. Wellingborough, England: Patrick Stephens, 1988.

Behe, George, and Michael Goss. *Lost at Sea*. New York: Prometheus Books, 1994.

Biel, Steven. *Down with the Old Canoe: A Cultural History of the Titanic Disaster*. New York: W. W. Norton, 1996.

Bonsall, Thomas. *Titanic*. New York: Gallery Books, 1987.

Braynard, Frank O. *Story of the Titanic, Postcards*. Toronto, Ontario: Dover Publications, 1988.

Braynard, Frank O., and William H. Miller, Jr. *Picture History of the Cunard Line 1840–1990*. New York: Dover Publications, 1991.

Bullock, Shan F. *A Titanic Hero: Thomas Andrews, Shipbuilder*. Riverside, Conn.: 7 C's Press, 1973.

Culver, Henry B., and Gordon Grant. *Forty Famous Ships*. New York: Garden City Publishing, 1936.

Cussler, Clive. *Raise the Titanic*. New York: Bantam, 1977.

Davie, Michael. *Titanic: The Death and Life of a Legend*. New York: Henry Holt, 1988.

Davis, Chris. *Titanic Lost and Found*. New York: Hearst, 1986.

Dodge, Washington. *The Loss of the Titanic*. 1912. Reprint, Riverside, Conn.: 7 C's Press, [n.d.].

Eaton, John P., and Charles A. Haas. *Titanic: Triumph and Tragedy*. New York: W. W. Norton, 1986.

————. *Titanic: Destination Disaster*. New York: W. W. Norton, 1987.

————. *Falling Star: Misadventures of White Star Line Ships*. New York: W. W. Norton, 1990.

Editors of *Reader's Digest*. *The Unsinkable Titanic*. Pleasantville, N.Y.: Reader's Digest Association, 1986.

Everett, Marshall. *Wreck and Sinking of the Titanic*. New York: L. H. Walter, 1912.

Eyman, Scott. *I Took a Voyage on the RMS Titanic*. Dublin, N.H.: Yankee Publishing, 1981. [The story of Marjorie Newell Robb, survivor of *Titanic*.]

Gannon, Robert. *What Really Sunk the Titanic*. New York: Popular Science, 1995.

Gardiner, Robin, and Dan Van der Vat. *The Riddle of the Titanic*. London: Orion, 1995.

Gracie, Col. Archibald. *The Truth about the Titanic*. New York: Mitchell Kennerley, 1913.

Harris, Rene. *Her Husband Went Down with the Titanic*. Book 1 of *America: An Illustrated Diary of Its Most Exciting Years, Memoirs and Memories*. New York: American Family Enterprises, 1973.

Further Reading *continued*

Harrison, Leslie. *A Titanic Myth*. London: William Kimber, 1986.

Hart, Eva, and Ronald C. Denney. *Shadow of the Titanic: Survivor's Story*. Dartford, England: Greenwich University Press, 1994. [Biography of Eva Hart, survivor of *Titanic*.]

Hutching, David F. *RMS Titanic: 75 Years of Legend*. 6th ed. Hampshire, England: Kingfisher Publications, 1990.

Hutchinson, Gillian. *The Wreck of the Titanic*. Tonbridge, England: Addax Publishing, 1994.

Lightoller, Cmdr. Charles H. *Titanic*. Riverside, Conn.: 7 C's Press, [n.d.].

————. *Titanic and Other Ships*. London: Ivor Nicholson and Watson, 1935.

Lord, Walter. *A Night to Remember*. New York: Holt, Rinehart and Winston, 1955.

————. *The Night Lives On*. New York: William Morrow, 1986.

Louden-Brown, Paul. *The White Star Line: An Illustrated History 1870–1934*. Coltishall, England: Ship Pictorial Publications, 1991.

Lynch, Don, and Ken Marschall. *Titanic: An Illustrated History*. Toronto, Ontario: Madison Press Books, 1992.

MacInnis, Dr. Joseph. *Titanic in a New Light*. Charlottesville, Va.: Thomasson-Grant, 1992. [IMAX companion.]

Maddocks, Melvin. *The Great Liners*. Alexandria, Va.: Time-Life Books, 1978.

Marcus, Geoffrey. *The Maiden Voyage*. New York: Manor Books, 1977.

Marshall, Logan. *Sinking of the Titanic and Great Sea Disasters*. New York: L. T. Myers, 1912.

McCaughan, Michael. *Titanic*. Belfast: Ulster Folk and Transport Museum, 1982.

Mowbray, Jay H. *Sinking of the Titanic*. New York: Geo. W. Bertron, 1912.

Ocean Liners of the Past: Olympic and Titanic. 3rd ed. Wellingborough, England: Patrick Stephens Limited, 1988.

Oldham, Wilton J. *The Ismay Line*. Liverpool: Charles Birchall and Sons, 1961.

Padfield, Peter. *The Titanic and the Californian*. New York: John Day, 1965.

Pellegrino, Charles. *Her Name, Titanic*. New York: McGraw-Hill, 1988.

Rostron, Sir Arthur H. *Home from the Sea*. New York: Macmillan, 1931.

Russell, Thomas H. *Sinking of the Titanic*. Chicago: Homewood Press, 1912.

Smith, Sen. William Alden. *Loss of the Steamship Titanic* [Report as conducted by the British government]. 1912. Reprint, Riverside, Conn.: 7 C's Press, 1975.

Smith, Sen. William Alden, and Sen. Isidor Rayner. *Titanic Disaster: Report of the Committee on Commerce, United States Senate*. 1912. Reprint, Riverside, Conn.: 7 C's Press, 1975.

Spedden, Daisy Corning Stone. *Polar the Titanic Bear*. Toronto, Ontario: Madison Press Books, 1994.

Stenson, Patrick. *"Lights": The Odyssey of C. H. Lightoller*. London: The Bodley Head, 1984.

Thayer, John B. *The Sinking of the S.S. Titanic*. 1940. Riverside, Conn.: 7 C's Press, 1974.

Thresh, Peter. *Titanic*. [n.p.]: Magna Books, 1992.

Wade, Wyn Craig. *The Titanic: End of a Dream*. New York: Penguin Books, 1986.

PERIODICALS

Boston Daily Globe, 16 April 1912, morning edition.

Boston Daily Globe, 16 April 1912, evening edition.

Bride, Harold. "Thrilling Tale by Titanic's Surviving Wireless Man," *New York Times*, 28 April 1912.

"The Great Liners: Posters from a Golden Age," *Daily Echo*, Southampton, England, 19 November 1994.

Credits and Acknowledgments

Archive Photos
Denis Cochrane
George Fenwick
Charles A. Haas and John P. Eaton
The Irish Picture Library/Father Browne, S.J. Collection
The Mansell Collection
National Maritime Museum, London
Public Archive of Nova Scotia
Popperfoto
RMS Titanic, Inc.
Ulster Folk and Transport Museum
Woods Hole Oceanographic Institution

[...]ect photographs are by Philipp Scholz
[...]ann unless otherwise noted.

[...] Matter
[...]AP
[...]UFT
[...]MC
[...]RMST

[...]r One: ORIGINS
[...]E
[...]C
[...]eft and center) HE
[...]ottom right) MC
[...]eft top) DC
[...]ight top) HE
[...]ight) HE
[...]E
[...]P
[...]E
[...]odd Gipstein, ©NG

[...]r Two: DESIGN AND CONSTRUCTION
[...]FT
[...]E
[...]op left) UFT
[...]ll others) DC
[...]FT
[...]op right) HE
[...]ll others) UFT
[...]eft) UFT
[...]ight) DC
[...]ottom right) UFT
[...]ll others) HE
[...]eft) UFT
[...]ight) HE
[...]E
[...]op) UFT
[...]enter and bottom) HE
[...]op) UFT
[...]ottom) HE
[...]C
[...]FT

44 DC
45 (Top) Todd Gipstein, ©NG
(Bottom left) LP3 Conservation/RMST
(Bottom right) RMST
46 (Left) HE
(Right) DC
47 IPFB

Chapter Three: DEPARTURE
49 DC
50 IPFB
51 (Left) DC
(Center) HE
52 (Left top) PF
(Bottom left) HE
(Right) MC
53 (Top) AP
(Bottom) MC
54 (Right) HE
55 UFT
56 (Center) AP
57 (Left) John P. Eaton
(Right top and bottom) HE
58 Simon Fisher, *On Her Trials*, oil on canvas, 1995. From the collection of John Booth, Westbury, Wiltshire.
61 PF/AP
66 (Left) DC
68 (Left) HE
(Right) Todd Gipstein, ©NG
69 IPFB
70 IPFB
71 IPFB

Chapter Four: LIFE ON BOARD
76 (Top, bottom center and left) UFT
77 (Top left) UFT
80 (Top) UFT
81 UFT
82 (Top right) HE
84 (Top) NMM
86 (Top) HE
(Center) DC
(Bottom left) MC
(Bottom right) PF/AP
87 (Bottom left and right) NMM
94 DC
95 HE
96 (Top right) HE
97 (Top right) HE
98 (Bottom left) AP
99 (Top left) HE
100 (Top) HE
101 (Top left) NMM
102 (Top and bottom right) HE
103 UFT
104 HE

106 (Top) HE
107 (Top left) HE
108 (Top) UFT
109 (Top right) HE

Chapter Five: NIGHT OF APRIL 14, 1912
112 From the collection of Mrs. J. Tyler.
113 HE
114 HE
115 DC
116 (Bottom right) HE
117 ©Rand McNally
118 (Left) HE
(Top right) DC
119 (Top right) DC
123 HE
124 DC
126 (Left) AP/Express Newspaper
(Top and bottom right) HE
127 HE
129 HE
130 DC
131 DC
134 (Left) HE
(Right) PF

Chapter Six: RESCUE
137 AP
138 (Top right) HE
(Bottom left) GF
140 (Left) AP/APA
(Right) GF
141 HE
142 (Top left and right, bottom left) GF
(Bottom right) HE
143 GF
144 (Left) GF
(Right) HE
145 (Left) GF
(Right) HE
146 (Top, bottom left and right) HE
(Center) GF
147 HE
148 (Top, center and bottom) HE
(Right) MC
149 (Top left) MC
(Top right) AP
(All others) HE
150 HE
151 HE
152 (Left) DC
(Top right and center) HE
(Bottom right) PANS
153 (Left) HE
(Right) DC
154 (Top right and left) Todd Gipstein, ©NG
(Center) HE

(Bottom left) PANS
(Bottom right) HE
155 PANS

Chapter Seven: AFTERMATH
156 MC
157 MC
158 (Top left) DC
(Bottom right) MC
(All others) HE
159 HE
160 HE
161 MC
162 (Top and bottom) HE
(Center) DC
163 (Left and top right) DC
(Bottom right) HE
164 HE
165 HE
166 (Left) HE
(Right) John P. Eaton
167 HE
168 (Left) Todd Gipstein, ©NG
(Right) DC
169 AP/Bert & Richard Morgan

Chapter Eight:: LEGEND
170 DC
171 Garrett White
172 (Left) DC
(Right and center) DC
173 DC
174 DC
175 DC

Chapter Nine: DISCOVERY
176 Kristof Emory, ©NG
177 DC
178 RMST
179 Kristof Emory, ©NG
180 (Top left and right) Kristof Emory, ©NG
(Bottom left and right) AP/WH
181 Kristof Emory, ©NG
182 AP/WH
183 Kristof Emory, ©NG

Chapter Ten: RECOVERY AND CONSERVATION
184 RMST
185 RMST
186 RMST
187 RMST
188 LP3 Conservation
189 (Top) LP3 Conservation
(Bottom) Todd Gipstein, ©NG
191 Kristof Emory, ©NG
192 Kristof Emory, ©NG
194 (Top left) Todd Gipstein, ©NG

Index